I0901113

POSTCARD HISTORY SERIES

Tennessee's Dixie Highway

The Cline Postcards

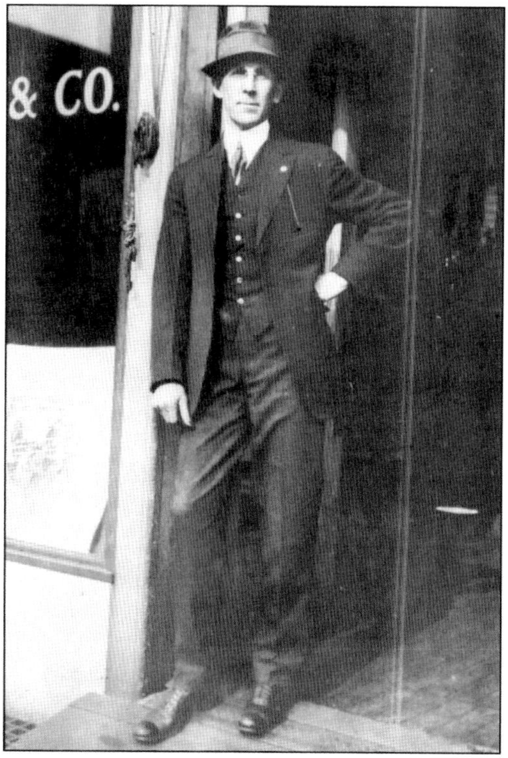

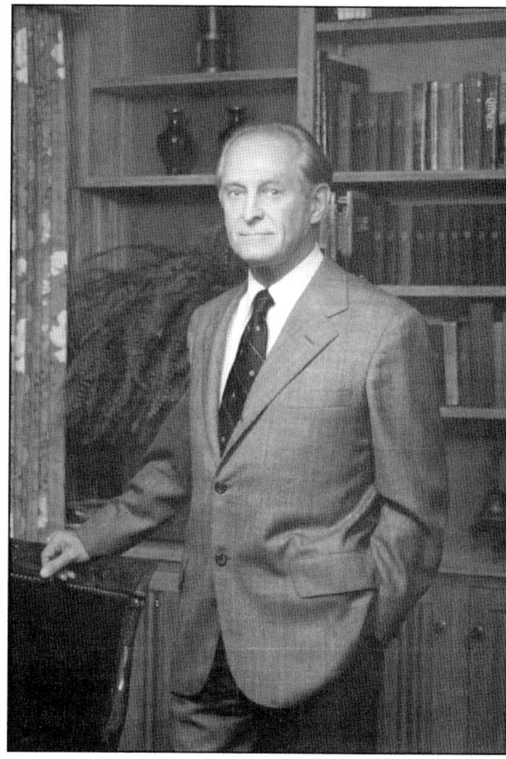

Walter M. Cline Sr. (left) and Walter M. Cline Jr. (right), both photographers, traveled the country documenting small towns across the South and beyond. Their efforts produced an enduring legacy of real-photo postcards for collectors and historians. The Clines used a distinctive numbering system that differentiates their postcards from others'. (Both, courtesy of Cathy Cline.)

On the Front Cover: US 25W, in the Cumberland Mountains between LaFollette and Jellico, was not originally chosen to be a part of the Dixie Highway. The section of road was added when designation was revoked for the highway from Cumberland Gap through Tazewell and Maynardville. (Courtesy of the author.)

On the Back Cover: Wynn's Craft-o'-th'-Hills, five miles north of LaFollette on US 25W, was considered one of the country's largest roadside craft markets. (Courtesy of the author.)

POSTCARD HISTORY SERIES

Tennessee's Dixie Highway
The Cline Postcards

Lisa R. Ramsay and Tammy L. Vaughn
Foreword by Cathy Cline and Haley Cline Morgan

ARCADIA
PUBLISHING

ISBN 978-0-7385-8769-1

Published by Arcadia Publishing
Charleston, South Carolina

Printed in the United States of America

Library of Congress Control Number: 2011921949

For all general information contact Arcadia Publishing at:
Telephone 843-853-2070
Fax 843-853-0044
E-mail sales@arcadiapublishing.com
For customer service and orders:
Toll-Free 1-888-313-2665

Visit us on the Internet at www.arcadiapublishing.com

Dedicated to the Clines for their contribution to preserving the history of countless communities and attractions along the Dixie Highway and beyond

Contents

Foreword

Our father, Walter M. Cline Jr., passed away when we were young adults just beginning our independent lives. Since his death, we have often wished that something could be written about him and our grandfather to bring attention to their talent and dedication to photography.

Our grandfather, Walter Matson Cline, was more of a dreamer than a businessman. Although he embraced modern technology such as the airplane, which he used for aerial photography, he also loved the romance of the early frontiersman. No doubt his sensitivity in this regard, as well as his excellent gunsmithing and sharpshooting skills, enabled him to become close friends with the wary residents of the remote areas of the Tennessee Appalachians. He also was a close friend of Sgt. Alvin York, whom doubtlessly also found himself straddling the divide between the simpler times of a frontier lifestyle and the demands of a modern world.

Our father inherited his father's talent and his mother's business acumen, which enabled him to build one of the largest and most successful photofinishing and postcard businesses in the South. In his early years of being married to our mother, before we were born, they traveled extensively throughout the Southeast and Southwest taking postcard photographs.

Both our grandfather and our father were extremely familiar with the Great Smoky Mountains. Our grandfather spent many happy years hunting with the locals in the mountains before the national park was created. As a result, he gained an extensive knowledge of the region, which he shared with our father, enabling both of them to take photographs that cannot be easily duplicated from the best possible locations. While photographing in the Smokies, our parents met a young Fess Parker on the set of *Davy Crockett*. They became good friends and, through Mr. Parker, our father met Walt Disney. Impressed with our father's work, Disney offered him a job. Our father declined, preferring to remain, like his father, his own boss.

Both our grandfather and our father loved to travel. At the age of 14, our father began driving our grandfather on photography excursions. He would have accompanied his father as his photography assistant on the numerous trips over the Dixie Highway that resulted in the early photographs contained in this book. We hope you enjoy your trip back through time on the Dixie Highway through our family's work.

—Cathy Cline and Haley Cline Morgan

ACKNOWLEDGMENTS

An undertaking of this size requires the assistance of a multitude of people. We received support from family, friends, other Arcadia writers, librarians, archivists, state park personnel, innkeepers, and many others. First and foremost, we would like to thank the Cline family for their help and encouragement. A special thank you goes to Cathy Cline and Haley Morgan for writing the foreword. Additionally, we would like to acknowledge the other Cline cousins—Bert Caldwell, Katherine Ives, and Toni Junkin—who were early advocates of the idea.

We want to recognize Lisa's sister, Joan McRay, for presenting the motivation to begin the project. The initial collection, consisting of Jellico postcards, began because of the love one sister has for the other and has culminated in this volume. Both of Lisa's sisters, Joan and Pam Anderson, helped in the early stages with research. Without the continual push from fellow collector Jim Laughlin, the idea might still be in its infancy. Laughlin also provided some images and the information for Camp Forrest.

The Arcadia authors who offered advice were Devora E. Butler, Bill Jakes, Mitch Kinder, and Leslie Sharp. The librarians and archivists who provided information were Steve Cox of the Lupton Library, Many Langmann and Jim Reece of Chattanooga–Hamilton County Library, Anne Bridges of the John C. Hodges Library, Barbara Milsaps of Harriman Public Library, Susan Drexler of the George Eastman House, Robert Vejnar of Emory & Henry College, Shirley Ford of Guernsey County District Public Library, and Teresa Berry of the University of Tennessee Libraries. State park personnel answering our inquiries were Mark Morgan of Norris Dam State Park, Kim A. Moore of Cove Lake State Park, and Kim Coons of Chickamauga and Chattanooga National Military Park. Additional thanks go to Marlene Payne of the Chattanooga History Center, lecturer Tammy Ingram, Robert and Audrey Hart, Suzie Thurber, and Eddie Archer.

Our final thanks go to Tammy's aunt, Robbie Barnett, for her willingness to proofread the book and to our editors, Maggie Bullwinkel and Brinkley Taliaferro, for their enthusiastic guidance.

All images were taken by Walter M. Cline Sr. or Jr. and are courtesy of the author, Lisa R. Ramsay, unless otherwise noted. Unfortunately, records could not be found to clarify which photographer was responsible for each picture.

INTRODUCTION

"Roads tell the greatness of a nation," said Pres. Theodore Roosevelt in 1903, when he spoke to National Good Roads Convention members on a stop at the Louisiana Purchase Exposition, held in St. Louis. Up until the push to improve the roadways began, most Southern states had little more than dirt roads, which were often treacherous during adverse weather. Many factors influenced the beginnings of the Good Roads Movement. In 1896, the federal government instituted the Rural Free Delivery (RFD) service, offering mail delivery to farmers and freeing them from hours spent traveling to and from town for mail pick up. In response to the US Post Office Department's refusal to accept applications for delivery where the roads were not passable throughout the year, farmers began to improve their local roads and joined Good Roads associations. In 1897, the first RFD route was established in Tennessee. Another significant factor in creating the movement for better roads was support from organizations like the League of American Wheelmen, a national bicyclist group wanting better riding conditions for its tours. Events in Southern states were largely avoided due to poor riding surfaces. During the early 1900s, Good Roads association membership grew throughout the South and in other parts of the country. Probably the most influential factor in the progress toward better roads was the mass production of the automobile that began in 1908. The price reduction made it possible for middle-class Americans to buy a car. With car sales skyrocketing, more citizens developed the desire to travel.

Carl G. Fisher, known as the father of the Lincoln Highway and one of the founders of the Indianapolis Motor Speedway, was the originator of the idea to build a highway linking the North and the South. The Dixie Highway Association, headquartered in Chattanooga, convened in 1915 to chart a highway route from Chicago to Miami. Ultimately, it was extended north to Canada. Instead of mapping one direct road, two separate routes were decided upon in order to serve a larger number of communities. In Tennessee, the western route started in Springfield and then traveled through Nashville, Murfreesboro, Shelbyville, Tullahoma, Winchester, Monteagle, Jasper, Whitwell, and finally Chattanooga. The eastern portion of the highway entered Tennessee at Jellico, then traveled through LaFollette, Jacksboro, Coal Creek (now known as Lake City), Clinton, Knoxville, Kingston, Rockwood, Dayton, and again to Chattanooga. In 1916, Harriman successfully petitioned to be added to the eastern route.

Slow progress on the Dixie Highway in Tennessee often frustrated Fisher and other members of the Dixie Highway Association. One of the most difficult sections to complete was between Monteagle and Jasper. The high elevation caused numerous problems and great expense. The state was finally able to satisfactorily complete the section by 1925, giving drivers new access between the towns.

With the completion of the Dixie Highway, towns became more accessible and tourism was brought to some small towns for the first time. Walter Cline, a prominent Chattanooga photographer, had a personal interest in developing tourism in the area and was a member of the Chattanooga Automobile Club, which was an avid promoter of the Dixie Highway project. During his lifetime, Cline took numerous photographs of towns and sights along the highway.

Walter Matson Cline was born in Guernsey County, Ohio, on April 21, 1873, to Isaac and Sarah (Matson) Cline and grew up in the town of Cambridge, Ohio. Cline began his career in photography 20 years before there were any thoughts of a Dixie Highway. By the age of 17, when he was still in high school, Cline's interest in camera work was already well established. He taught an iron millworker friend to read and write in exchange for the purchase of a $10 camera he had seen in a *Youth's Companion* magazine advertisement. He prized his first photograph, a snow scene in Cambridge, so much that he kept it throughout his life. Beginning work when he was only 18 years old, Cline was first employed by a studio in his hometown. He then worked in Pittsburgh, Pennsylvania, for two years, then in various Ohio cities and in Birmingham, Alabama, for a period of time. On his way home to Ohio, he stopped in Chattanooga, taking pictures with his Kodak camera because he was very impressed with the scenic beauty of the area. Upon returning to Cambridge, Cline partnered with Nathaniel T. Bell in a studio called Bell & Cline. Their photographs won local recognition at the Guernsey County Fair in 1898.

Along with his mother and sister, Cline moved in 1904 to the Chattanooga area, where he worked for Elsworth L. Mudge and, later, Amos W. Judd. Within six years, he purchased the business of his former employer Mudge and established Cline Studios. In the years following, he added Cline Photo Service and the W.M. Cline Company, a scenic photography business, to his endeavors. He became a well-respected commercial and landscape photographer, traveling throughout the country. In addition to being a still photographer, Cline produced some scenic film work for movie companies like Paramount, Pathé, and Universal. Some have estimated that the number of photographs he took of the Chattanooga area is in excess of 75,000, with nearly 3,000 being used in a local tourism campaign during the 1930s.

In January 1914, Cline married Lucy Haley of Chattanooga. They had two children, Walter Matson Jr., born in December 1914, and Sara Antoinette, born in March 1916. The photography business became a family endeavor for Cline, with his son following in his footsteps. Their styles are so similar that it can be difficult to distinguish the father's photographs from the son's, and this publication contains works from both.

In addition to his love of photography, Cline Sr. had a passion for old American muzzle-loading firearms. His collection numbered close to 100 different weapons. Considered one of the foremost authorities on the subject, he helped organize the National Muzzle Loading Rifle Association, serving as president for five years. He sold one of his rifles, called "Long Tom," to the production company of the film *Sergeant York*, released in 1941. Cline Sr. gained further recognition for an article about muzzle loaders written for *American Rifleman* magazine. This led to the book that he was working on prior to his death, *The Muzzle-Loading Rifle: Then and Now*, which was completed by his wife and published posthumously. Cline Sr.'s unfortunate and untimely death occurred on April 12, 1941, when a pistol he was preparing for an event accidentally discharged, killing him instantly. The National Muzzle Loading Rifle Association created the Walter Cline Range in Friendship, Indiana, to honor him.

Cline's wife took over the business at Cline Studios, and his son continued successfully in the commercial photography business. With his father's guidance, Cline Jr. had already established the W.M. Cline Company as a thriving postcard business in 1938. By 1951, his business had become one of the South's leaders in photographic processing, with plants in Atlanta and Knoxville and branches in Nashville, Memphis, Gatlinburg, Asheville, Charlotte, Atlanta,

Birmingham, and Huntsville. Cline Jr. sold the company to Fox-Stanley Photo Products in 1978 for approximately $5 million. Cline Jr. was a traveler like his father. He raced sports cars and was an avid downhill skier and hiker and an ardent mountain climber, becoming a well-known authority on the southern Appalachians. In 1964, he climbed the Matterhorn in Switzerland, a goal he had set for himself as a high school student after reading Edward Whymper's *Scrambles Amongst the Alps in the Years 1860–69.* Cline Jr. died from chronic lymphocytic leukemia in 1984 at the age of 69, one year older than his father was at the time of his death.

Cline postcards are popular among today's collectors for the same reason they were purchased by travelers—people can relate to them. Bryan College, one of the photographs included in this collection, was named after William Jennings Bryan, who was the prosecuting attorney in the famous Scopes evolution trial that took place in Dayton, Tennessee, in 1925. *Str. Gordon C. Greene*, the steamboat pictured on the Tennessee River, appeared in the movie *Gone with the Wind.* Another postcard shows the lovely home of Grace Moore, who was nominated for an Academy Award for Best Actress in 1934. Many of the postcards included in this book were taken in the 1930s, a time when the Dixie Highway made traveling through Tennessee much easier.

A visitor traveling the old Dixie Highway routes will find many charming small towns, with antique stores and beautiful old homes, some of which are listed in the National Register of Historic Places. Several towns on the Dixie Highway are located on or near lakes popular for fishing, swimming, and other outdoor activities. Those interested in the Civil War will find museums along the Dixie Highway route, some containing artifacts from that war. Cline, being interested in the Civil War himself, took photographs of such places as Hazen's Monument at Stones River Battlefield in Murfreesboro and Ochs Memorial at Point Park on Lookout Mountain. Living the majority of his life in Chattanooga, many of his postcards were of popular attractions such as Lookout Mountain and Rock City.

Cline's Tennessee postcard pictures along the Dixie Highway routes recall the history of the communities on today's US Routes 41, 27, and a handful of other numbered highways. The first chapter of this book focuses on Tennessee's western route from Nashville to Chattanooga. The second concentrates on Chattanooga and the surrounding area. The third chapter covers the eastern route from Chattanooga to Jellico, and the final section consists of miscellaneous Cline cards. Some towns, like Springfield and Knoxville, are noticeably absent from the pages, as postcards from these areas could not be located.

The Dixie Highway affected many different communities. This collection of Cline postcards shows a small portion of the work done in Tennessee, offering a glimpse of what life was like in the 1930s and 1940s and some of the attractions these towns still have to offer. In today's fast-paced environment, interstates are easier to travel and small towns are often bypassed. Perhaps readers will find that the fastest road isn't always the best one to take.

One

From Nashville to Chattanooga

Before the completion of the Dixie Highway in 1927, traveling from Chicago to Miami could be an adventurous undertaking. Some roads were paved, while others were impassible. Many areas had no gas stations, and motorists often became stranded. Food and shelter were not always readily available. The completion of the highway made traveling safer and more enjoyable. It brought tourism to some towns for the first time and also gave these same areas easier access to other locations.

Because so many communities wanted to be part of the Dixie Highway, both eastern and western routes were constructed. In addition, some of the routes changed throughout the years. The map and routes used in this book are from the ***Dixie Highway*** magazine of September 1919. In Tennessee, the western route headed south from Springfield through Nashville, Murfreesboro, Shelbyville, Tullahoma, Winchester, Cowan, Monteagle, and Jasper to Chattanooga.

This first chapter follows Walter Cline's camera lens south along the western route of the Dixie Highway, starting in Nashville, with visits to the Hermitage and the Parthenon. From there, the journey continues on US 41 to the Sam Davis home in Smyrna and then to Murfreesboro, which has many attractions, including the Stones River battlefield. From Murfreesboro, the Dixie Highway goes south on Highway 231 to Shelbyville, a town famous for Tennessee walking horses. Traveling along the present-day US 41A to Tullahoma, Cline documented an important part of Tennessee history at Camp Forrest, a facility that has not existed since 1946. Farther south, atop the Cumberland Plateau, is Sewanee, the University of the South. Also along the plateau, Monteagle and the surrounding areas offer a variety of interesting and often beautiful attractions, including Wonder Cave, the "million dollar view," and Foster Falls. The chapter concludes with scenes of Jasper, the Sequatchie Valley, and the Tennessee River leading into Chattanooga.

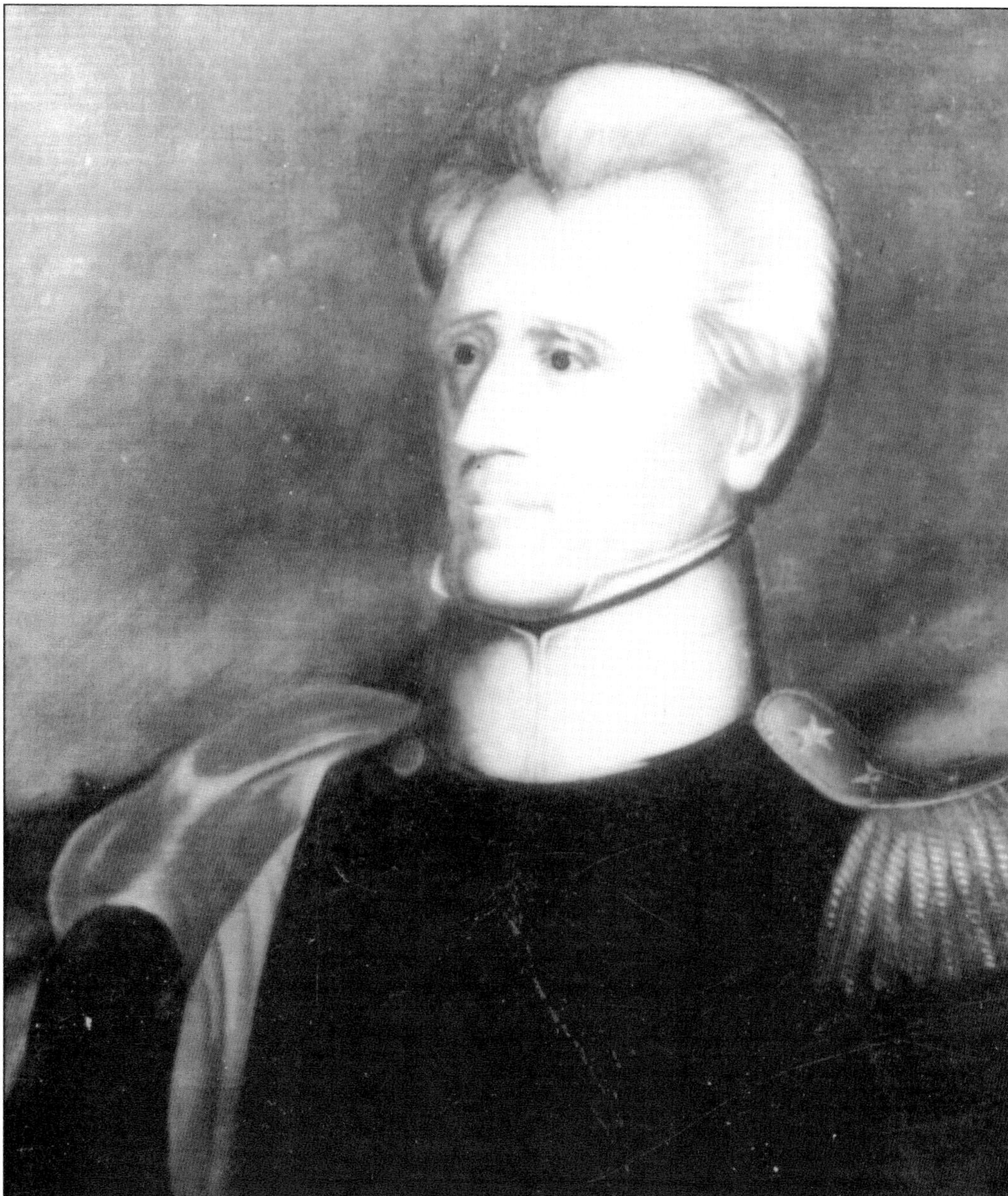

Andrew Jackson was the seventh president of the United States, serving two terms from 1829 to 1837. The son of poor Scots-Irish immigrants, he was the first president born in a log cabin. He was also the first Democratic president, the first president to ride a train while in office, and the first and only president to pay off the national debt. Orphaned at 14, Jackson was known for his toughness, earning the nickname of "Old Hickory" when he fought as a general in the War of 1812. Jackson met his future wife, Rachel Donelson Robards, when he lived at her mother's boardinghouse in Nashville after being appointed district attorney for the area. He married Robards in August 1791, but they later discovered the marriage was not legal because the divorce from her previous husband had not been finalized. After the divorce was finally granted, they remarried in January 1794. He and his wife lived on two farms in the Nashville area, Poplar Grove and Hunter's Hill, before purchasing the Hermitage in 1804.

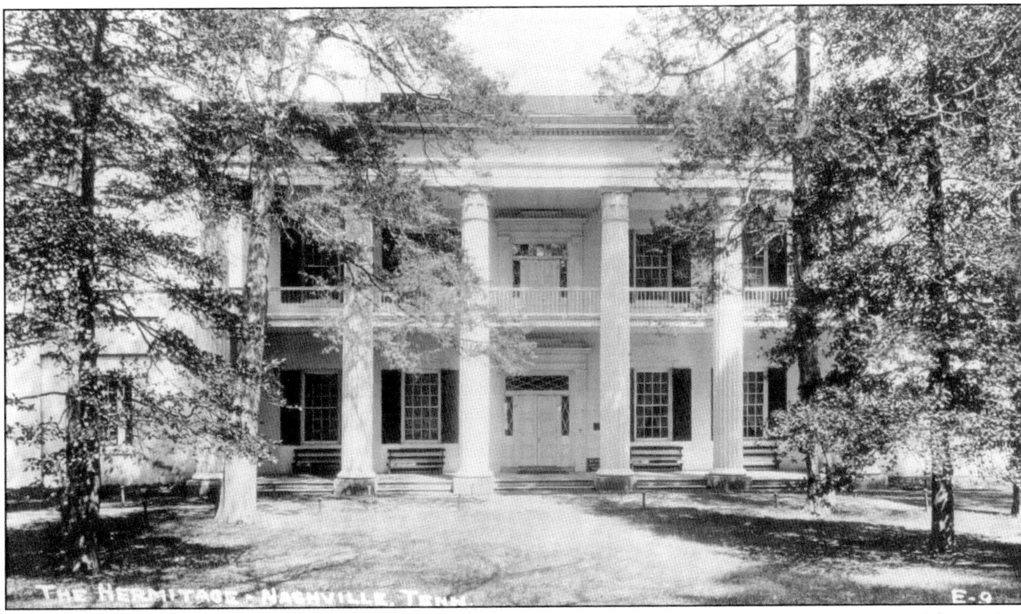

The Hermitage, home to Andrew Jackson and his family, has over 1,000 acres and is located 11 miles east of downtown Nashville. It has been managed by the Ladies' Hermitage Association as a museum since 1889. Andrew Jackson and his wife, Rachel, lived in a log cabin when they first bought the cotton plantation. In 1819, they built a large Federal-style two-story brick home. It had four rooms upstairs, four rooms downstairs, and a beautiful garden on the east side of the house. In 1831, the mansion was remodeled and several rooms were added. It was severely damaged by a chimney fire in 1834 and was remodeled again in 1837 in a Greek Revival style. Philadelphia classical-style furniture was purchased to replace items destroyed in the fire.

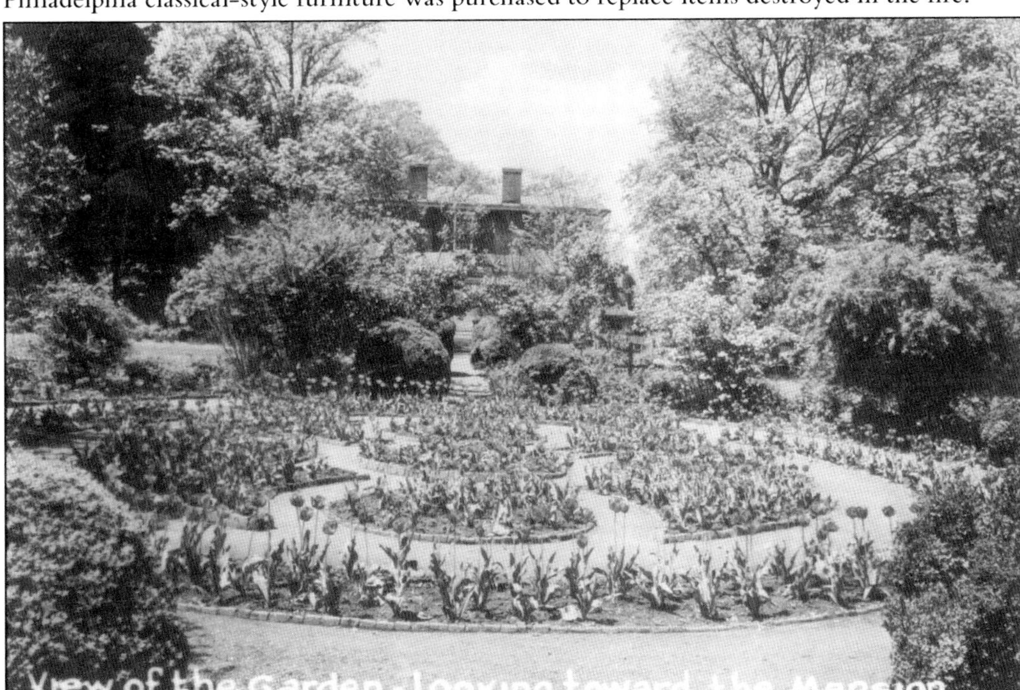

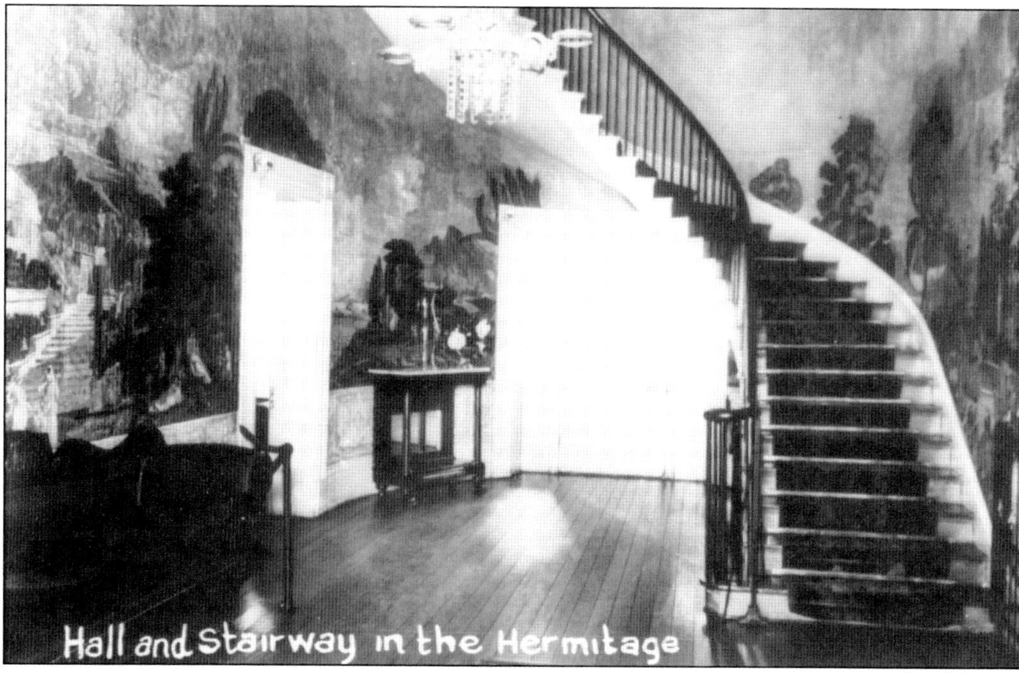

The Hermitage mansion contains much of the original furniture and decorations purchased during the 1837 remodeling. The beautiful cantilevered elliptical staircase pictured above was built during the renovation. Several of the wallpapers from that period still remain on the walls today. A collection of the family's portraits, as well as some of Jackson's swords, can be seen along with other items throughout the house. When viewing his bedroom, visitors can see the bed on which Andrew Jackson died. His office contains books and newspapers he read. Because of the age of the furnishings, each room is behind protective glass.

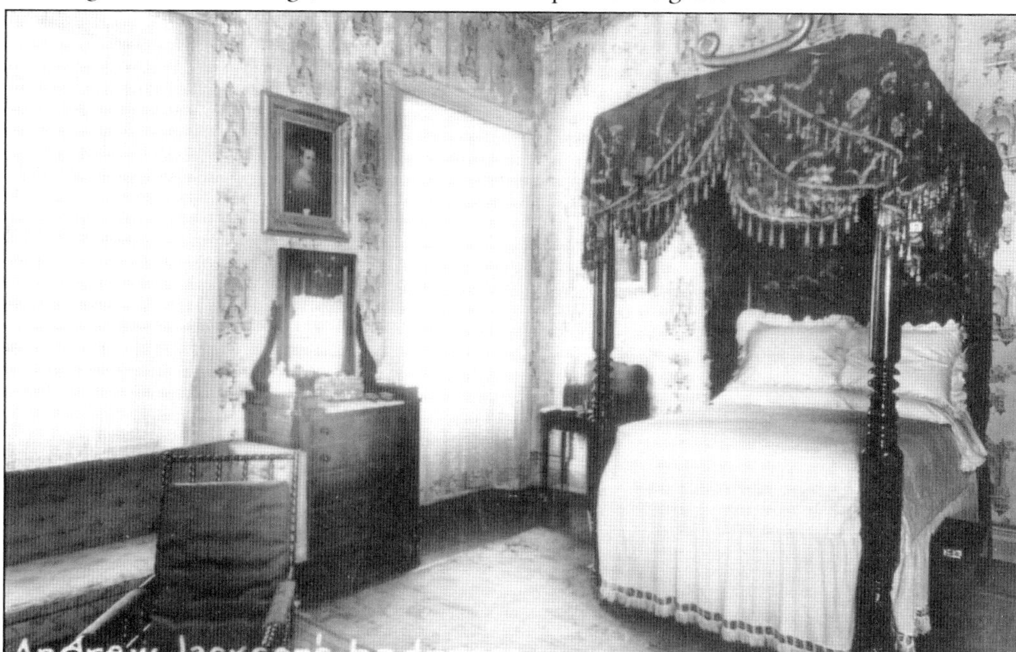

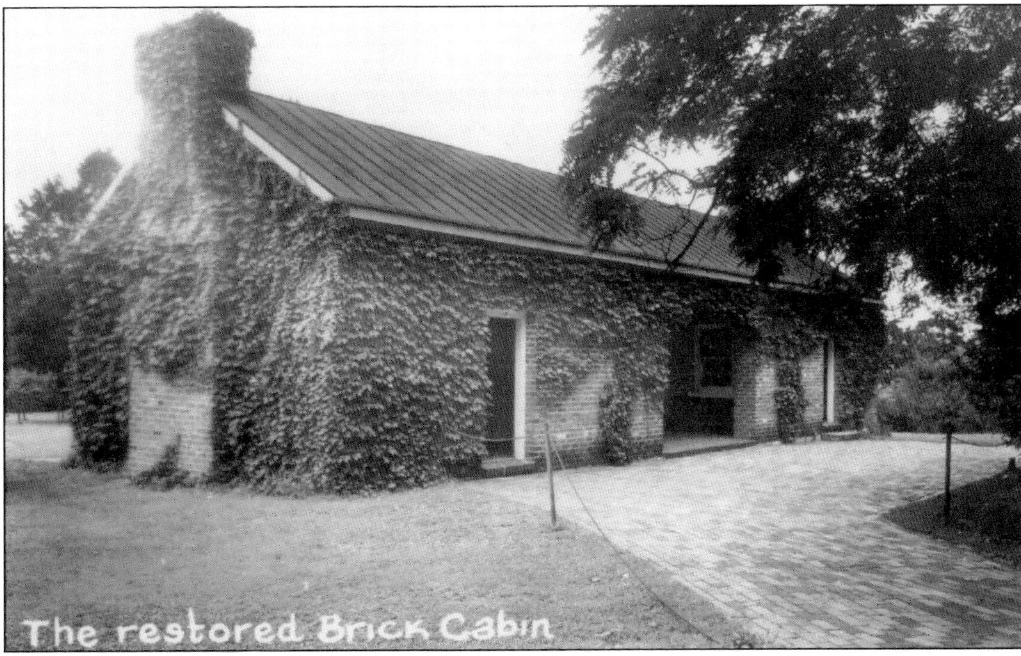

After walking up the cedar-lined driveway and touring the mansion, visitors can also explore the surrounding grounds. The Ladies' Hermitage Association has restored many of the Hermitage's original buildings. There are 32 historic buildings on the plantation, including the log cabin where Rachel and Andrew Jackson lived before the mansion was built, which was later used as slave quarters.

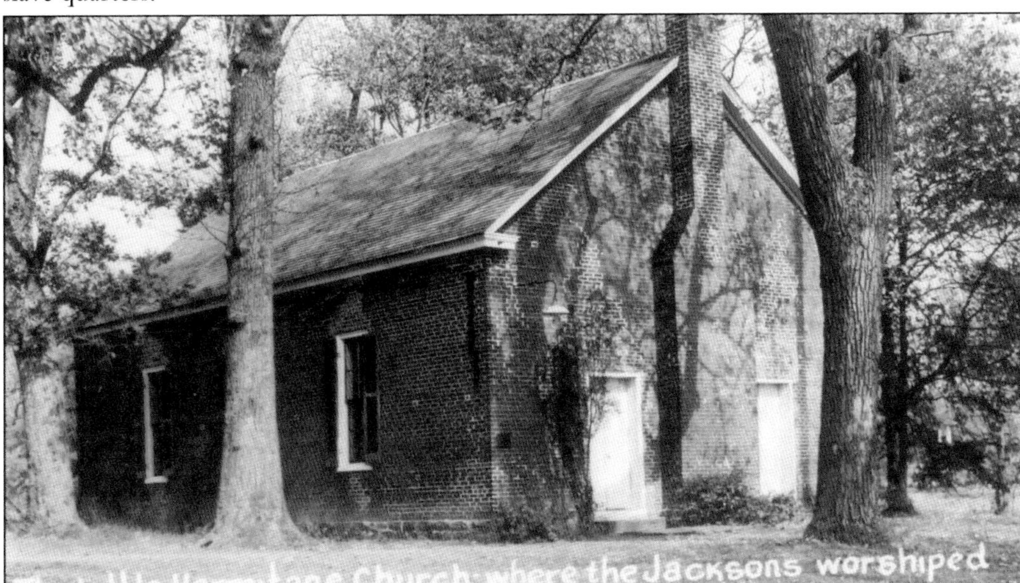

In 1823, Jackson and his neighbors built a small church on land he had donated. Originally named Ephesus Church, it measured 30 feet by 50 feet. In 1839, the building went through a major renovation and was renamed the Hermitage Church in honor of Andrew Jackson. The Ladies' Hermitage Association bought the church in 1965, after it was gutted by a fire. It is now used for weddings and other events.

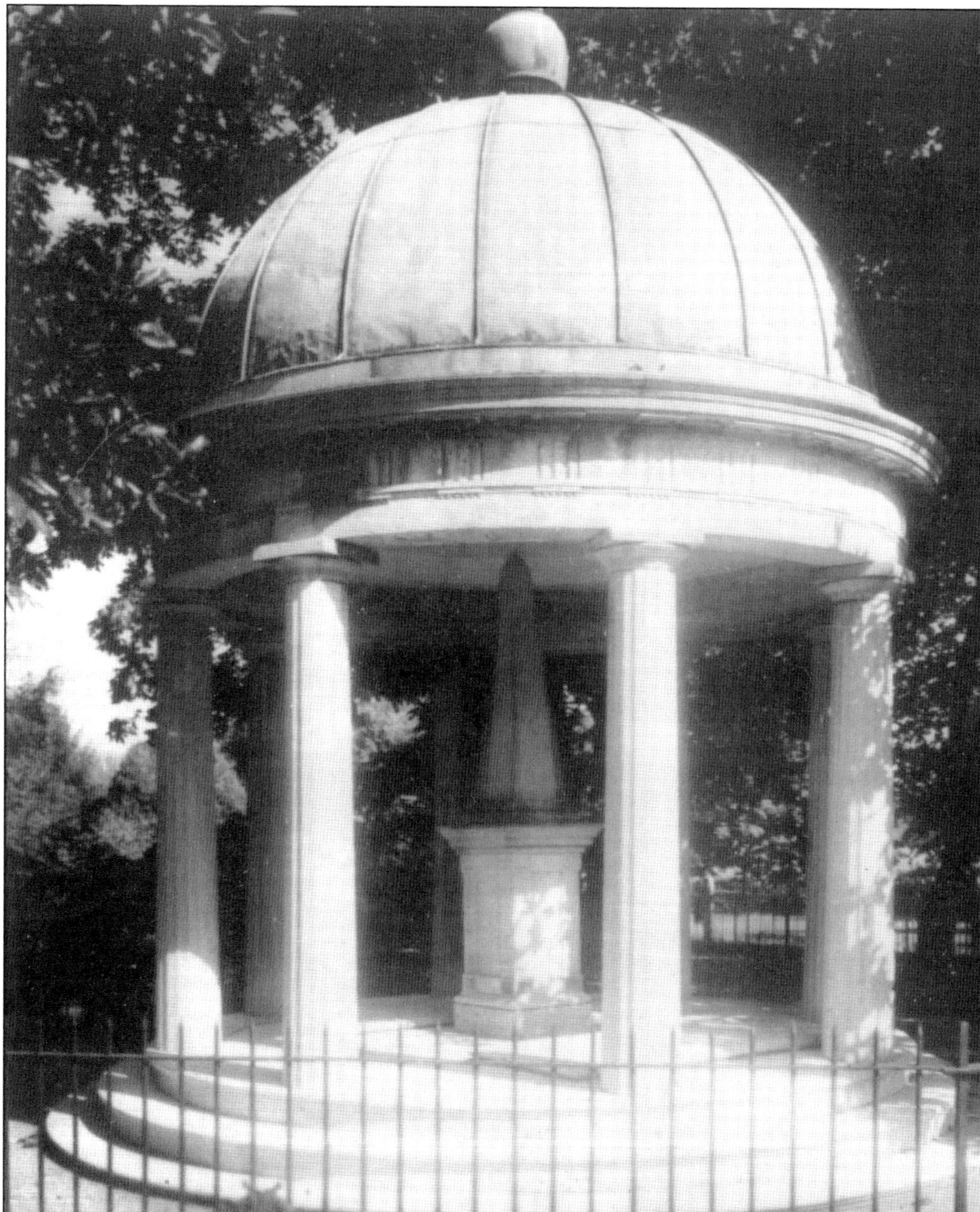

Andrew Jackson's wife, Rachel, died on December 22, 1828, shortly before his inauguration as president of the United States. Since their beautiful garden was one of her favorite places, he had her buried there, using a small frame house as a temporary marker. In 1831, he had the mansion remodeled and a limestone tomb built as a permanent monument. The domed tomb had a copper roof and was built in the style of a Greek temple. Next to the tomb was a small family cemetery. After his second presidential term was over, in 1837, Jackson spent the next eight years at the Hermitage, visiting his wife's grave as long as his health would allow. When he died, his body was laid to rest beneath the tomb next to his beloved Rachel. His inscription was elegant and simple, stating "General Andrew Jackson, March 15, 1767—June 8, 1845."

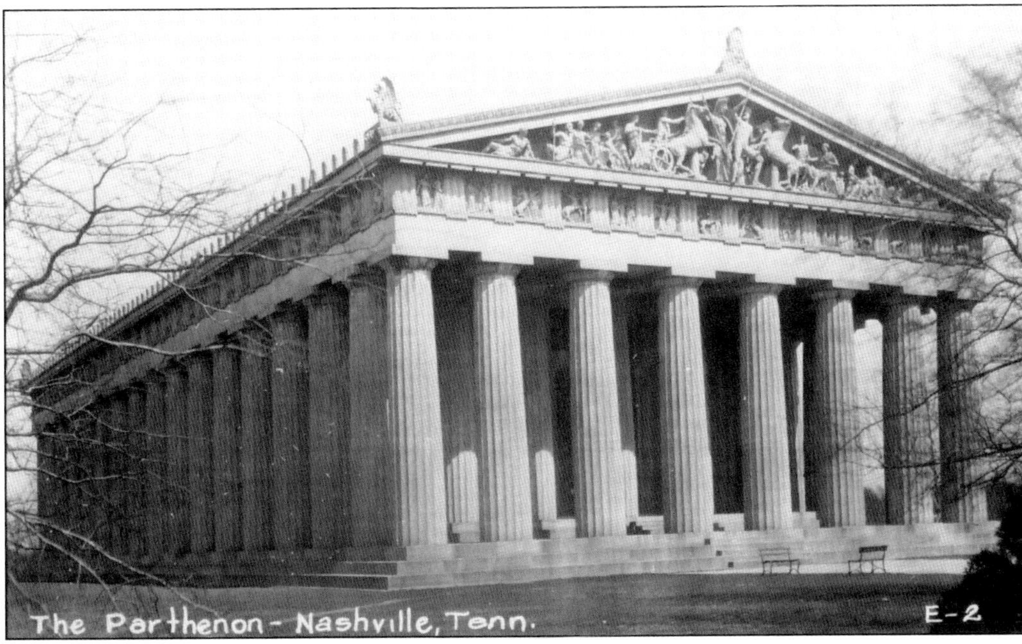

Because of its many colleges and universities, Nashville was once known as the Athens of the South. In reference to the nickname, a full-scale replica of the ancient Greek temple was built for the Tennessee Centennial Exposition of 1897. Meant to be a temporary exhibit, the Parthenon was constructed of inexpensive materials.

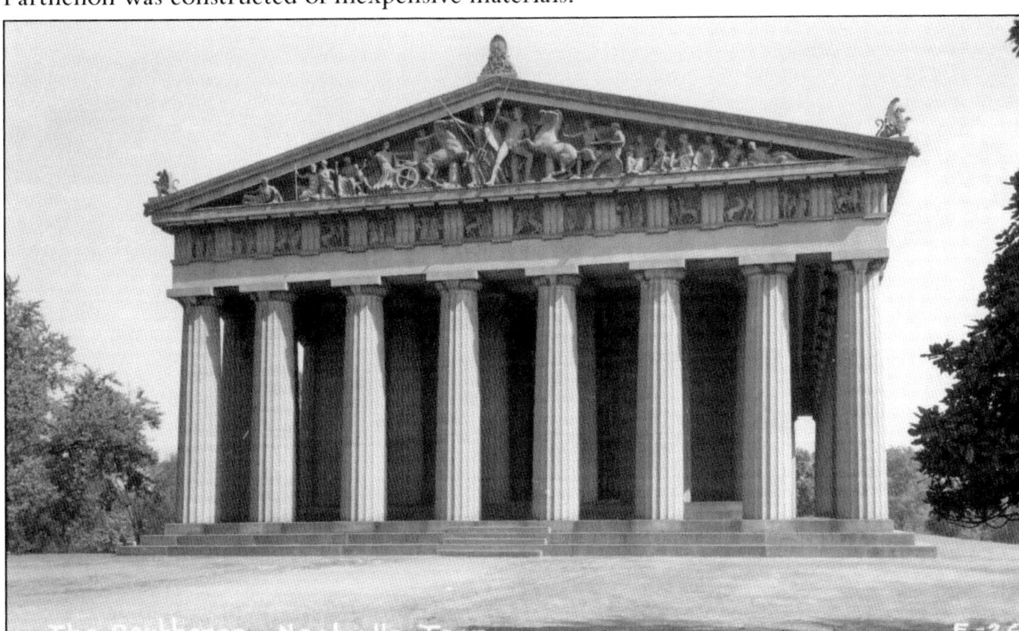

After the huge success of the six-month exhibition, all exhibits were eventually removed—except the Parthenon. Five years after the exposition, the recently formed Nashville Board of Parks created Centennial Park, with the Parthenon as the centerpiece. The building deteriorated over the years, and parts of it were removed for safety reasons. In 1920, Nashville decided to reconstruct the Parthenon using concrete and other permanent materials.

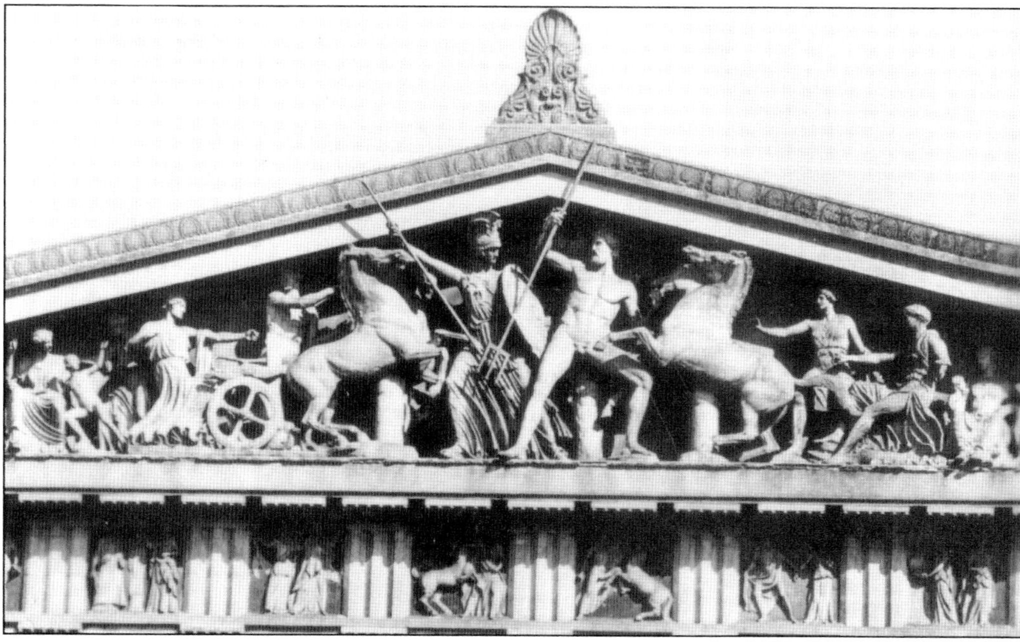

Construction of the exterior of the building was completed by 1925. Sculptures on the west gable of the roof depict a struggle between Athena and Poseidon for control of Athens. The east pediment depicts the birth of Athena from the head of Zeus. The sculptors for the pediments were Belle Kinney, a native of Nashville, and her husband, Leopold Scholz.

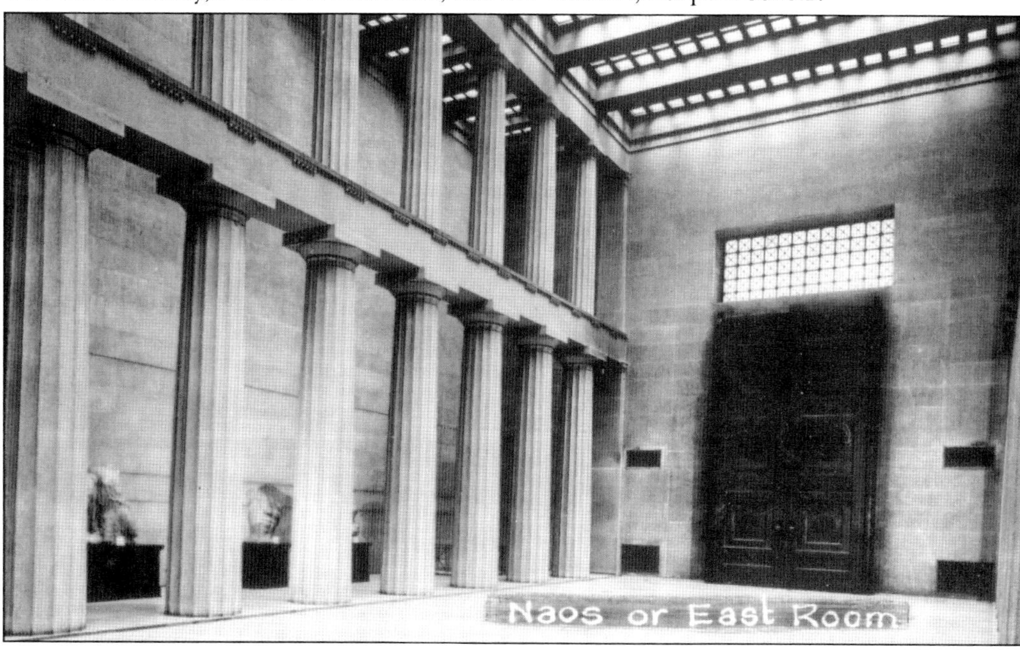

Construction of the interior of the Parthenon was completed by 1931. The Parthenon has two sets of bronze doors; each door is 24 feet high, seven feet wide, and weighs over seven tons. The interior consists of two rooms, the Naos on the east side and the Treasury Room on the west. Galleries were built to display a large number of paintings on loan from Europe and various parts of the United States.

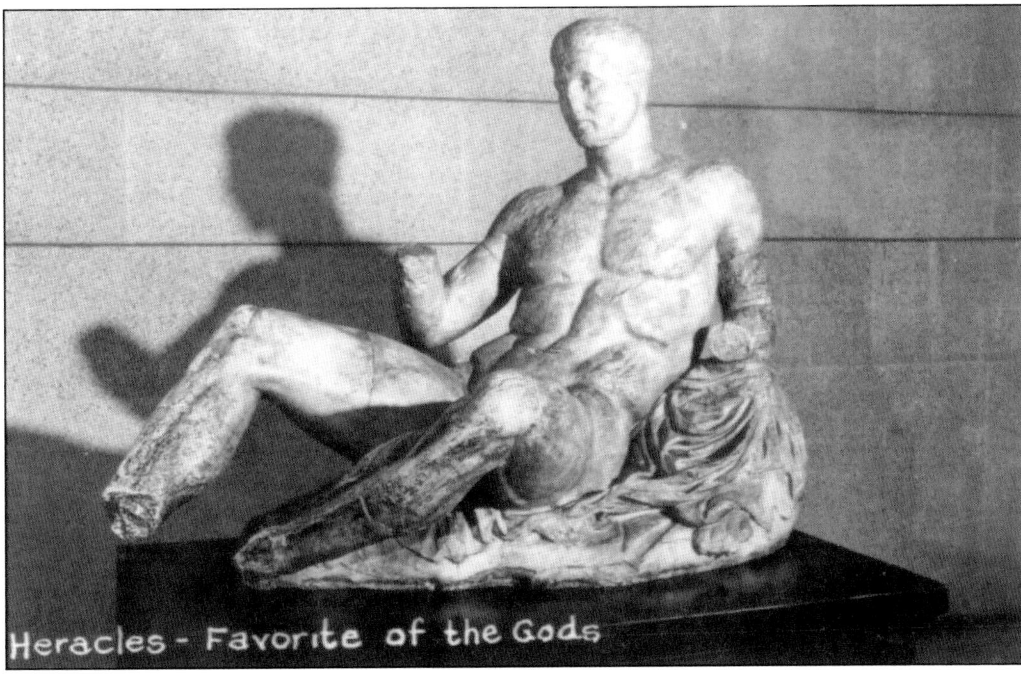

The statues in these postcards are from the east pediment, where Greek gods witnessed the birth of Athena. An explosion in 1687 damaged much of the original Greek Parthenon. The Turks, who had conquered Athens in 1456, were defending Athens from the invading Venetians and using the Parthenon as a powder house when the explosion occurred. Lord Elgin, a British ambassador, obtained several of the salvaged statues from the Turkish government in 1801 and later sold them to the British government. Nashville purchased casts of these statues from the British Museum to make replicas for the Nashville Parthenon. Because of financial restraints, the Parthenon did not have a replica of the 42-foot statue of Athena when it reopened in 1931. After donations were collected for several years, the statue of Athena was finally unveiled in 1990.

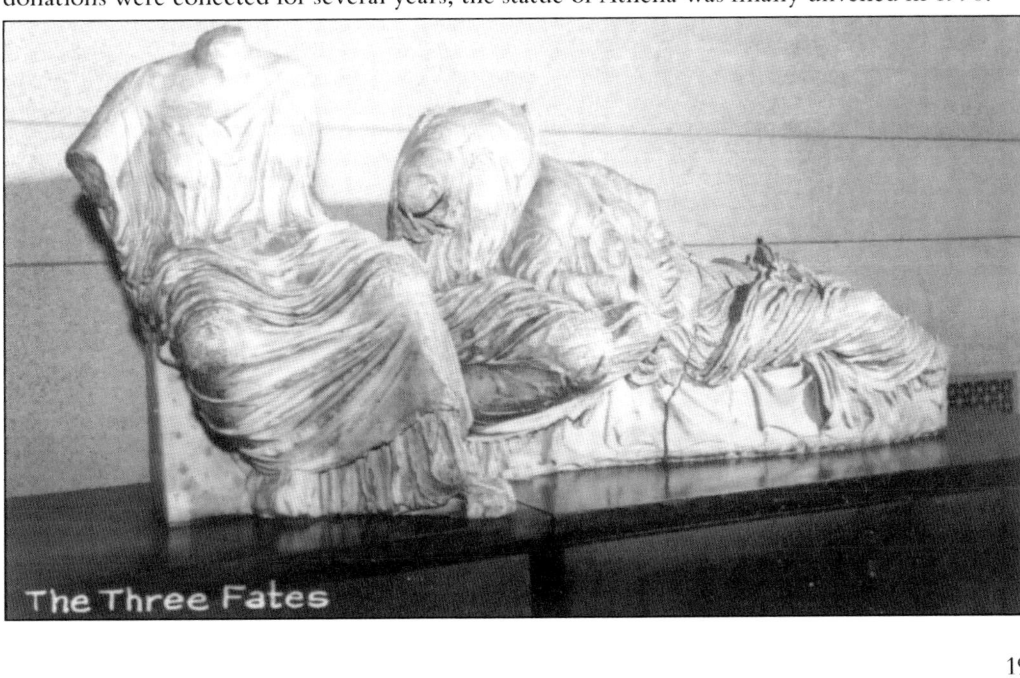

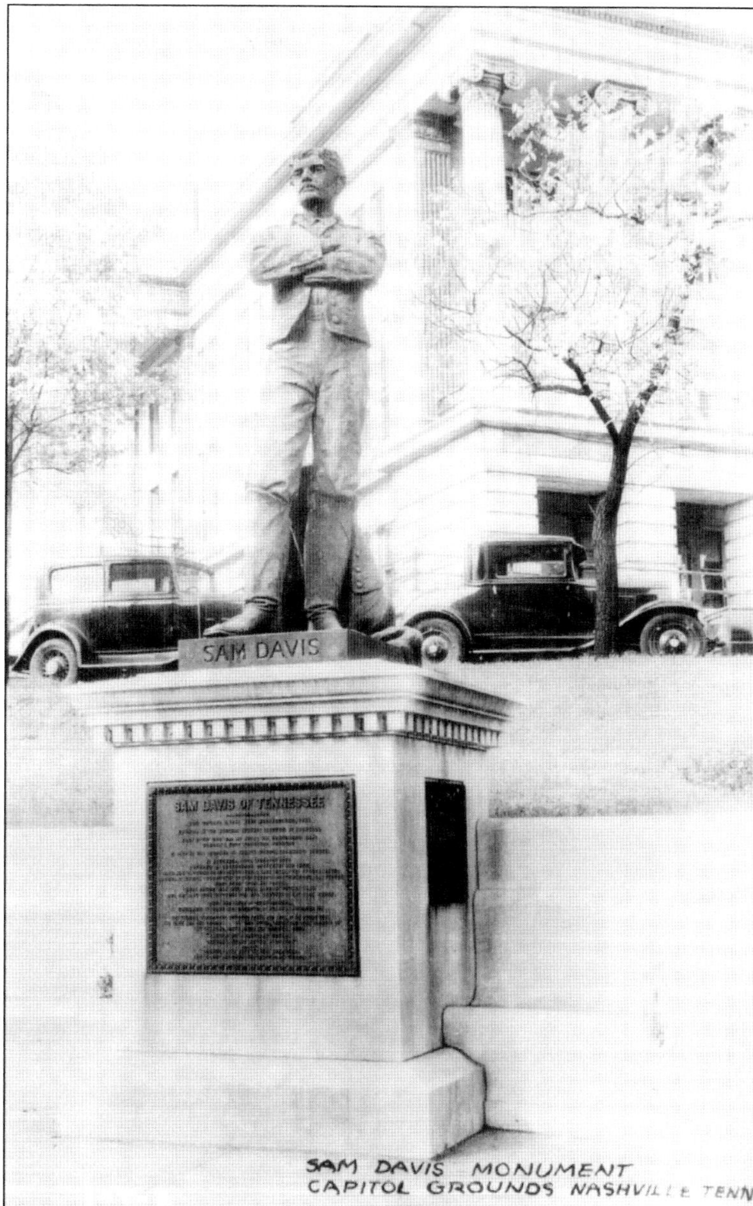

A statue of Confederate war hero Sam Davis sits on the grounds of Tennessee's state capitol in Nashville. Nashville did not become the permanent state capital until 1843; it was originally located in Knoxville in 1796. Over the next several years, the capital was moved between Nashville, Knoxville, and Murfreesboro. A narrow vote by the legislature finally made Nashville the permanent location. The capitol was built on a piece of land donated to the state that was known as Campbell's Hill. Construction of the capitol started in 1845 and was completed in 1859. The building was designed by William Strickland, who died before it was completed. The statue of Sam Davis was unveiled on April 29, 1909. Still a popular tourist attraction today, visiting the capitol and grounds, as well as the nearby Bicentennial Capitol Mall State Park, is free to the public. The 19-acre park was established to commemorate Tennessee's 200th birthday and offers visitors a superb view of the capitol.

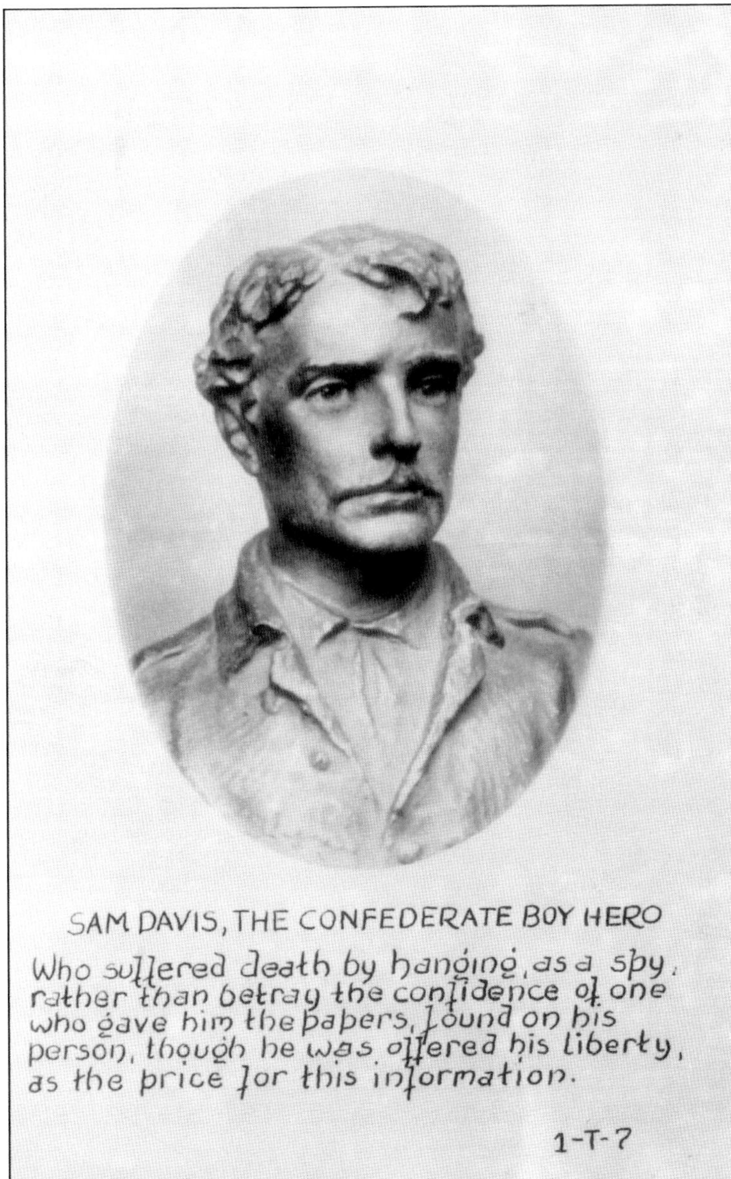

Known as the "Boy Hero of the Confederacy," Samuel Davis was born in 1842 and died in 1863. He attended the Western Military Academy in Nashville for a short time before enlisting in the 1st Tennessee Infantry Regiment, where he fought under Robert E. Lee in the Cheat Mountain campaign in western Virginia. The regiment also fought in the battles of Shiloh and Stones River. By 1863, a large part of middle Tennessee was occupied by the Union army. Davis joined a group known as Coleman's Scouts, whose purpose was to disrupt communications behind enemy lines and collect information on Union troop movements. Even though they wore Confederate uniforms, they were considered spies by the Union army. In November of 1863, Union soldiers captured Davis and discovered he had concealed documents containing information on Union troop movements. He was court-martialed as a spy and sentenced to hang. His last words before the sentence was carried out were, "I would rather die a thousand deaths than betray a friend or be false to duty."

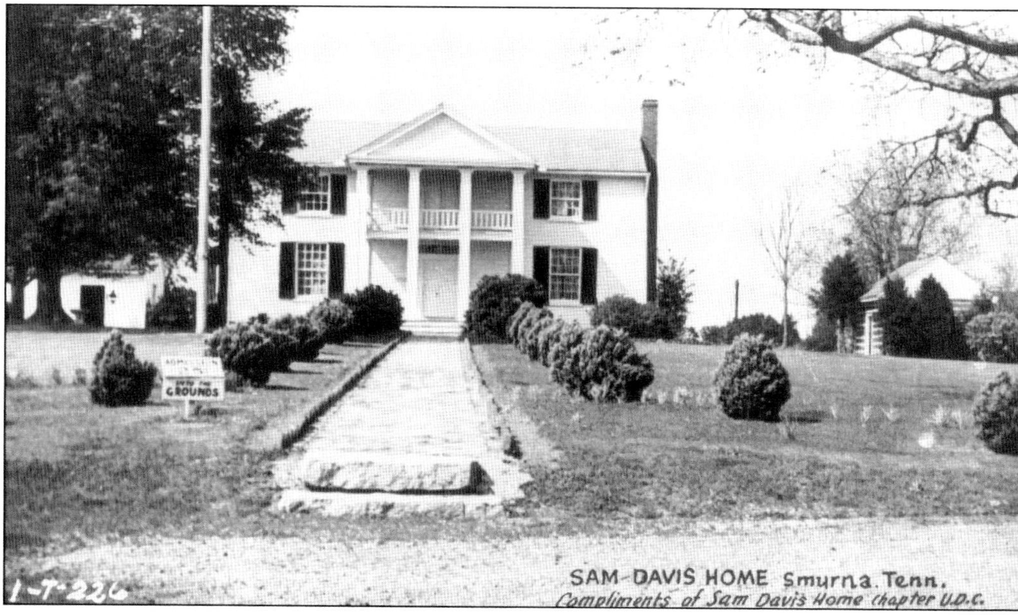

Charles Lewis and Jane Simmons Davis, an upper-middle-class couple, were the parents of Sam Davis. The home where he spent his childhood was built in 1810. The Davis family renovated the house in 1850. Visitors have been able to tour this beautiful home and grounds since 1930, three years after the State of Tennessee purchased the property for $16,000.

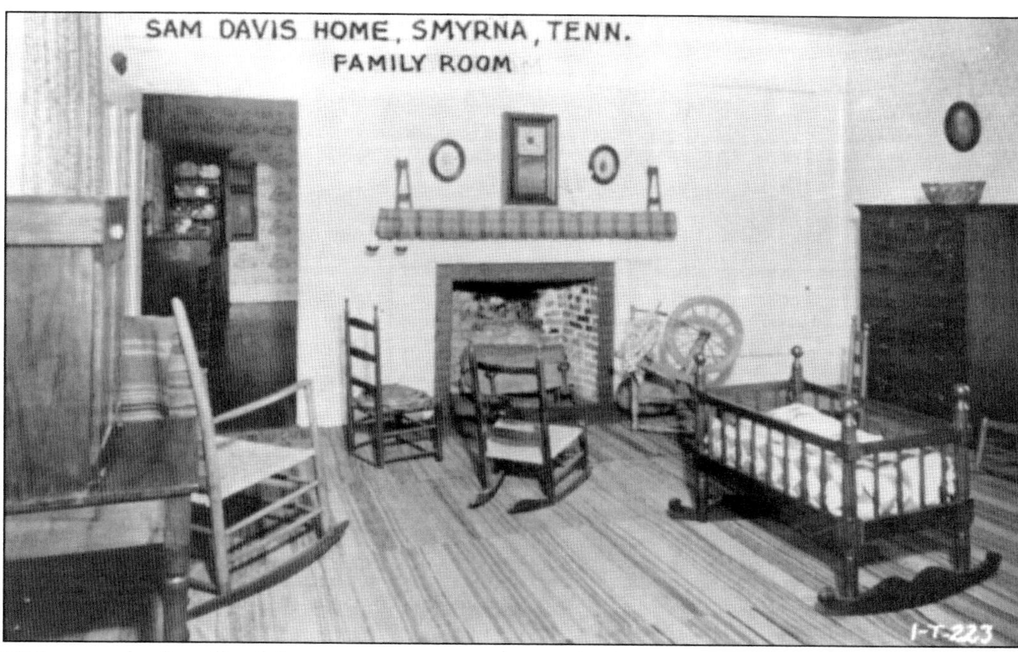

Visitors to the Sam Davis home can temporarily step back in time. The interior rooms contain over 100 pieces owned by the Davis family. Most of the woodwork, including all of the doors and floors, date back to the 1850 renovation. The house contains nine rooms, one of which has Confederate guns and other period pieces on display.

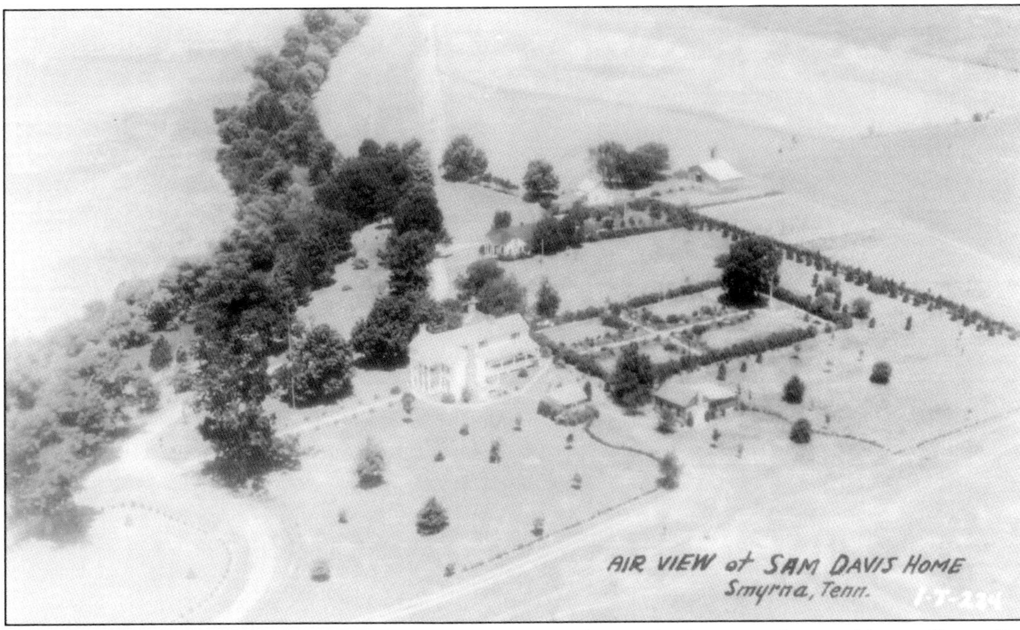

This postcard shows an aerial view of the Sam Davis home in Smyrna, located just a few miles from US 41 (part of the original Dixie Highway). Guided tours of the two-story house and grounds include many original buildings, such as the kitchen and smokehouse. Cotton is still grown on the 160-acre farm.

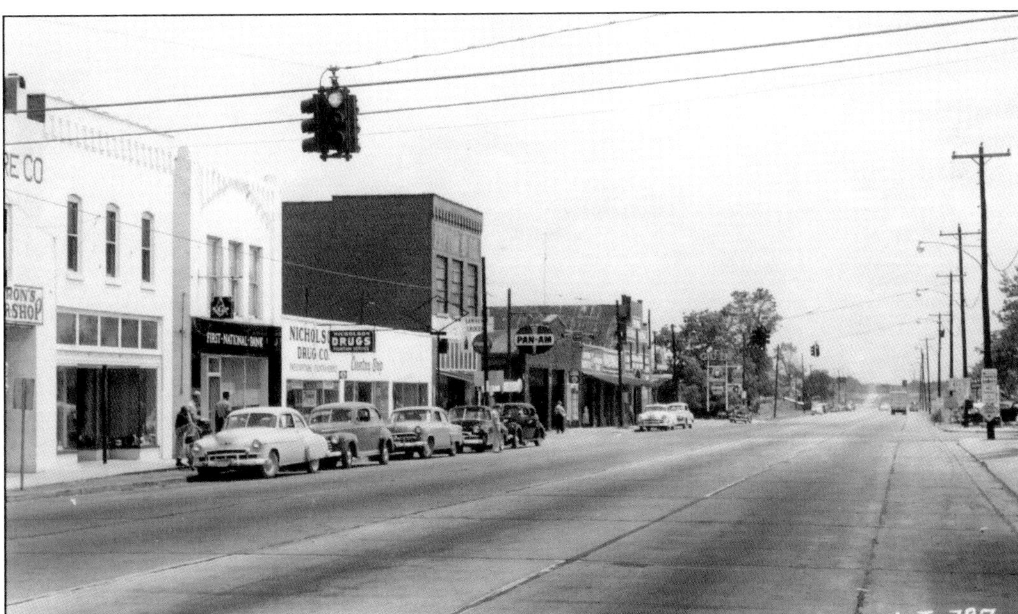

Smyrna began as a farming community in the mid-1800s. The picture above shows a portion of US 41 on the Dixie Highway in downtown Smyrna. Though the businesses have changed, many of the original buildings remain. Nearby is a train depot that once served as a railroad refueling station on the main line of the Nashville, Chattanooga & St. Louis Railway (NC&StL).

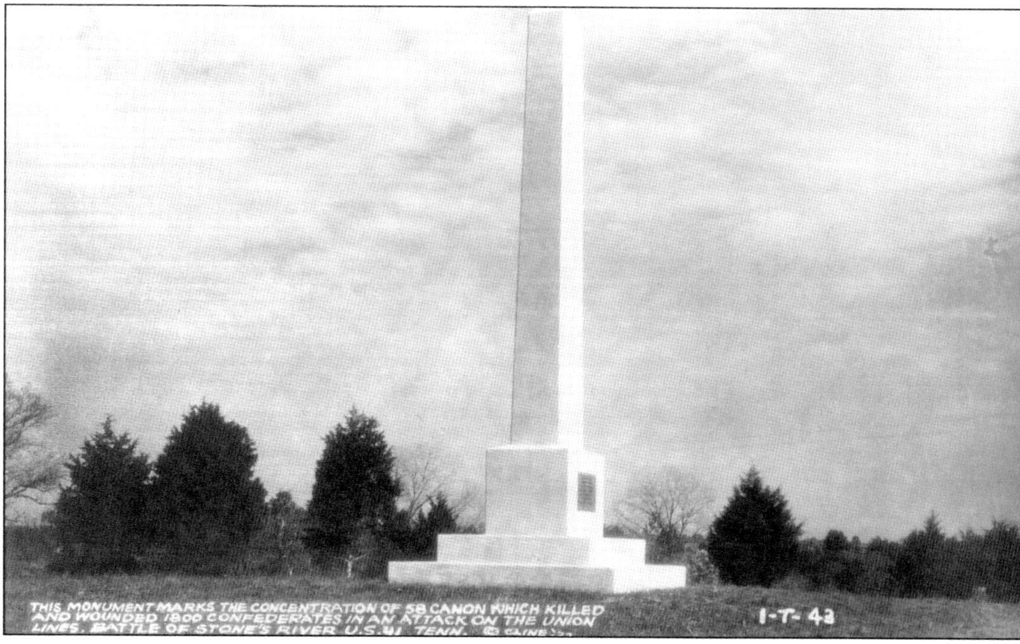

In 1906, the NC&StL railroad erected the 34-foot Artillery Monument to memorialize the battle that took place at Stones River on January 2, 1863. Gen. Braxton Bragg had ordered an attack of the enemy army in occupation of the rise overlooking McFadden's Ford on the east side of Stones River. The Confederates faced a barrage of cannon fire that killed or wounded 1,800 men. (Courtesy of Jim Laughlin.)

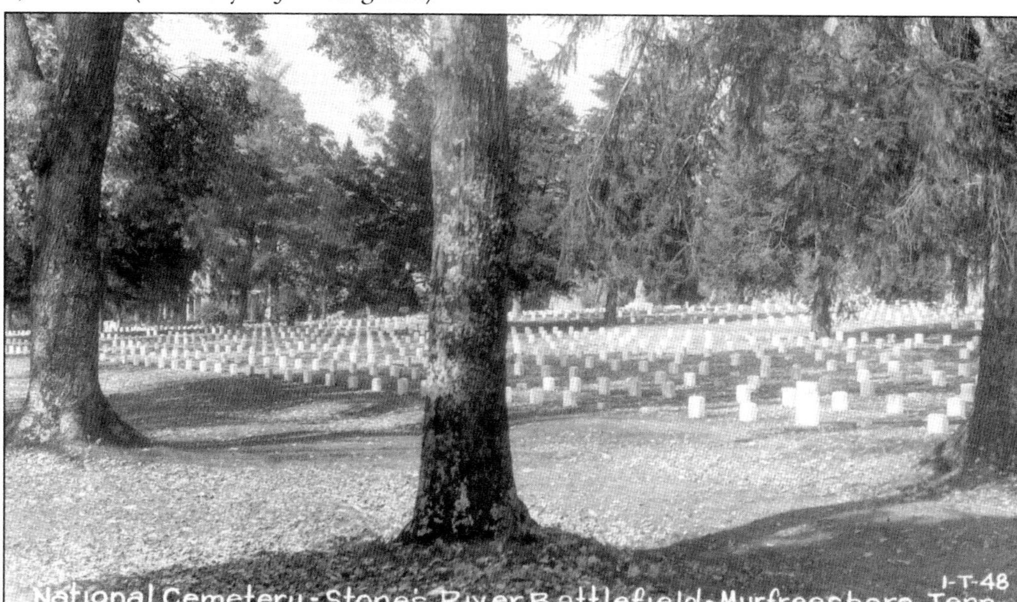

Stones River National Cemetery was established by military order in March 1864 to inter the Union dead. Casualties who had initially been buried on the Stones River battlefield or in Franklin, Shelbyville, Tullahoma, Cowan, and other areas within about 90 miles had to be moved to the new location. Most of the reburials were finished by 1867. There are 6,124 soldiers buried there.

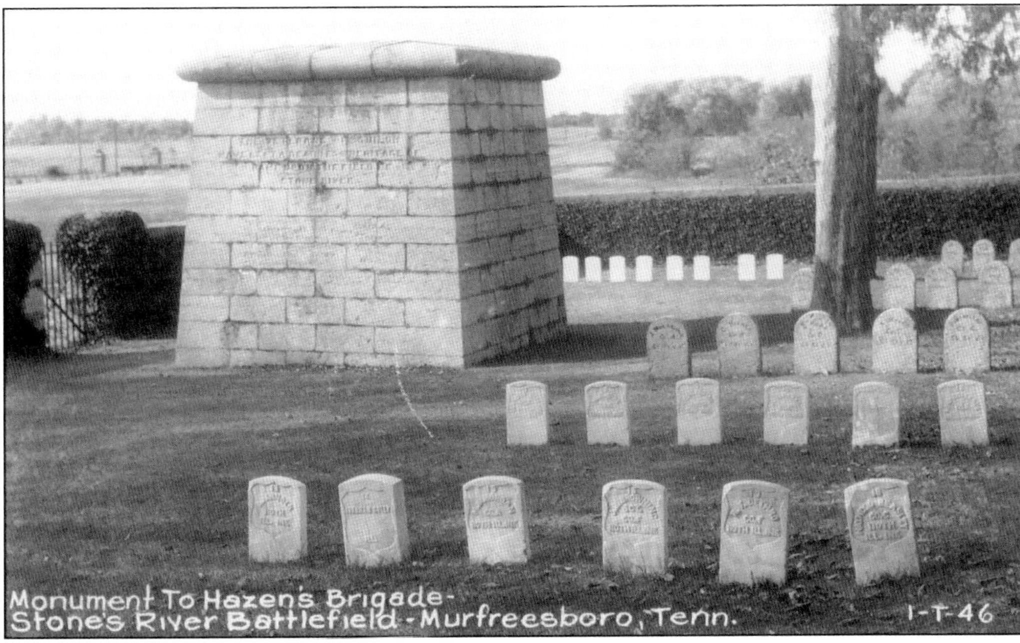

Hazen's Monument, at Stones River National Battlefield in Murfreesboro, is thought to be the first memorial created for soldiers of the Civil War. It was built after the Battle of Stones River, fought on December 31, 1862. A portion of the southern face of the monument reads: "Their faces towards heaven, their feet to the foe." In 1985, a time capsule of sorts was discovered during a restoration of the monument; nine Civil War artifacts were found inside.

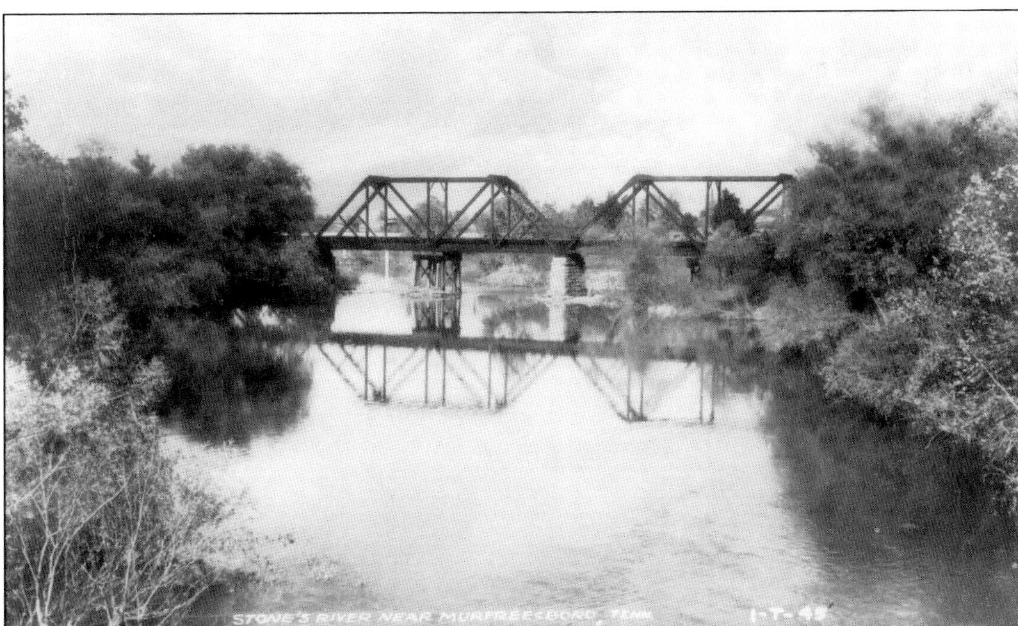

Going south along the Dixie Highway (US 41), this bridge, once known as the Nashville Turnpike Bridge, crossed the Stones River until it was replaced in 2005. The river was named for Uriah Stone, who was one of a small group of long hunters that discovered it in 1766.

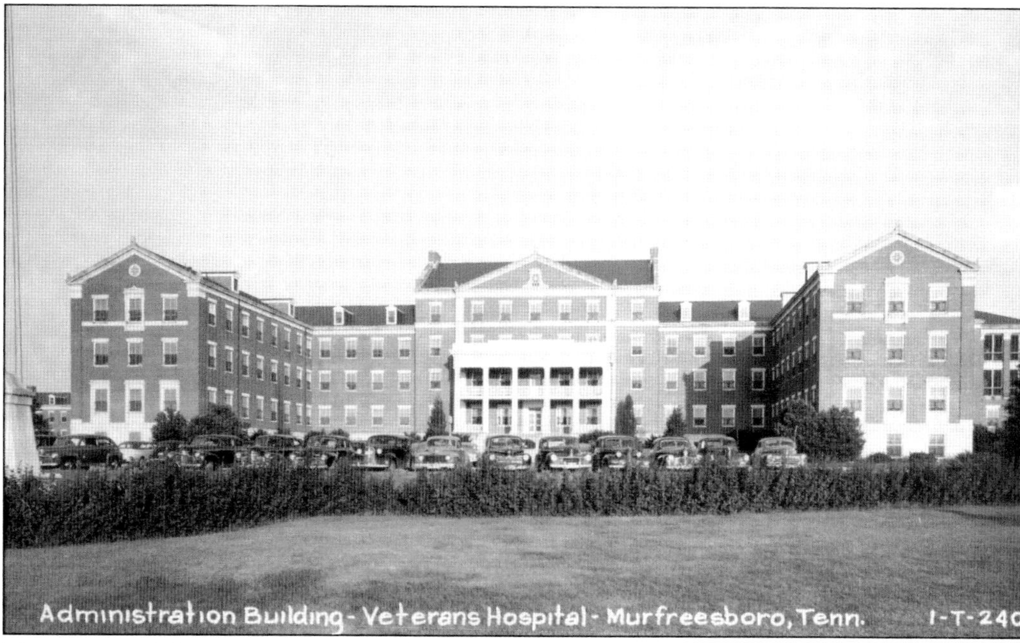

The Veterans Administration Hospital, as it was called when it opened in 1940, is now officially called the Tennessee Valley Healthcare System–Alvin C. York Campus and is a part of the Department of Veterans Affairs. The building of the hospital was funded jointly by the Public Works Administration (PWA), the Works Progress Administration (WPA), and the Veterans Administration (VA). It was the most important New Deal project in Rutherford County. Pres. Franklin D. Roosevelt authorized its construction in 1936, and the PWA, which was a part of the National Industrial Recovery Act of 1933, allocated $674,000 for the undertaking in 1938. When the facility opened, it was the second-largest VA hospital in the United States, with 21 classical and Colonial Revival-style buildings on the grounds.

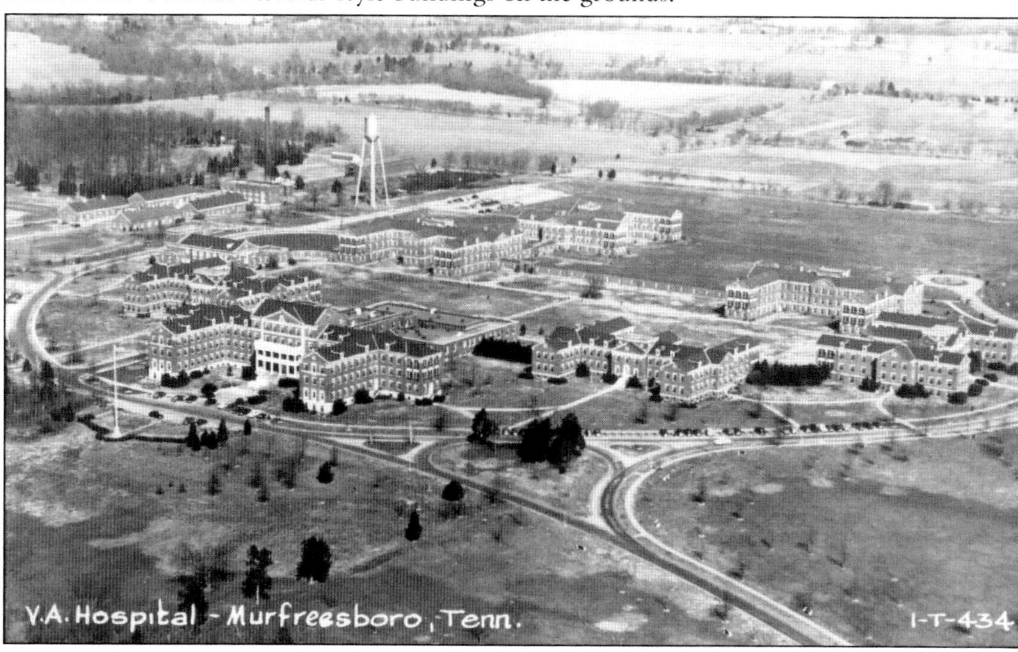

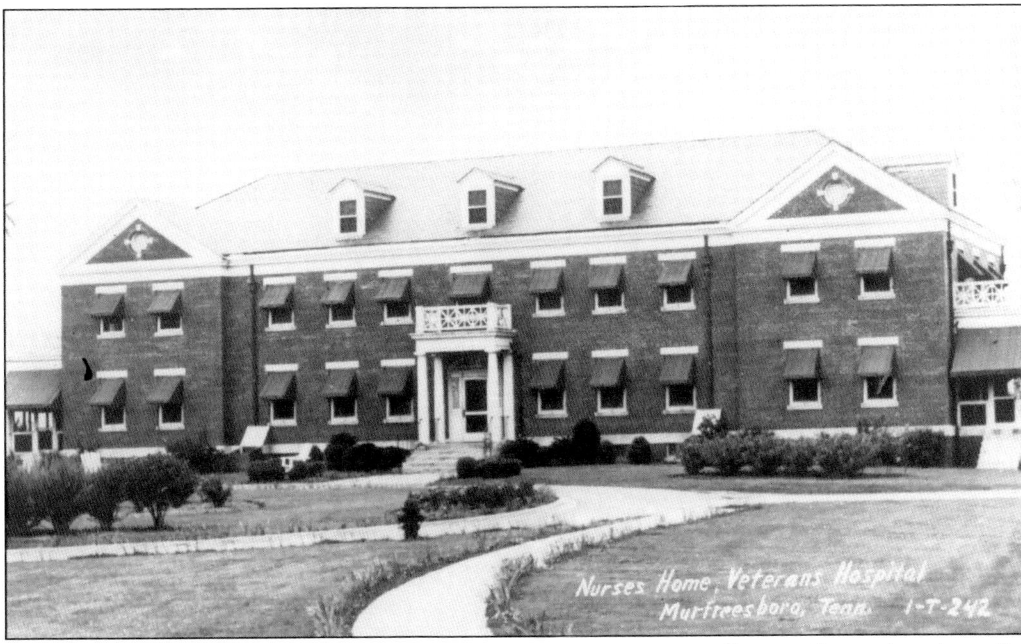

The acreage surrounding the veterans' hospital has been historically significant since just after the American Revolution. It was a part of the land grant given to Isaac Shelby by North Carolina for his work surveying middle Tennessee. Thomas Rucker purchased it from Shelby in 1801. When the Tennessee General Assembly selected a committee in 1811 to determine a new permanent location for Rutherford County's seat, Rucker's property narrowly lost the vote to land owned by William Lytle. A Tennessee Historical Commission marker in front of the hospital marks the surrounding area as the temporary Civil War encampment of Confederate Gen. Joseph Wheeler, cavalry commander of the Army of Tennessee. From this location, his brigade moved north to Walter Hill and then west to Jefferson to successfully raid Union leader Maj. Gen. William S. Rosecrans's army.

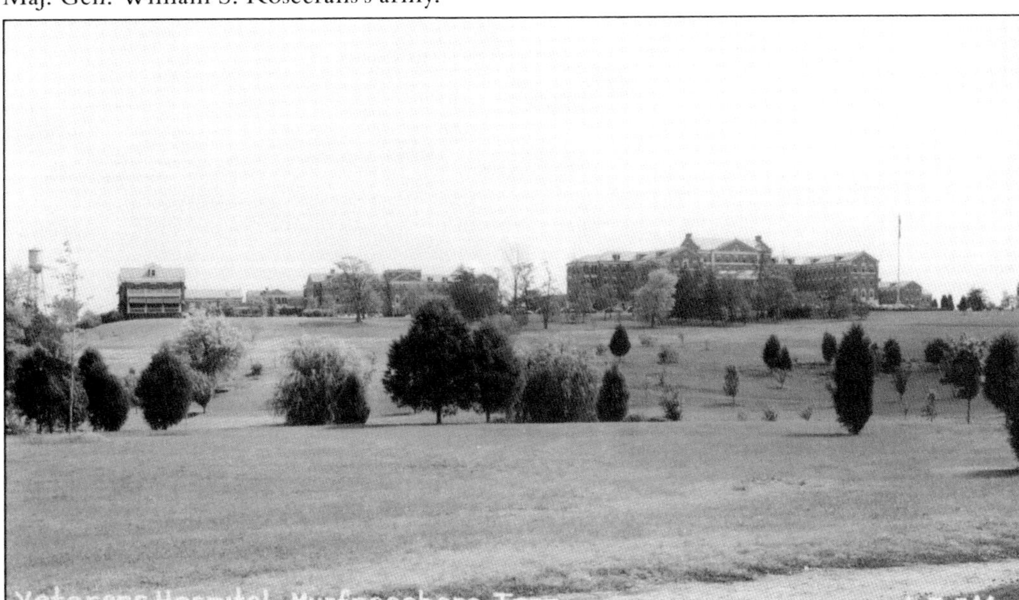

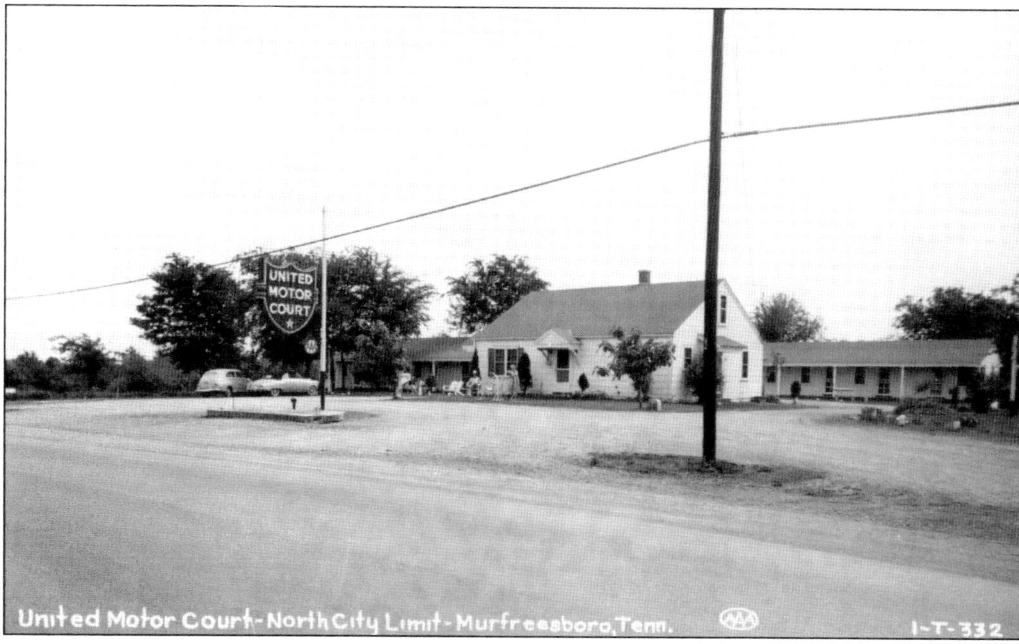

The United Motor Court was a popular rest stop along the Dixie Highway at the northern city limits of Murfreesboro. Organized in California in 1933, United Motor Courts was one of the most successful referral chains in the United States. The group promised "clean rooms, quality beds and good service." Many of them later withdrew from the group to form Quality Courts United, which is known today as Choice Hotels.

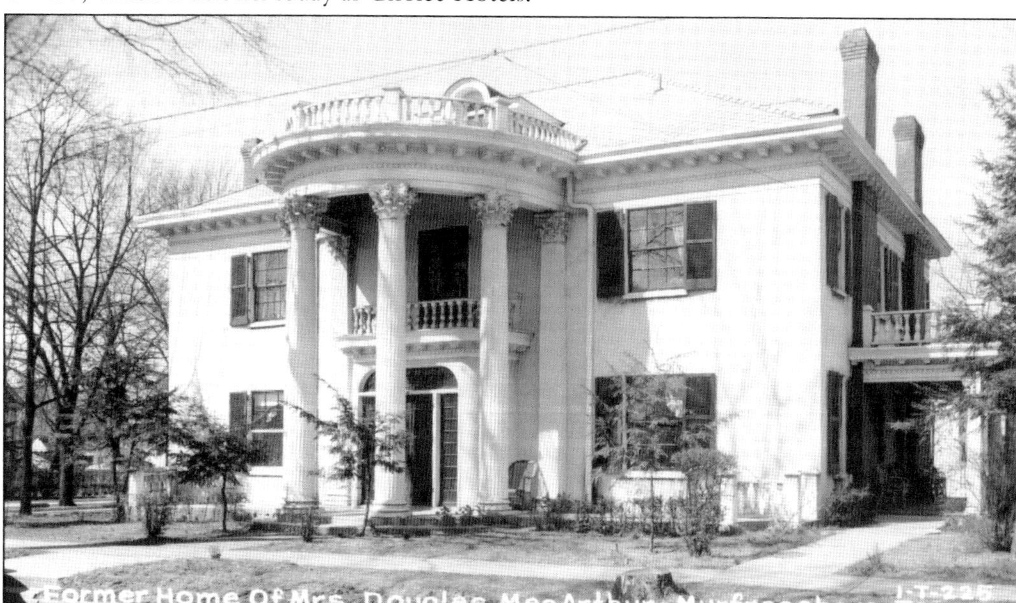

Faircloth, as many have referred to the childhood home of Jean Faircloth MacArthur, wife of Gen. Douglas MacArthur, was once located on East Lytle Street in Murfreesboro. She was the valedictorian in the final graduating class of Murfreesboro's Soule College in 1917. The house was demolished in 1975 to make room for more hospital parking. Jean MacArthur died in 2000 at the age of 101.

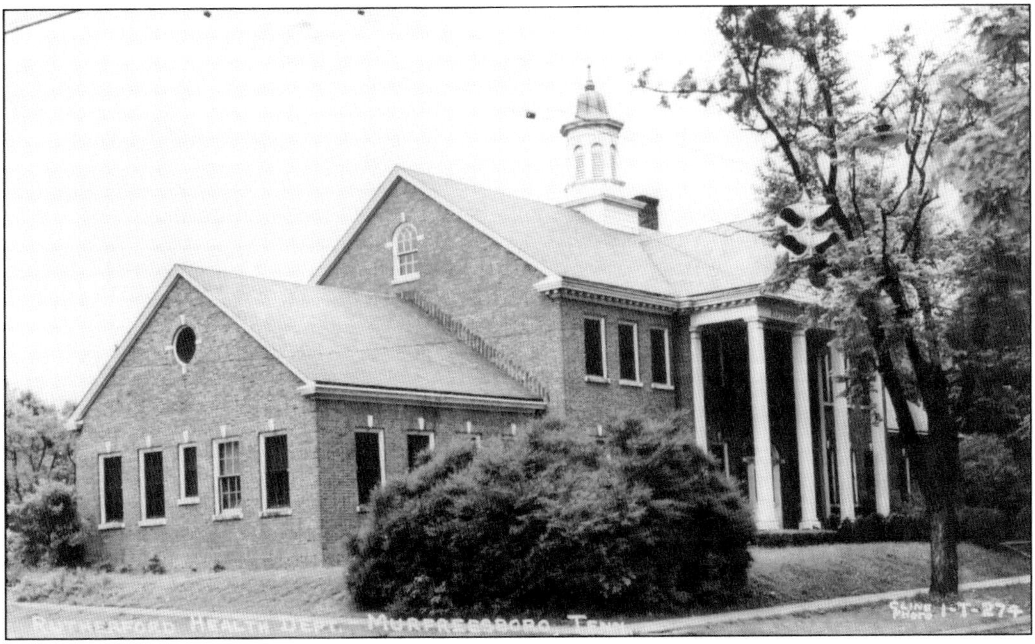

In 1931, the Commonwealth Fund of New York financed the construction of the Rutherford County Health Department building as part of its public healthcare improvement projects. Placed in the National Register of Historic Places in 1992, the building is thought to be one of the best examples of the Colonial Revival style of architecture in Murfreesboro.

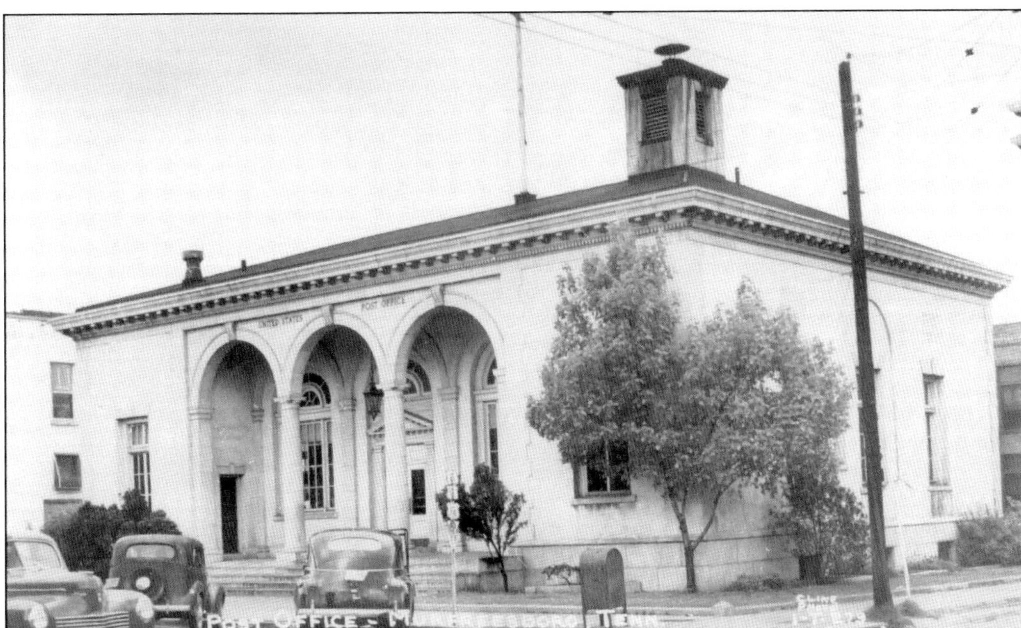

Originally built in Murfreesboro in 1909 as a post office, this Italianate structure once housed the Linebaugh Public Library and is now the Center for the Arts. It is located on West College Street, which was on the Dixie Highway. The library relocated here in 1962 and paid $1 per year to lease it until a new library building was constructed in 1992.

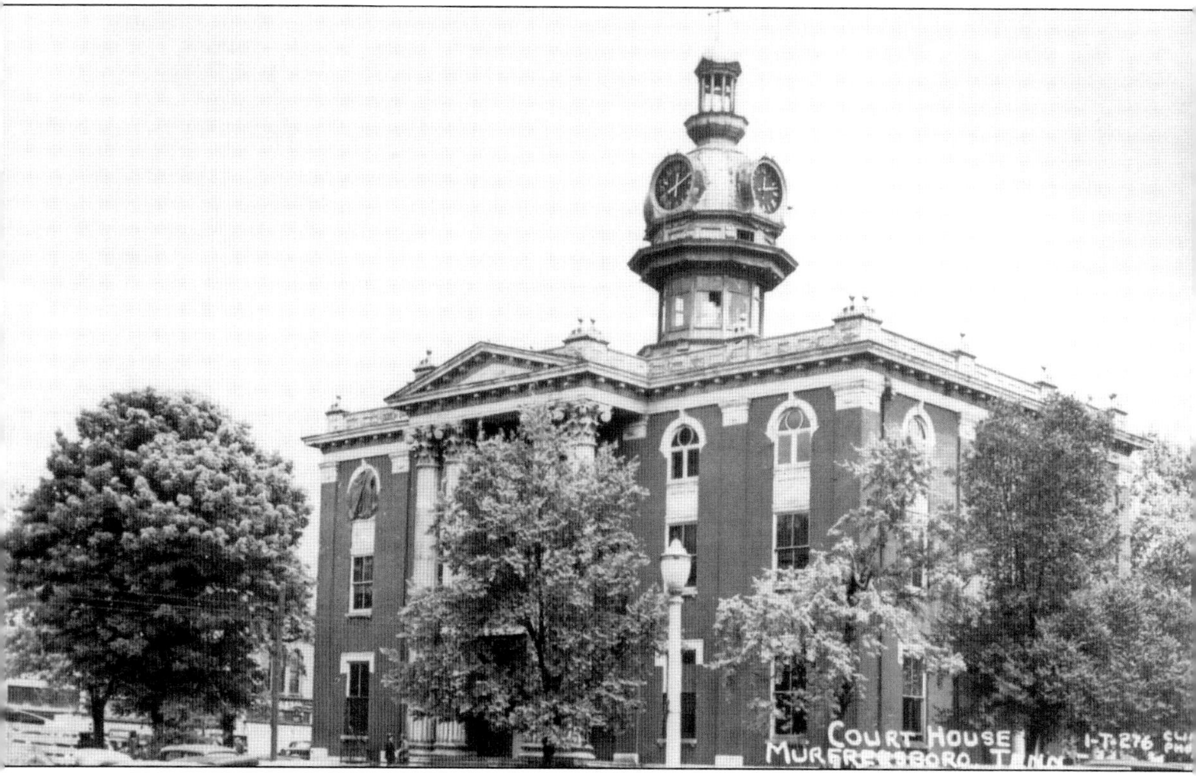

The Rutherford County Courthouse, built in 1859, is listed in the National Register of Historic Places. It is one of only six antebellum courthouses still standing in Tennessee. One of the more interesting stories involving the courthouse is that of the "Human Fly." In early April 1923, a young man arrived in Murfreesboro promising to climb the courthouse for donations. His ascent to the very top of the cupola was successful. Then, as he was descending, he fell from the top of the clock dial to the flat roof of the courthouse, breaking his neck and dying instantly. The *Nashville Banner* newspaper reported that a total of only $13 had been collected. According to local legend, his identity was unknown and he was buried in the pauper section of Murfreesboro's Evergreen Cemetery. However, the man was actually James A. Dearing (stage name Ray Royce), from St. Louis, Missouri. The body of the 26-year-old daredevil was returned to his family in St. Louis and buried on April 11, 1923, at St. Matthew Cemetery (block 6, number 2378).

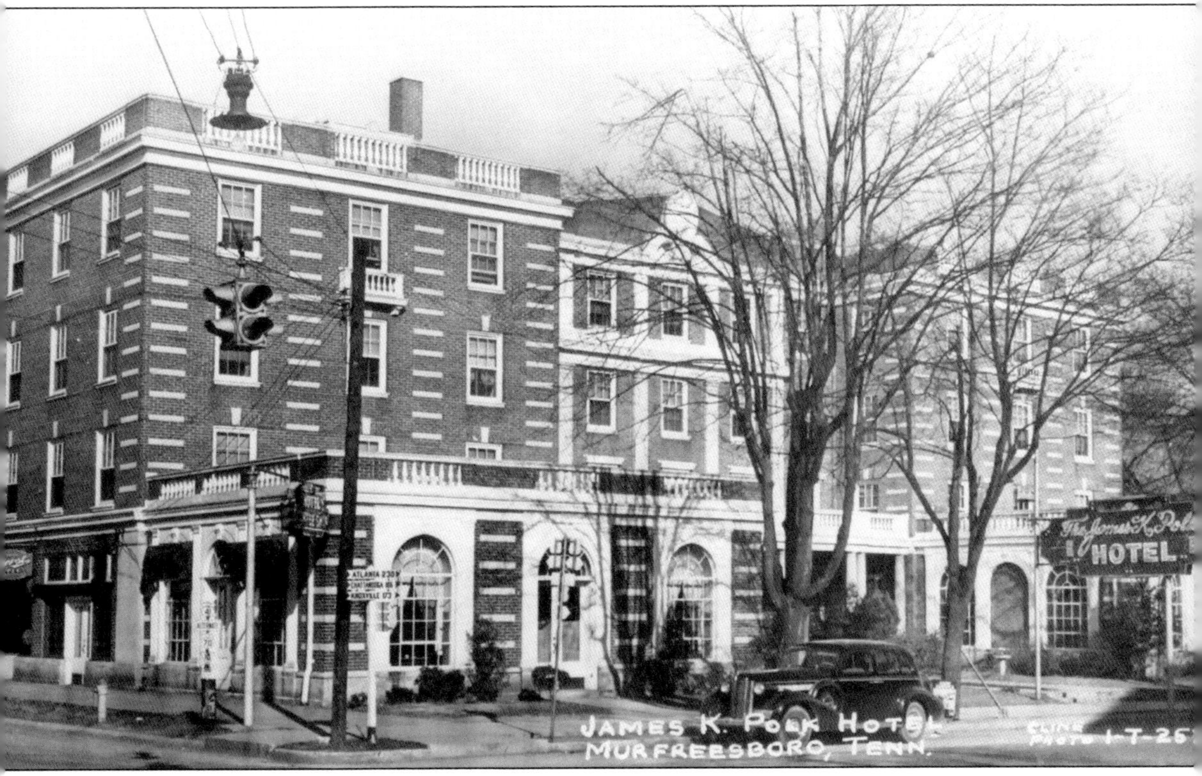

When the James K. Polk Hotel opened along the Dixie Highway (US 41) in 1929, it was Murfreesboro's largest building. Designed by Nashville architect Donald W. Sutherland, it was built in the Colonial Revival style using red textured brick and trimmed with Indiana limestone and white woodwork. According to the August 1933 issue of *Hotel Monthly*, Sutherland's intention was to create a structure that was appropriate to the surrounding area while simultaneously offering all the modern conveniences available. The 57-room hotel was built at a cost of $150,000 and furnished for an additional $65,000. The rooms had Beautyrest mattresses, Simmons springs, Hunter fans, and Bigelow carpet over Ozite (a carpet underlayment made of cattle hair). The furniture was from Lenoir, North Carolina. In 1938, Richard C. Shacklett moved his photography studio from his home on Maple Street to the James K. Polk Hotel. He worked there for the next two years. After a military stint and a number of years spent in Idaho, he returned to Murfreesboro in 1956 to open Shacklett's Photography, a business that remains on the square today.

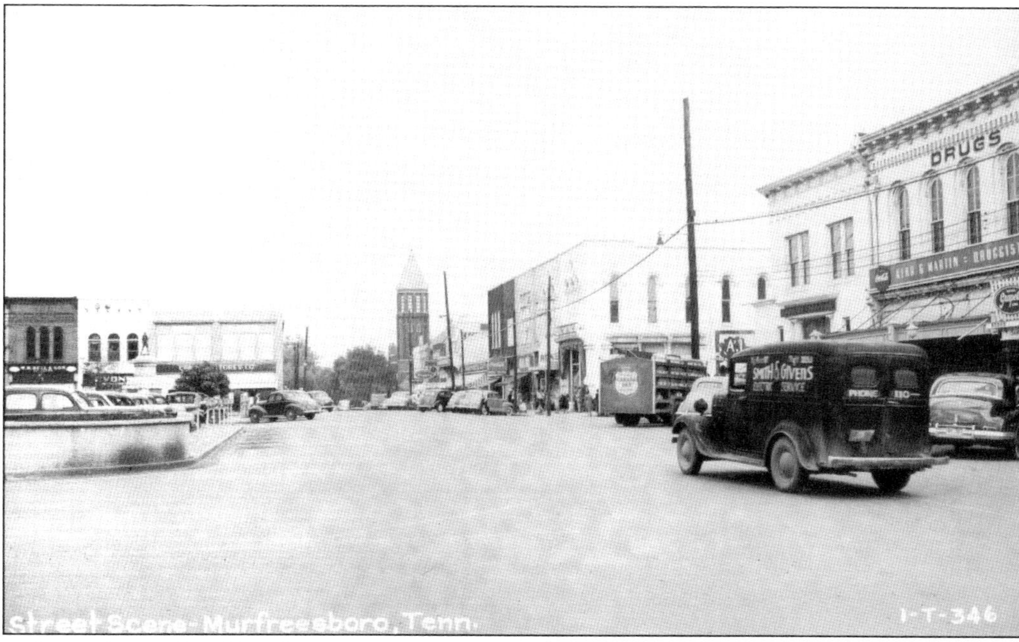

Bell Jewelers is the oldest known continually run retail business in Murfreesboro. William R. Bell opened the store (building pictured at far left) in 1879 at 8 North Public Square. After changing hands a few times, the company has been run by the Tidwell family for more than 35 years. It remained on the square until 1998, when the Tidwells relocated to Broad Street, providing more showroom space and convenient parking. (Courtesy of Jim Laughlin.)

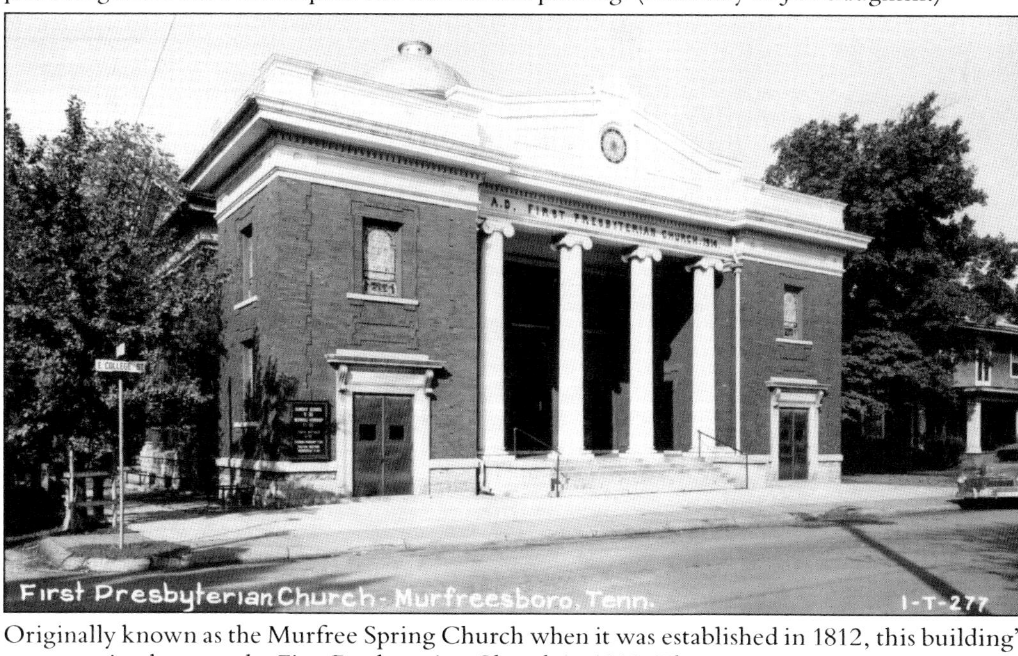

Originally known as the Murfree Spring Church when it was established in 1812, this building's congregation became the First Presbyterian Church in 1818. The congregation moved to a new building in 1868. When the building was seriously damaged by a tornado in 1913, the sanctuary was rebuilt in the Classical Revival style (shown above), and it was dedicated in October 1914. The church was added to the National Register of Historic Places in 2010.

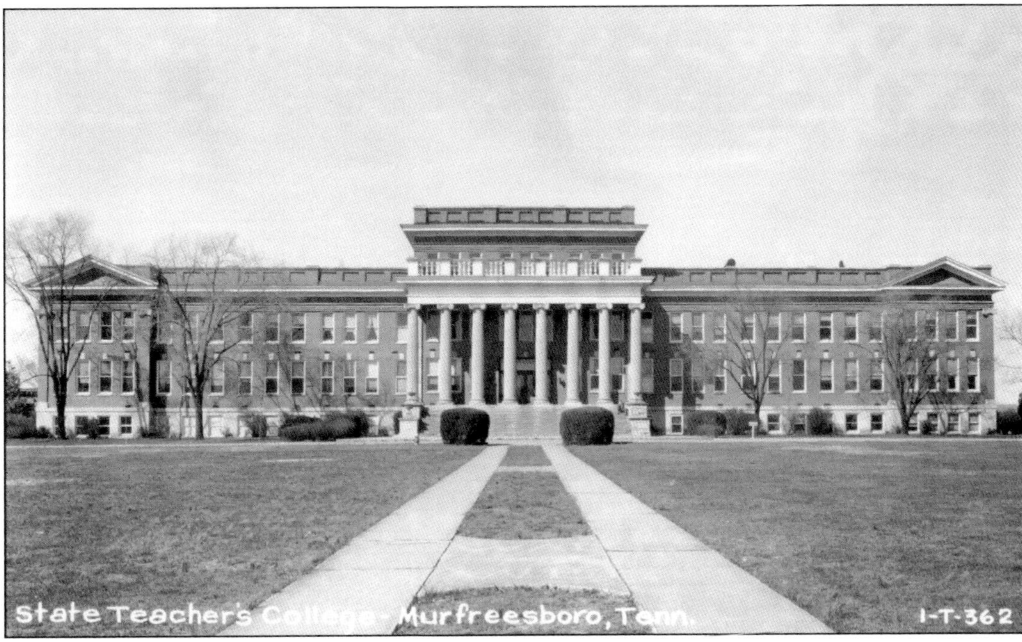

Middle Tennessee State University, as the institution has been called since 1965, celebrates its 100th anniversary in 2011. It began as Middle Tennessee State Normal School, one of three two-year teachers' colleges in the state. A school was built in each area of the state: east, middle, and west. Murfreesboro beat out eight other middle Tennessee towns vying for the school. The structure pictured above and below was one of the five earliest buildings constructed on the campus. It was originally the administration building and is now known as Kirksey Old Main (KOM). Clarence K. Colley, a Nashville architect, designed the building in the Classical Revival style, and it was erected by the George Moore & Sons construction company.

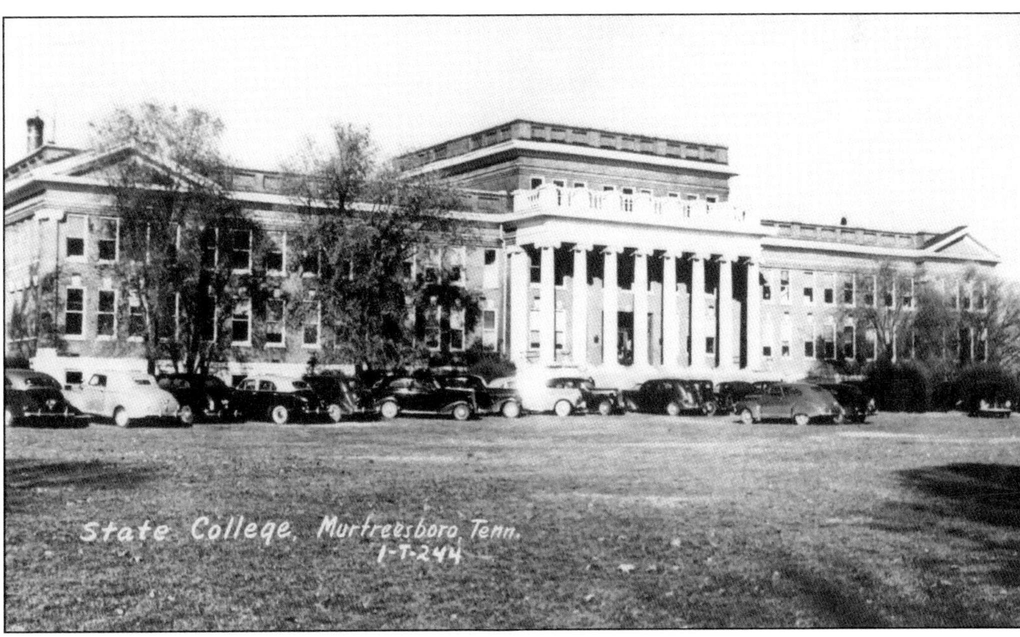

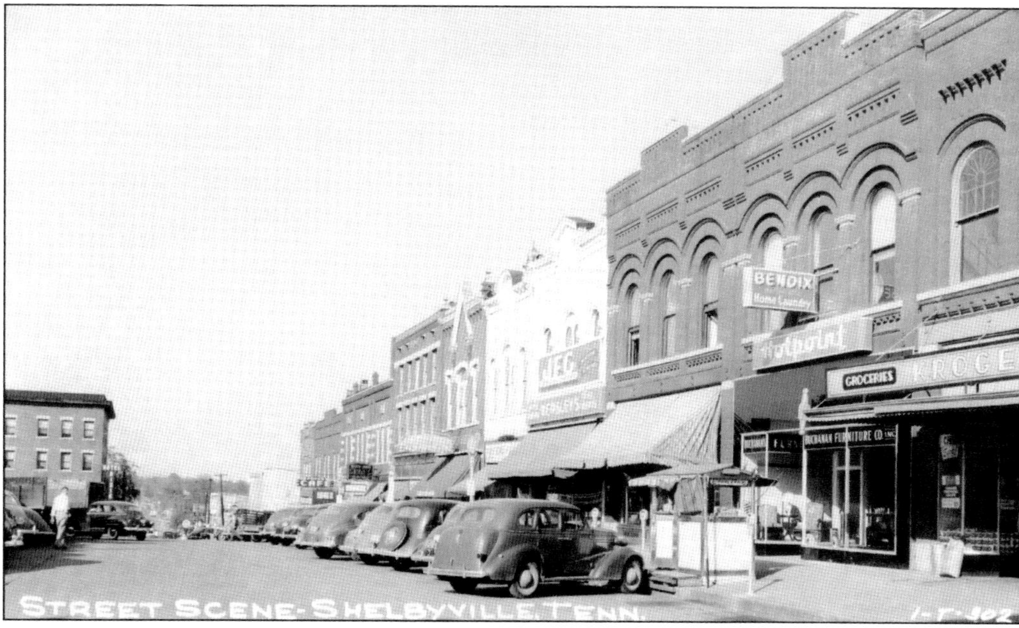

From Murfreesboro, the Dixie Highway continues south on US 231 to the town of Shelbyville. The buildings shown above are on Main Street, two blocks from US 231, and can still be seen today. Known as the "Walking Horse Capital of the World," Shelbyville has held the Tennessee Walking Horse National Celebration since 1939. It is also known as the "Pencil City" and is the home of the Musgrave Pencil Company. The town was established in 1810 and is the county seat of Bedford County, the birthplace of the Confederate general Nathan Bedford Forrest. The city itself is the birthplace of Oscar-nominated actress Sondra Locke.

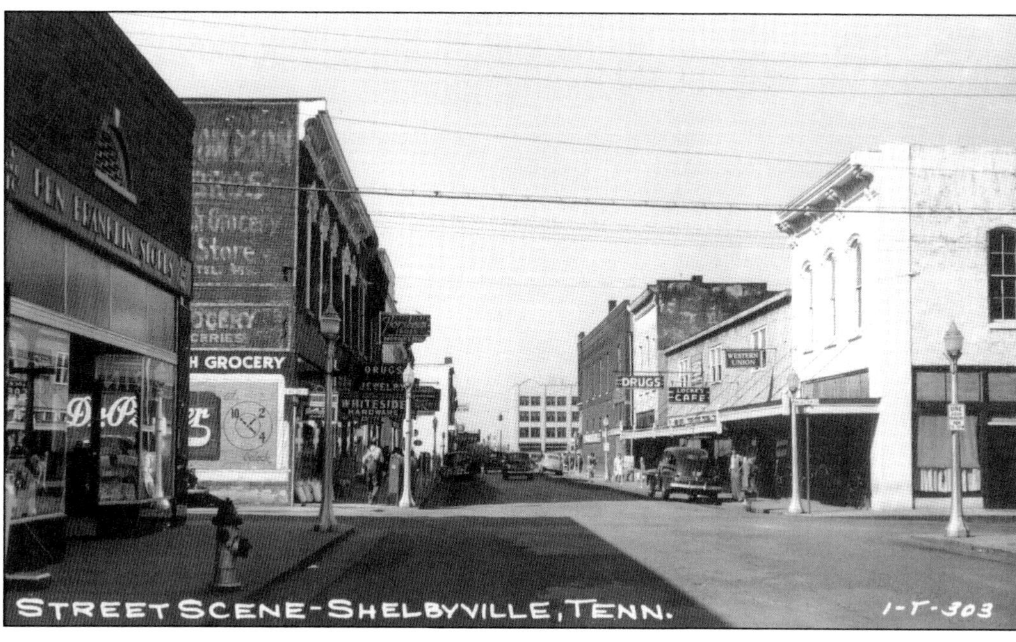

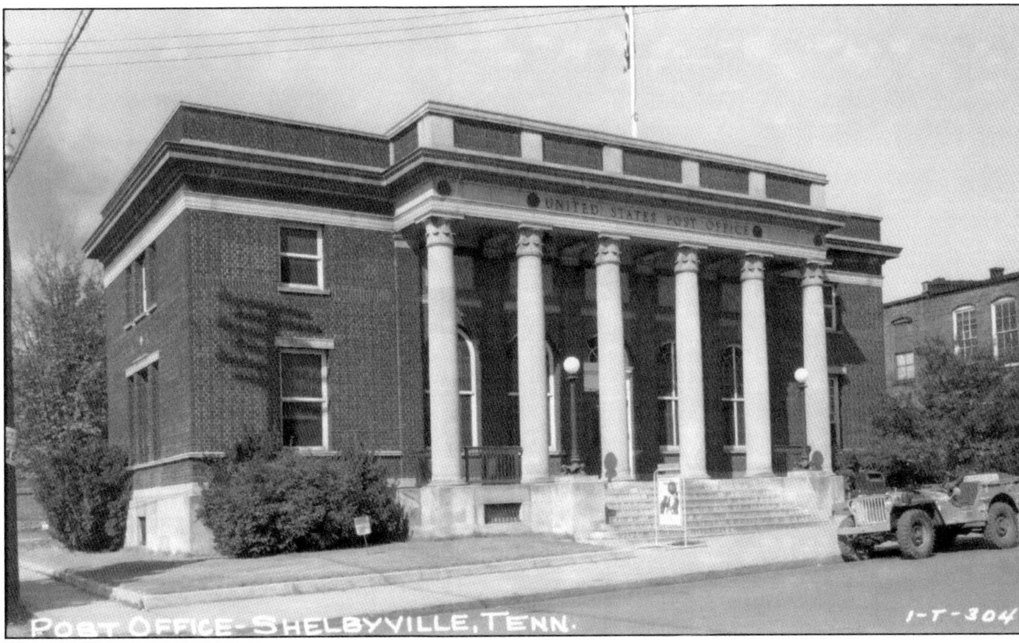

Built in 1914, the former post office at 100 South Main Street in Shelbyville is now the location of the Argie Cooper Public Library. On a side street adjacent to the library is the Fly Manufacturing Company building. The two-story industrial structure was built in 1927 and is now a cultural arts center with a museum. Nearby, on Spring Street, stands the Bedford County Jail, which was built in 1867 and is listed in the National Register of Historic Places. In the postcard below and located on the west side of the town square is the historic Gunter Building (on the left), former home of Cohn & Glazer's department store.

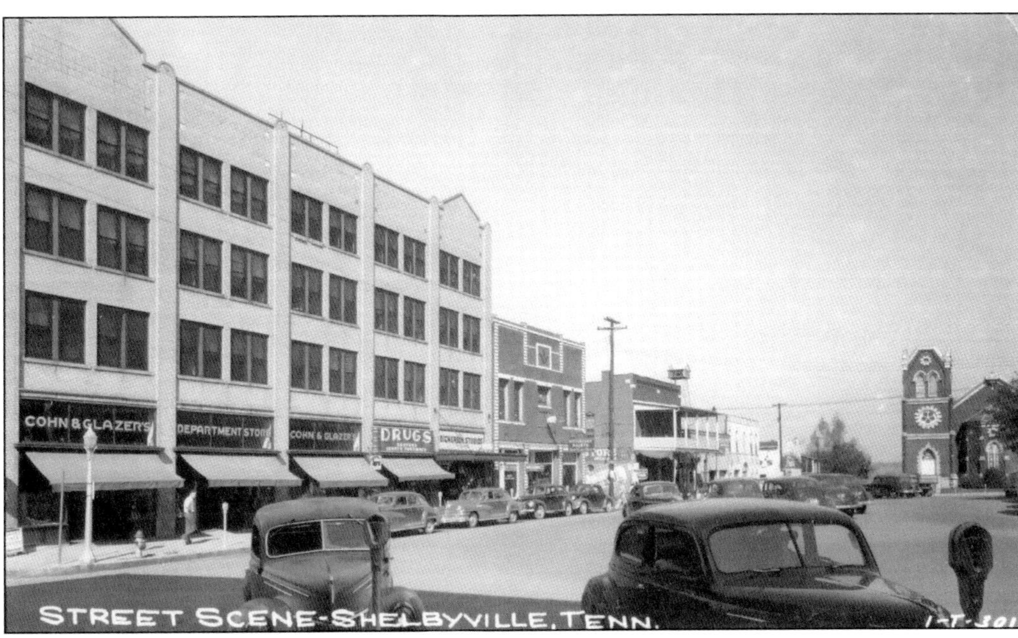

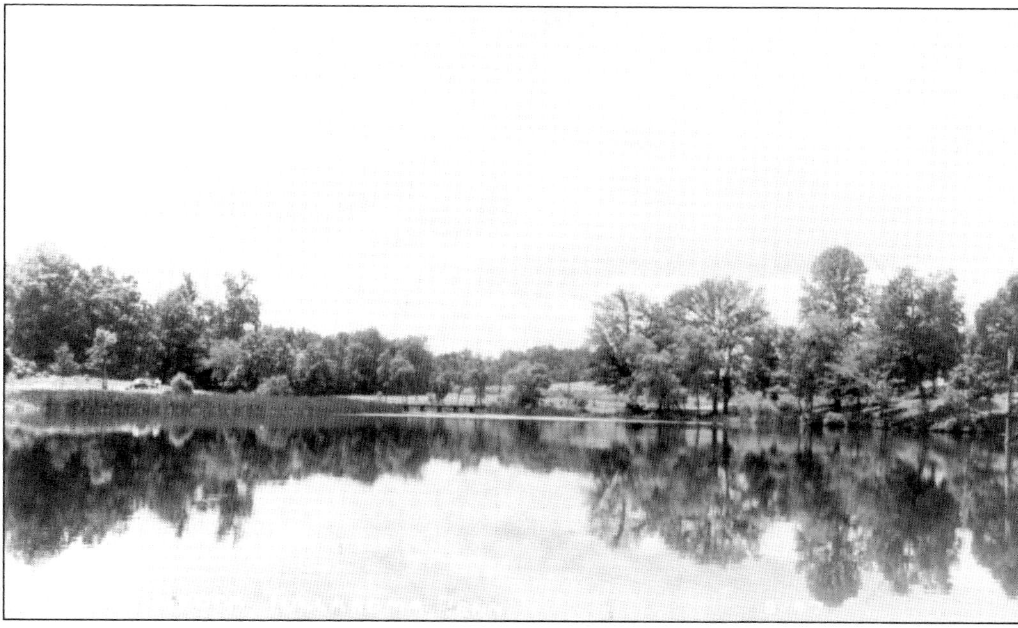

From Shelbyville, the Dixie Highway continues south on US 41A. A few miles from the highway, the beautiful and serene Ovoca Lake caught the photographer's eye. This small lake lies just north of Tullahoma in Coffee County. A cascading waterfall north of the lake is located on private land and is not accessible to the public.

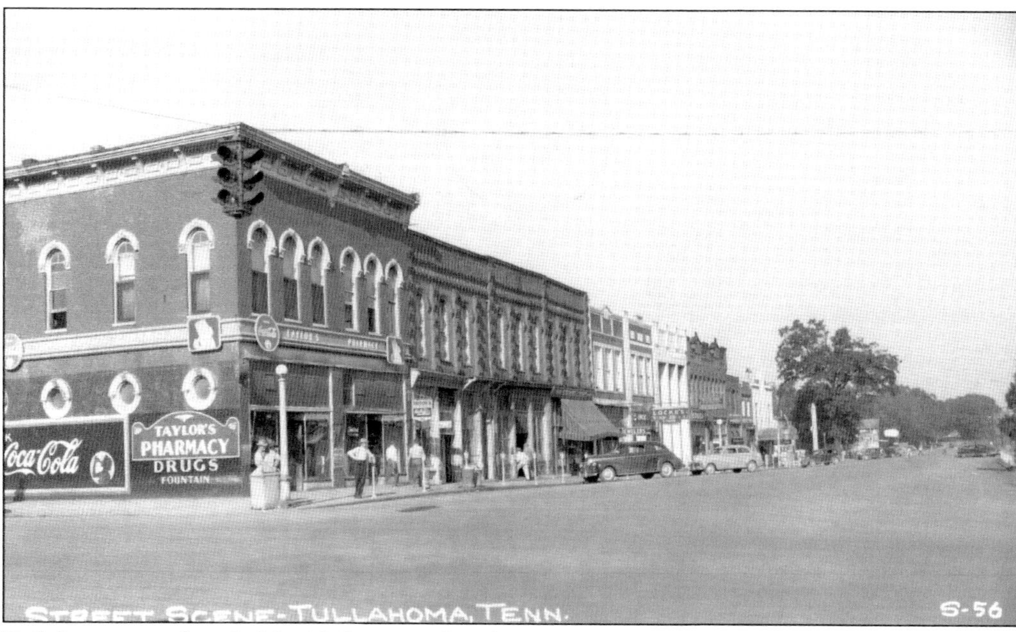

Tullahoma was founded in 1852 as a railroad community. The Union army destroyed much of the town during the Tullahoma campaign in 1863, when General Rosecrans forced the Confederate army out of Middle Tennessee. An interesting place to visit is the Baillet House. Built in the aftermath of the Civil War, it is the oldest brick building in Tullahoma and is part of the Tullahoma Fine Arts Center.

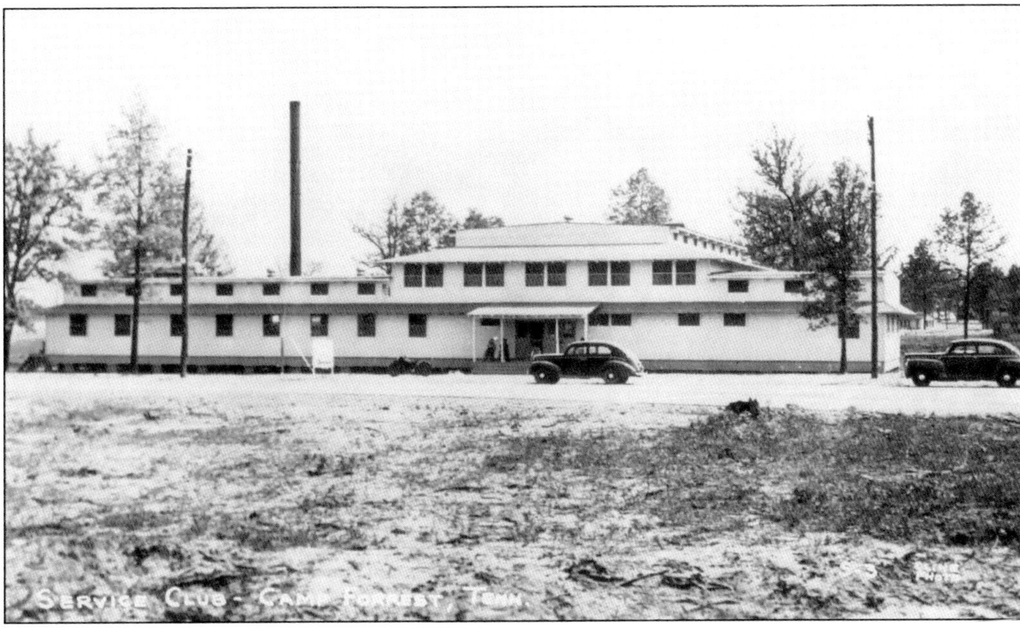

Camp Forrest, one of the Army's largest training bases during World War II, was active from 1941 to 1946. The post, originally named Camp Peay for Tennessee governor Austin Peay, was built east of Tullahoma as a National Guard camp in 1926. In 1941, it was renamed after Nathan Bedford Forrest, the Civil War Confederate general. A 1944 welcome guide informed incoming servicemen that the camp offered the expected conveniences: two service clubs, two guest houses that would accommodate 56 people each, a library, 38 post exchanges, a post office, a nearly new hospital, religious services with provisions for all faiths, four motion picture theaters, and recreation areas with swimming, archery, tennis, a sports arena, a nine-hole golf course, and shower facilities.

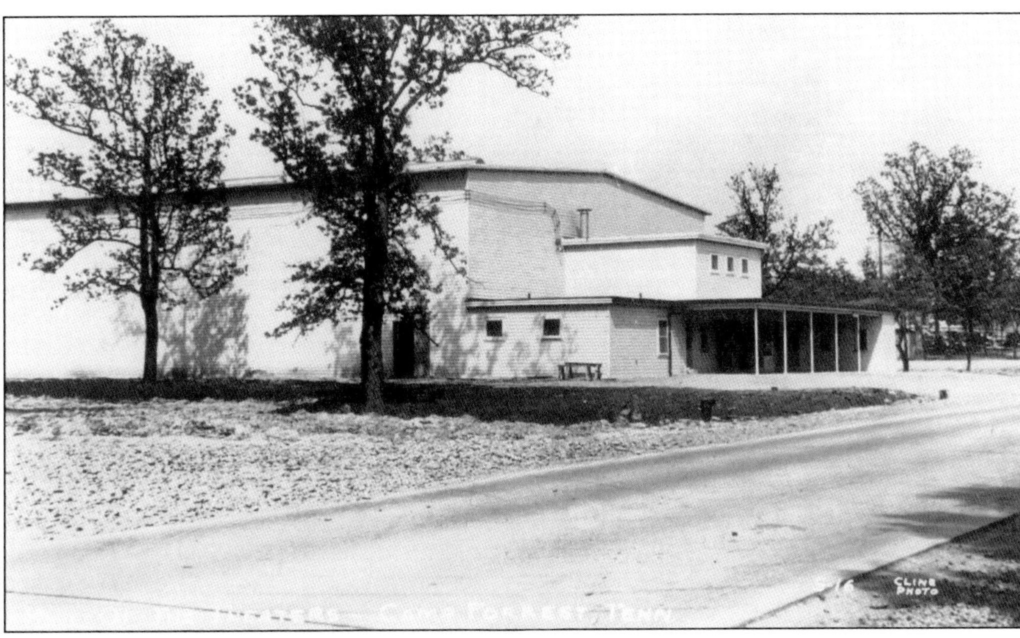

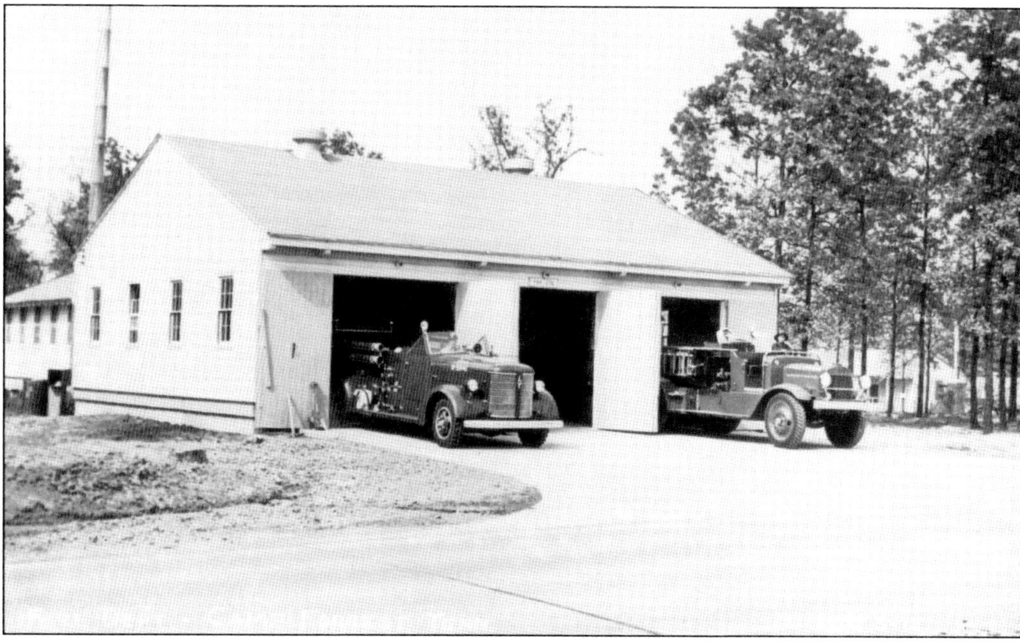

The Red Cross and Army Emergency Relief facilities were available to help servicemen with family, business, and financial matters. Camp Forrest was a training facility for infantry, artillery, engineer, and signal troops. It acted as host for troop maneuvers during the war, including those of the prominent Maj. Gen. George Patton and the 2nd Armored Division from Fort Benning, Georgia. Tullahoma residents were significantly impacted by the location of the camp. They had to deal with frequent traffic jams, roadblocks, crowded retail spaces, and soldiers who camped wherever space allowed. The population grew from 4,500 in 1941 to 85,000 people by the end of the war in 1945.

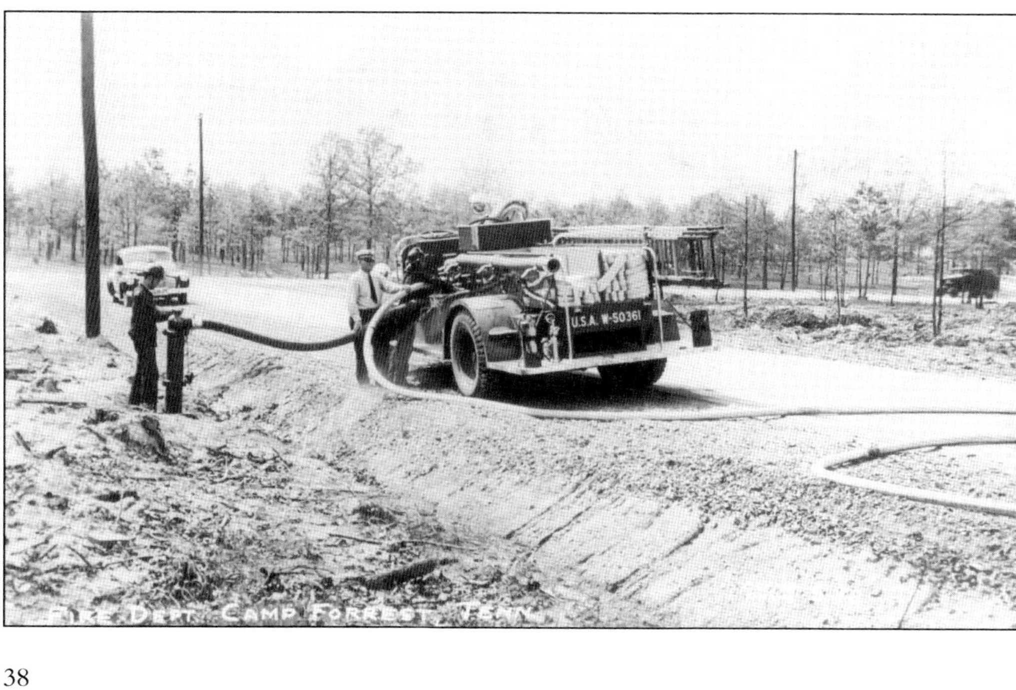

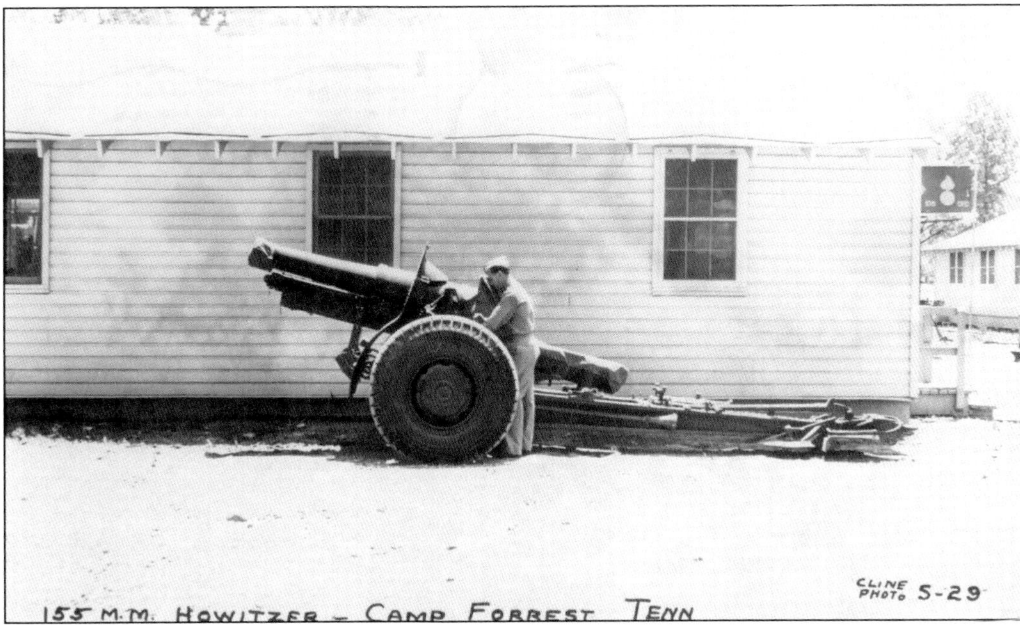

Unnoticed by many local residents, Camp Forrest became the first internment camp in the nation housing "alien enemies." About 800 Japanese civilians were confined at this detention center until late 1942. German and Italian prisoners of war (POWs) replaced them in 1943, when the camp was officially designated "Camp Forrest Prisoner of War Camp." The enlisted POWs became laborers in the hospitals and on local farms. The government enacted an Intellectual Diversion Program designed to change the Germans' attitude toward the American lifestyle and to foster an admiration for the United States. In 1946, after the war ended, Camp Forrest was declared surplus property, with buildings sold at auction, dismantled, and hauled away.

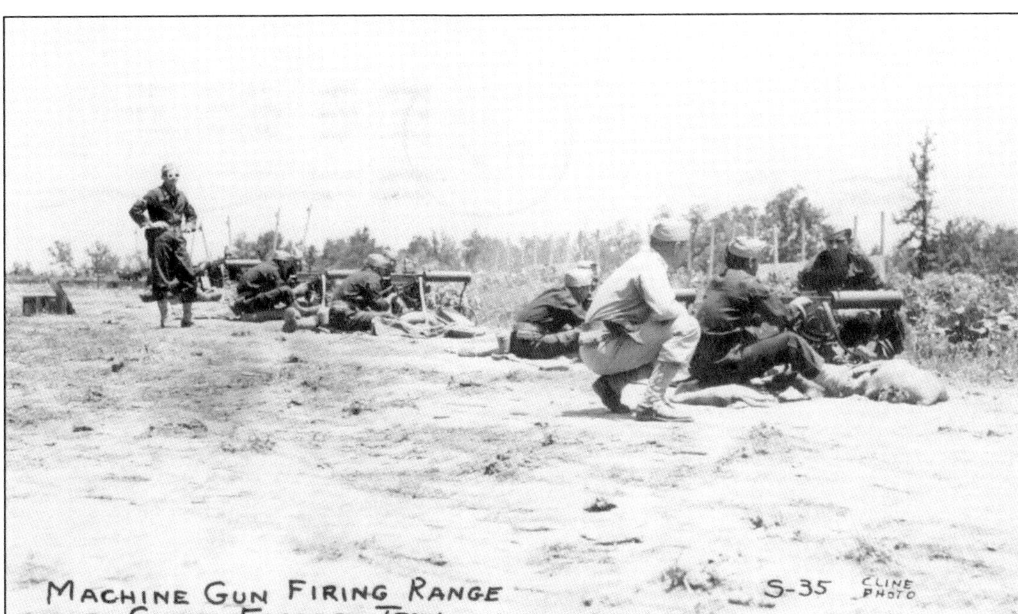

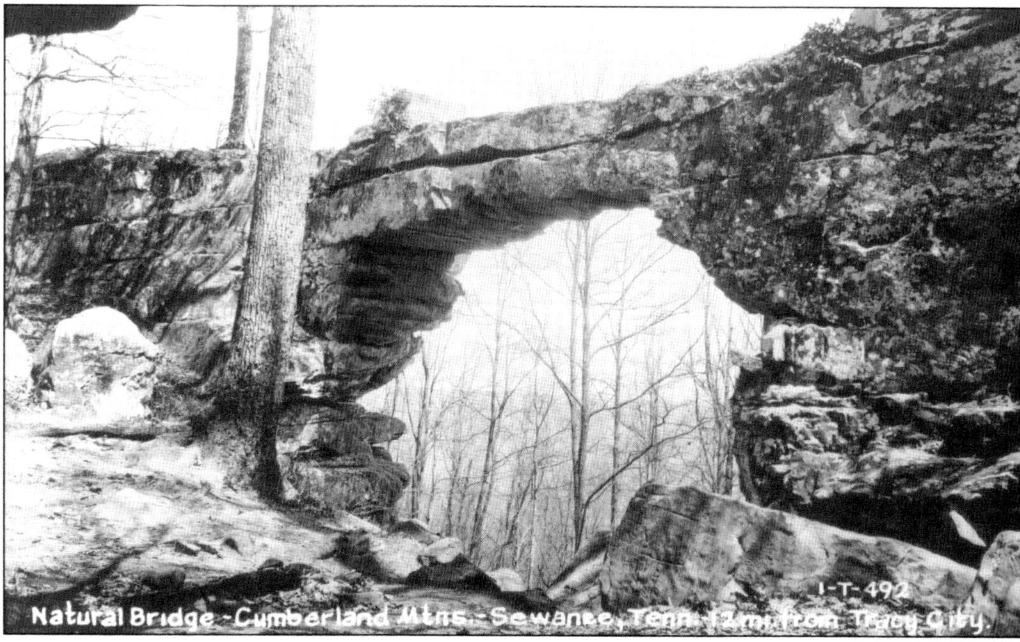

The Sewanee Natural Bridge is located a few miles off Highway 41A near Sewanee. Part of the South Cumberland Recreation Area, the natural sandstone arch is 25 feet high and 50 feet long. The three-acre natural area was donated to the state by the University of the South and is open to the public.

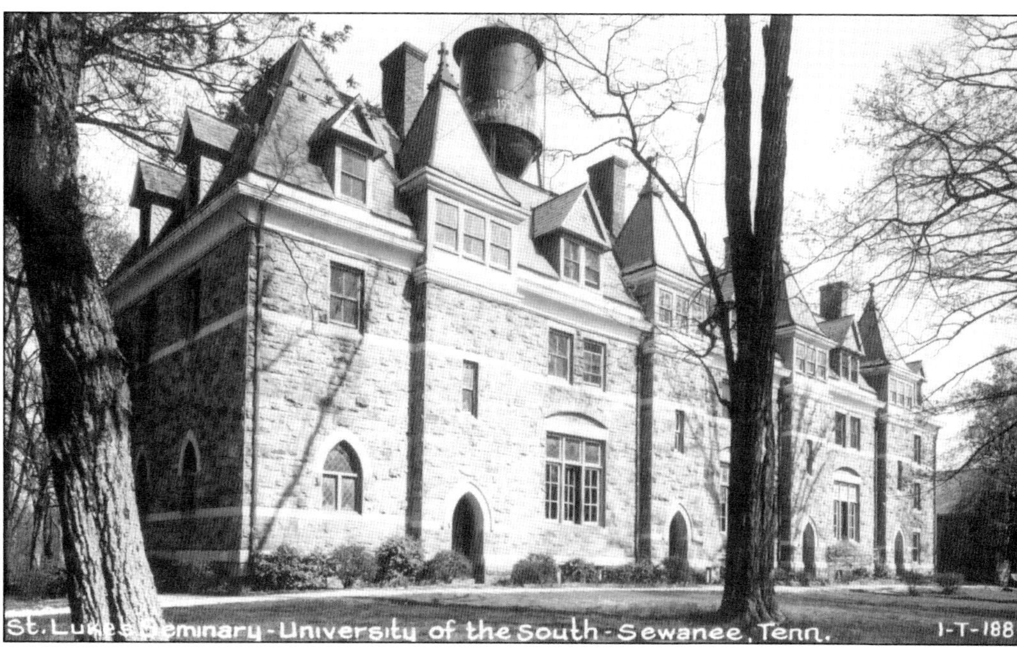

The University of the South, also known as Sewanee, was founded in 1857 by the Southeastern dioceses of the Episcopal Church. St. Luke's Hall was built in 1887 and is one of the oldest buildings on the university's campus. Once used as a home for the seminary, it is now a coed residence for approximately 100 students.

The University of the South is a liberal arts college and a seminary. The *Sewanee Review*, a highly respected literary journal, was first published at the university in 1892. William Porcher DuBose, a noted theologian, was dean of the college from 1894 to 1908. The campus is located at the top of the Cumberland Plateau on 13,000 school-owned acres known as the domain. The perimeter trail lies within the domain and is approximately 20 miles long. It is managed by the school's outing program and is open to the public for day use. One of many scenic sights available on the perimeter trail is the cross pictured at right. The war memorial cross was built in 1922 to honor soldiers in the Sewanee area who had served in World War I but was later rededicated to also include those in Franklin County who had served in wars since that time.

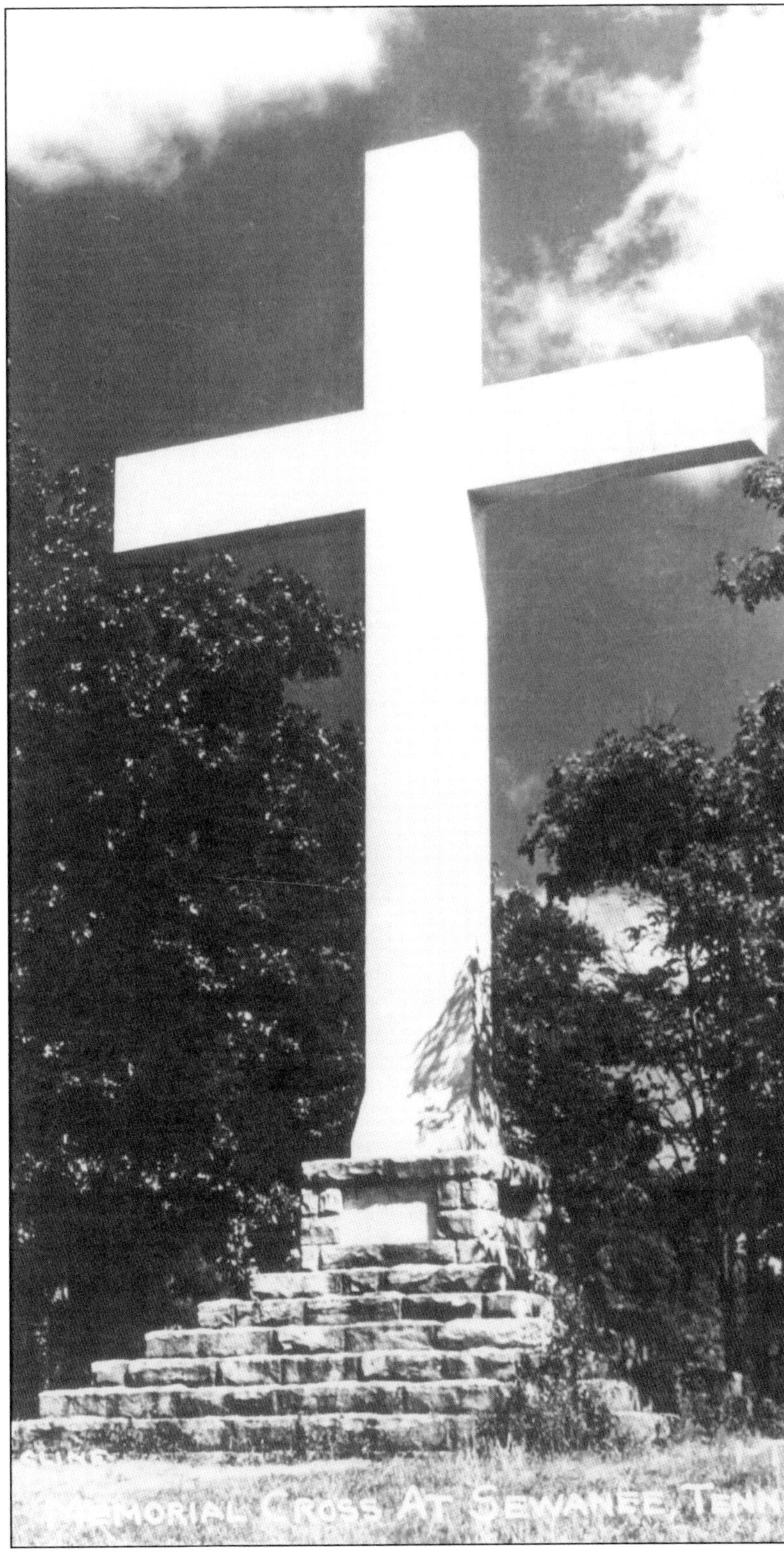

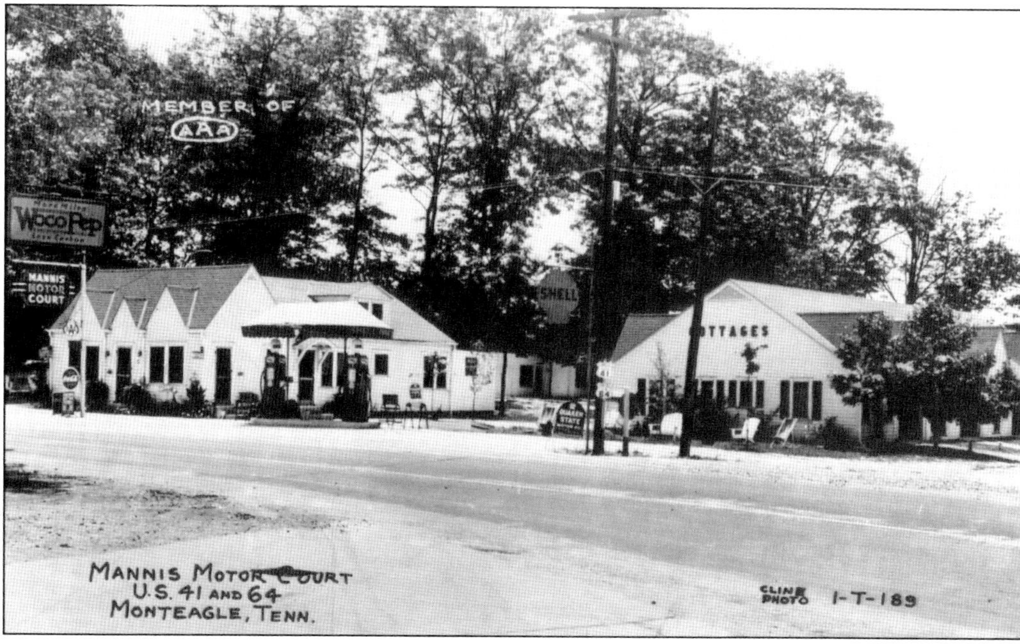

Settled by Swiss and Scots-Irish immigrants, Monteagle rests at an elevation of 2,100 feet and was the highest point between Chicago and Miami on the Dixie Highway. With its many nature trails and scenic overlooks, Monteagle was and remains a popular destination. After the completion of the Dixie Highway, restaurants and lodgings such as the cottage-style Mannis Motor Court were opened on US 41. The town is home to the Monteagle Sunday School Assembly, which was established in 1882 to promote intellectual and spiritual growth. The DuBose Memorial Church Training School, also located in Monteagle, is listed in the National Register of Historic Places.

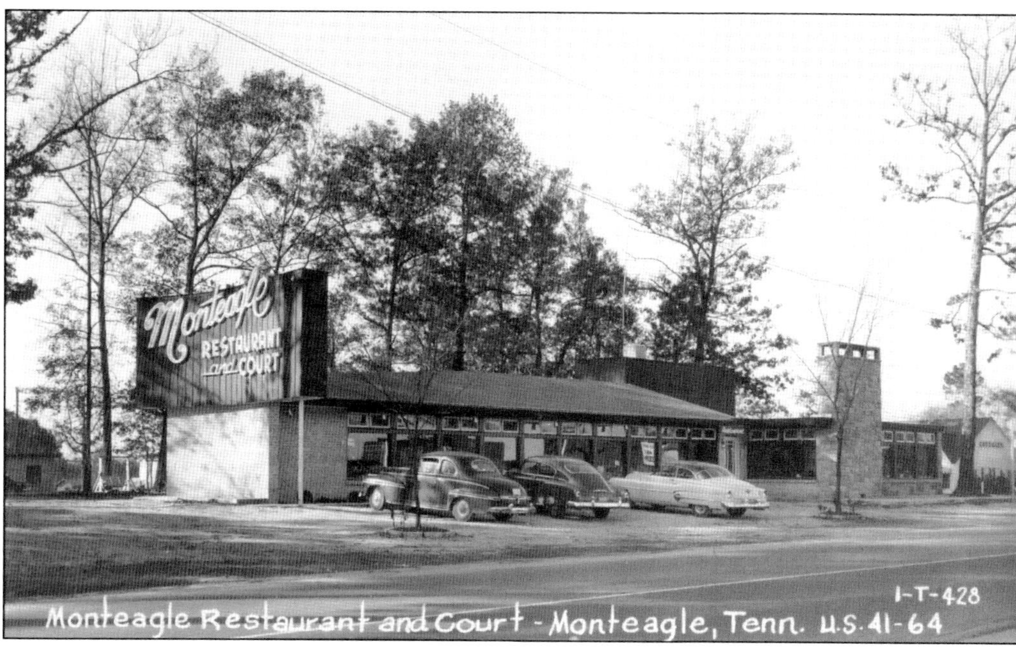

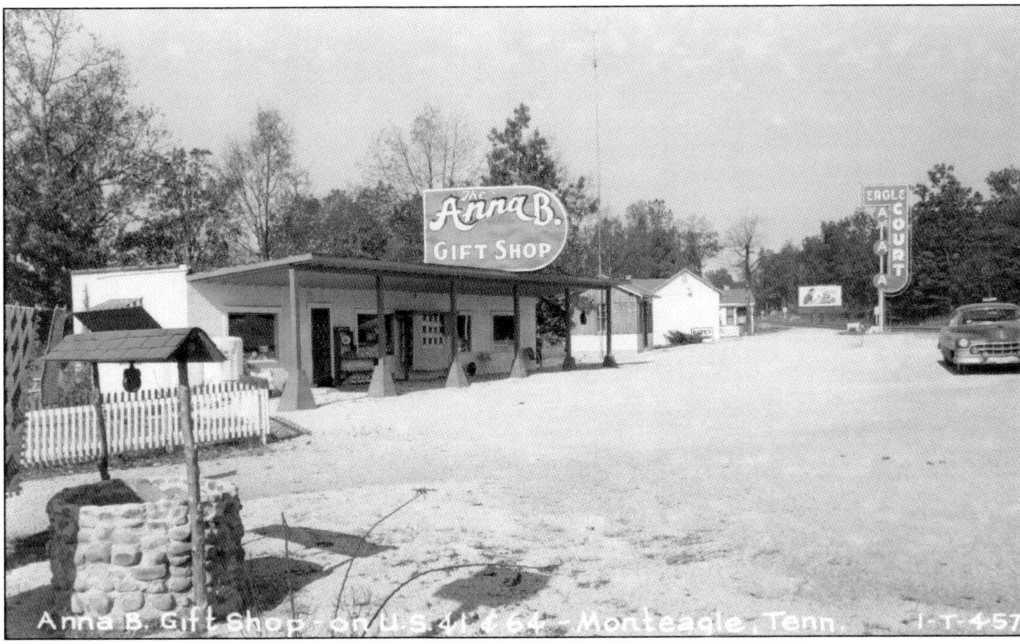

The Anna B. Gift Shop and adjacent Eagle Court were located on US 41 and US 64 on the Dixie Highway at Monteagle. Anna Bell and Ray C. Davenport opened the shop in 1945 and sold local crafts at the location for the next 30 years. The items sold included handmade quilts, dolls, pottery, and chairs, as well as canned sausages, hickory-smoked hams, and homemade candy. Craft shows were sometimes held on weekends, with local artists and craftsmen attending. A local author and teacher, May Justus, attended many craft shows and sold her books in the gift shop. The May Justus Memorial Library in Monteagle is named in her honor.

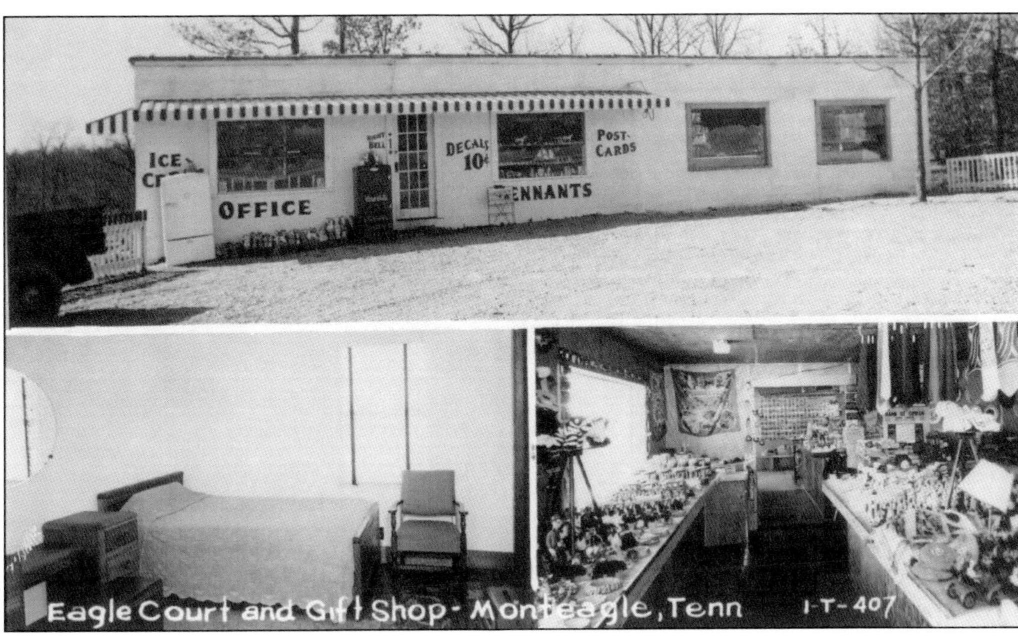

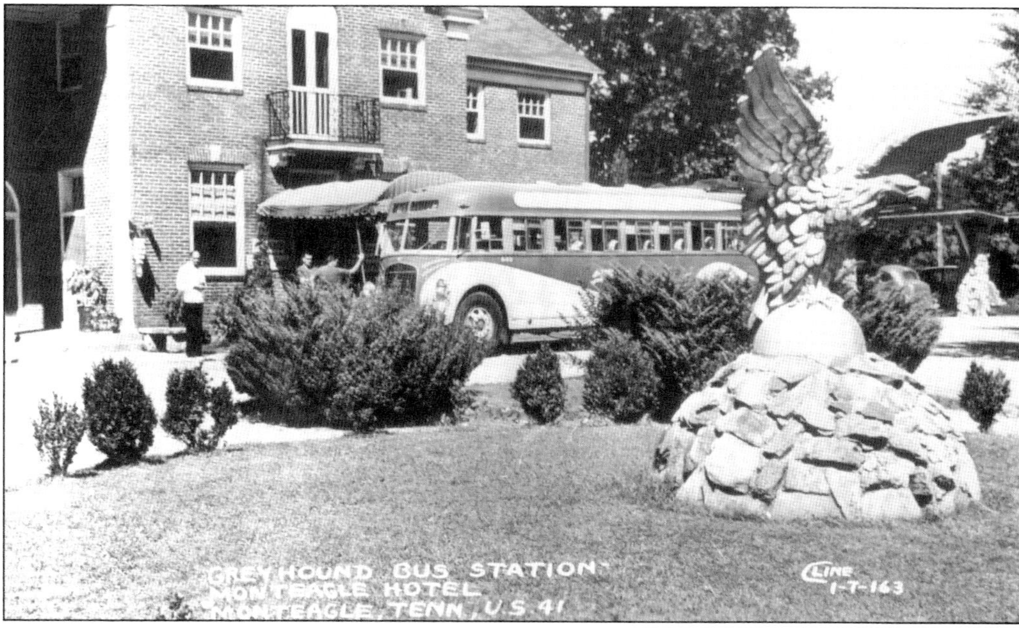

Monteagle Hotel was built in the early 1930s on the Dixie Highway (US 41). The two-story brick Colonial-style building had a circular driveway with a statue of a silver eagle atop a mound of rocks centered in the front. The dining room of the resort had knotty pine walls, hardwood floors, and a beautiful stone fireplace. Guests could enjoy listening to bands in the hotel's ballroom. In the mid-1940s, the town's railroad depot was moved to the Monteagle Hotel and used as a bus depot. On February 28, 1950, the Southeastern Greyhound bus station caught on fire. The fire quickly spread to the hotel and destroyed both buildings.

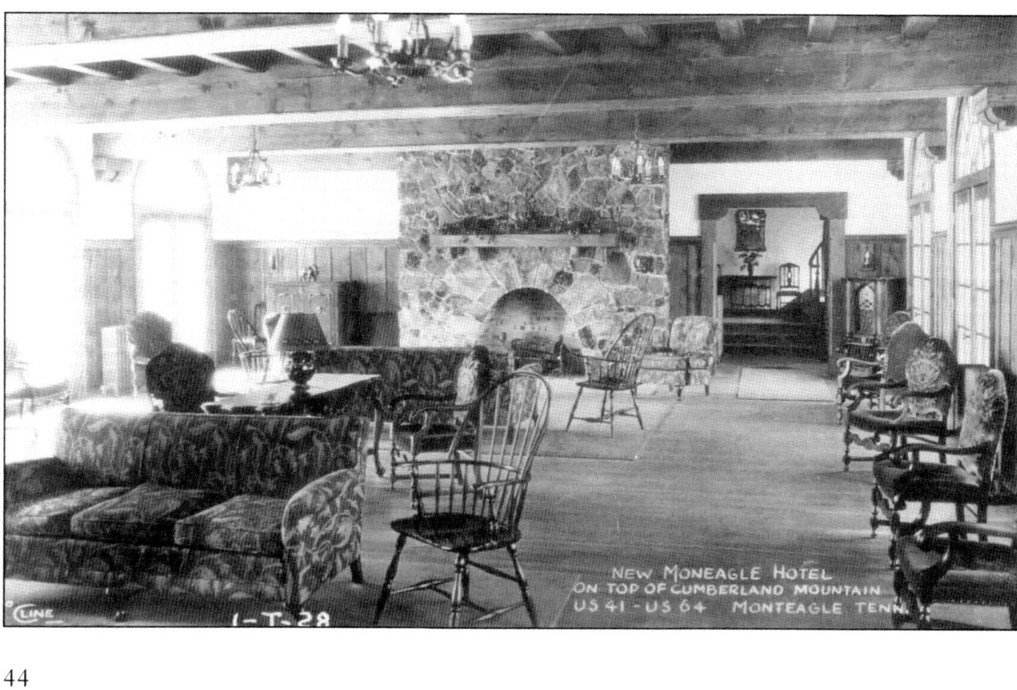

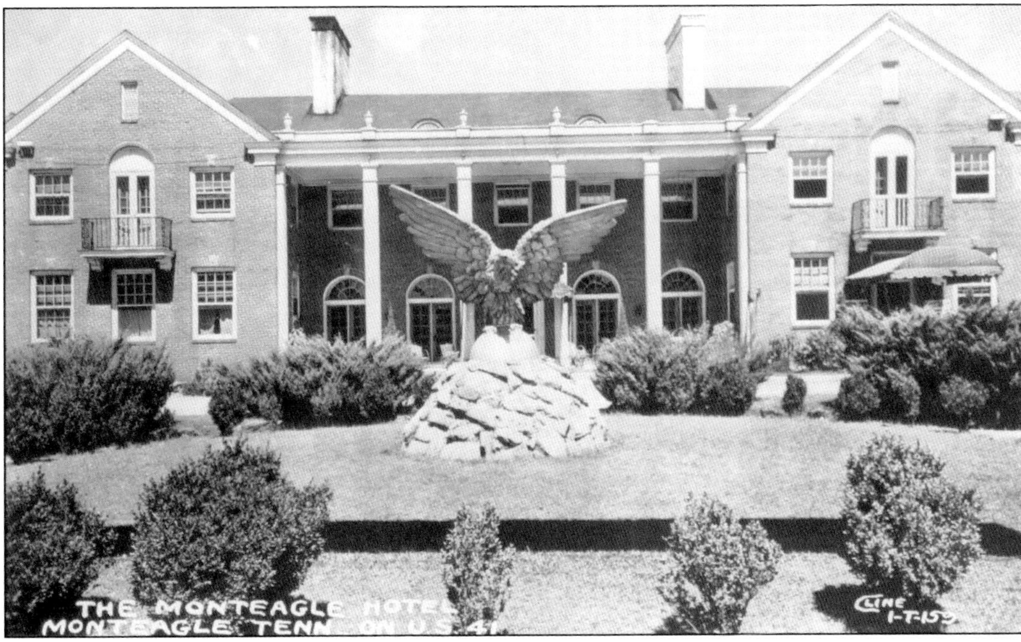

After the fire in 1950, the eagle statue still remained in front of the hotel. Since their team symbol was a golden eagle, some Tennessee Tech University students took the statue from the hotel grounds (without permission) for a pregame rally during the 1952–1953 school year. In 1958, the owner of the Monteagle Hotel, John W. Harton, donated the statue to the school at the request of Gov. Frank G. Clement. After being given a golden finish, the eagle was placed in the tower of Derryberry Hall on the Cookeville campus in 1961 and can still be seen there today.

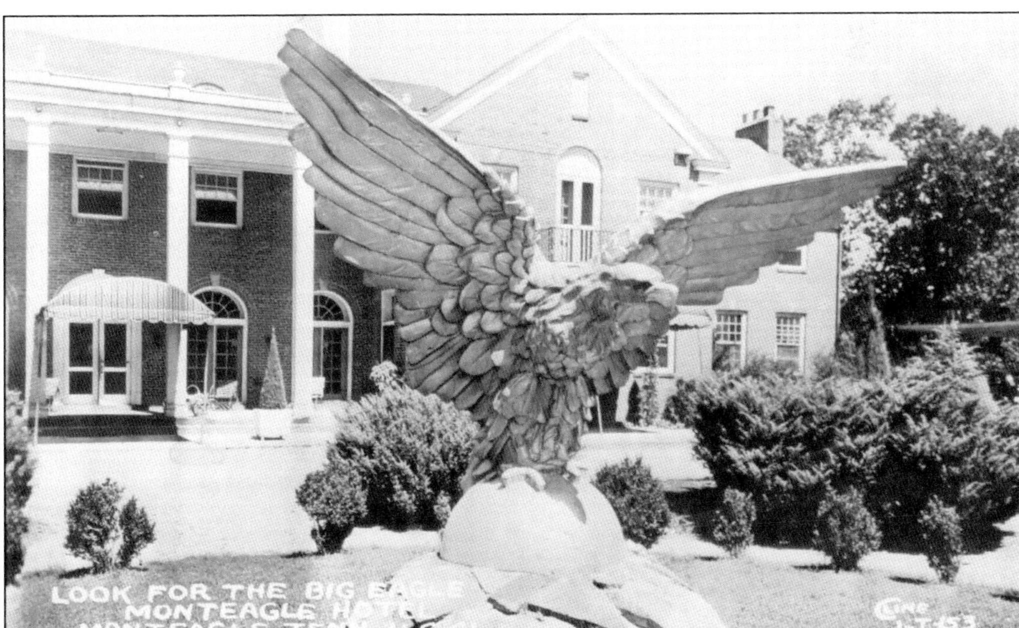

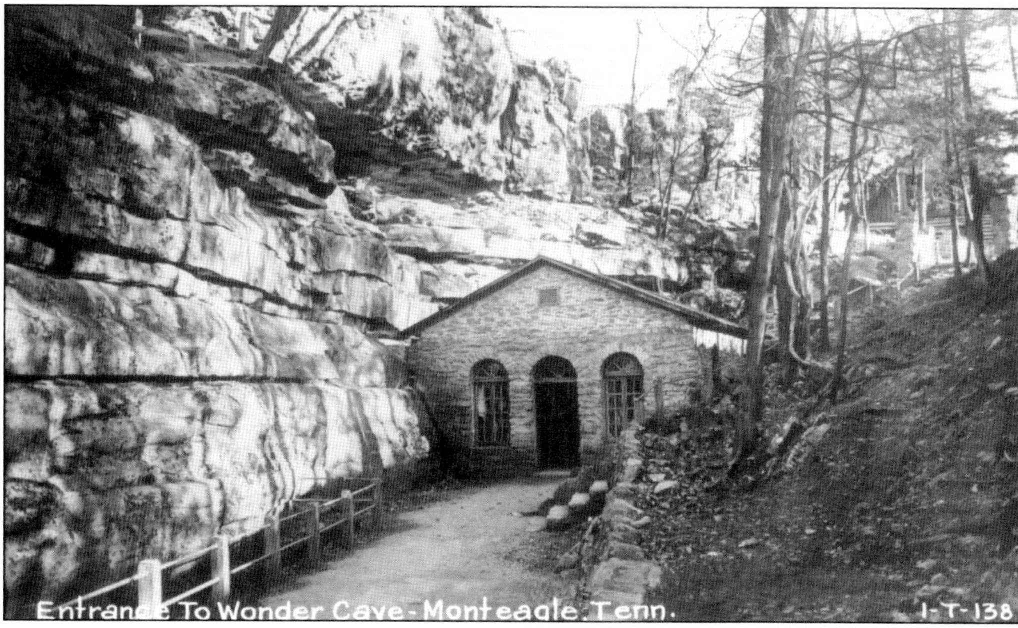

Robert A. Nelson, Will Fitzgerald, and Melville Anderson discovered Wonder Cave in 1897. After stopping for a drink of water from a spring, they spotted a small opening in the rock wall near the spring's mouth. Upon entering the opening, they found a large cave in pristine condition with a number of stalactites, stalagmites, and other unusual calcite formations. A year later, Robert M. Payne purchased the land and developed it into a commercial cave. In the early years, when the cave first opened, people often traveled by train to see it. The base of Monteagle Mountain, located less than four miles from the cave, was on a branch line of the Nashville, Chattanooga & St. Louis Railway (NC&StL) and was a major summer resort area. Easy accessibility from the resort made Wonder Cave a popular tourist destination.

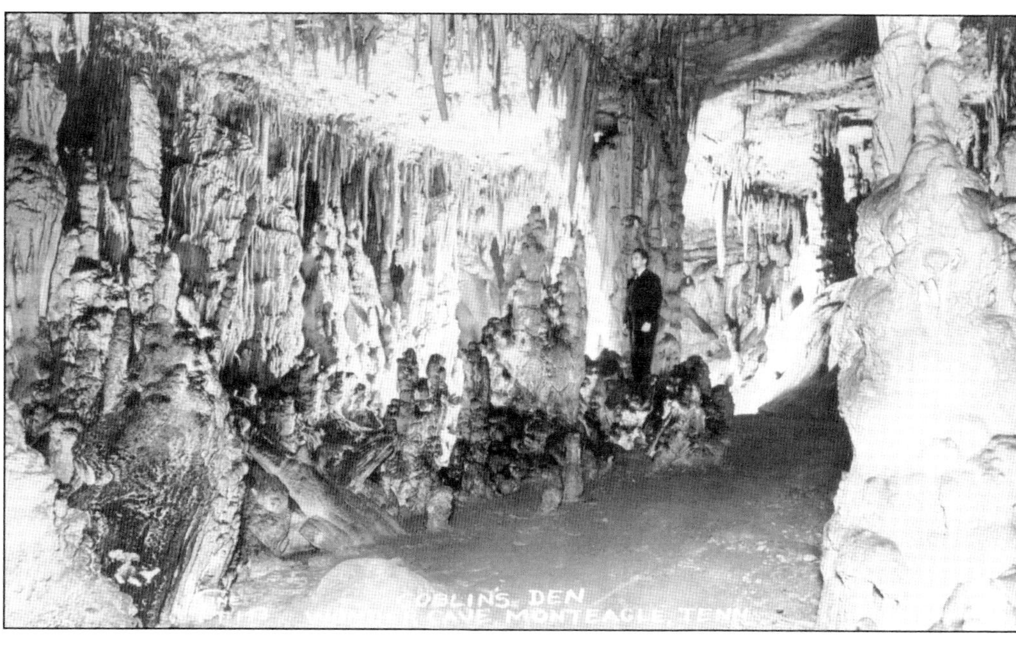

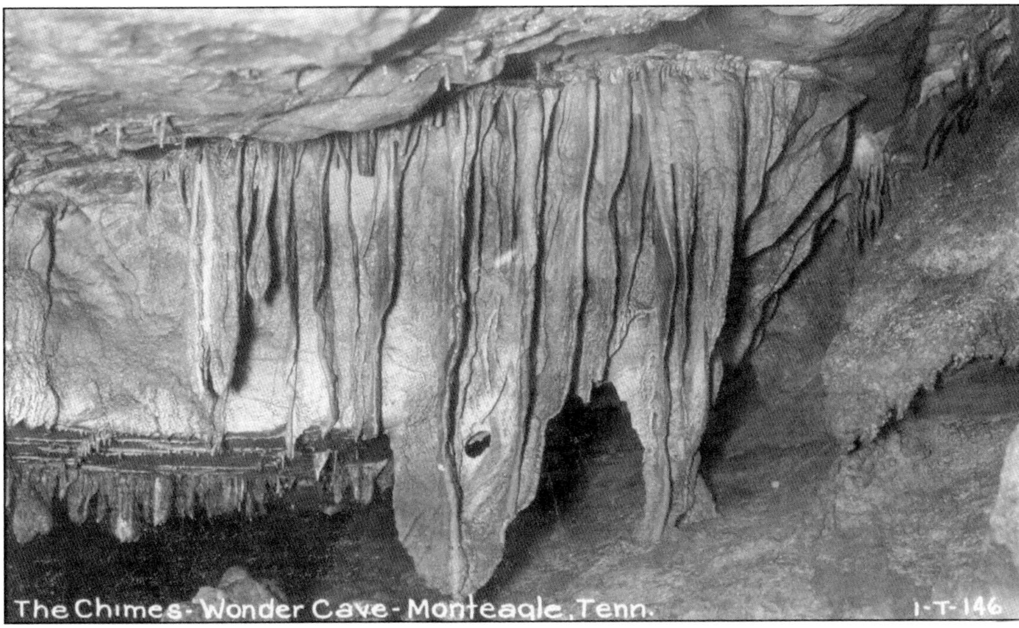

Years later, automobiles began to replace railways as the dominant means of transportation. Fortunately for the owners, Wonder Cave was located less than a mile from US 41, giving tourists even greater year-round accessibility. Billboards advertising the attraction were strategically placed on the highway. Attendance remained high throughout the years until the opening of Interstate 24 in the mid-1960s. The cave was located several miles from the interstate, and attendance soon began to dwindle. Wonder Cave finally closed in 1986. New owners opened a bed and breakfast in 1989, and it stayed open until 2000. The cave was occasionally open during that time but has been closed to the public since 2000.

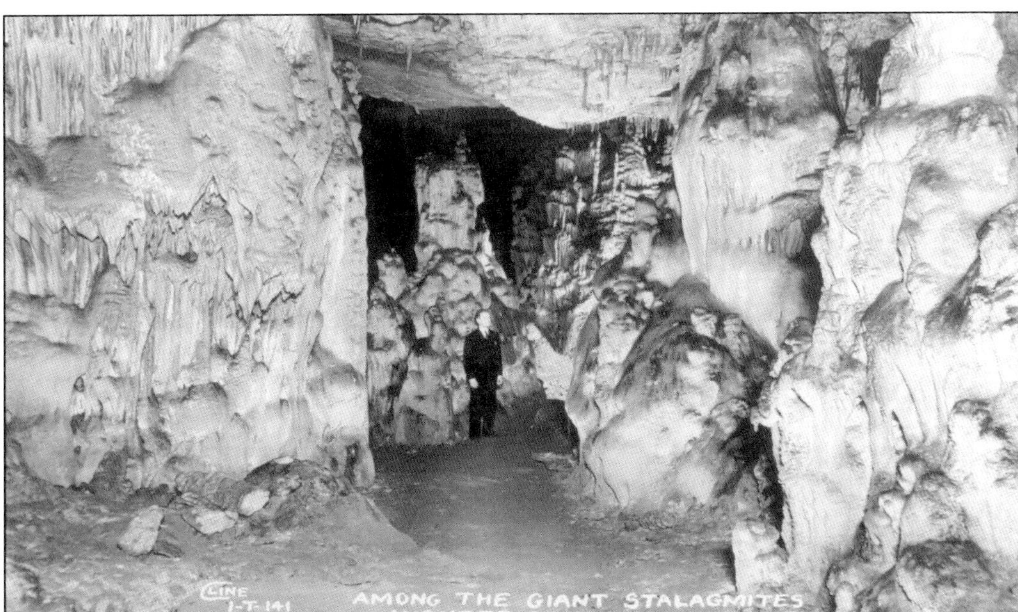

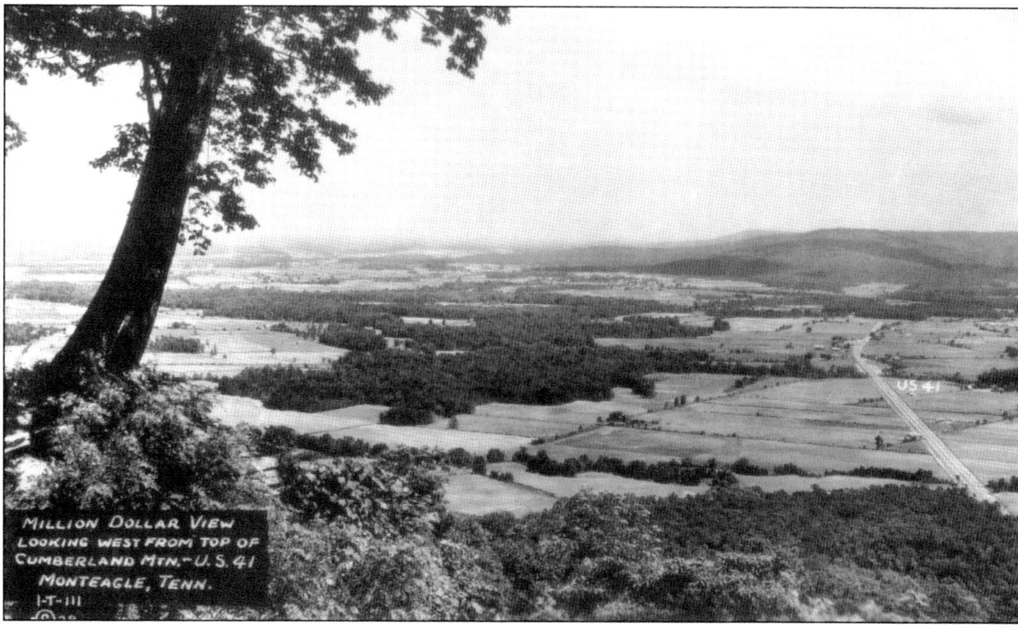

Not far from Wonder Cave is what Dixie Highway travelers dubbed the "million dollar view." Eagle Cliff has an elevation of nearly 1,800 feet and gives visitors a spectacular vantage point of the area. Wrenn's Nest, a privately owned 1908 Queen Anne–style house near the cliff, was originally owned by George Leonidas Wrenn and is now listed in the National Register of Historic Places.

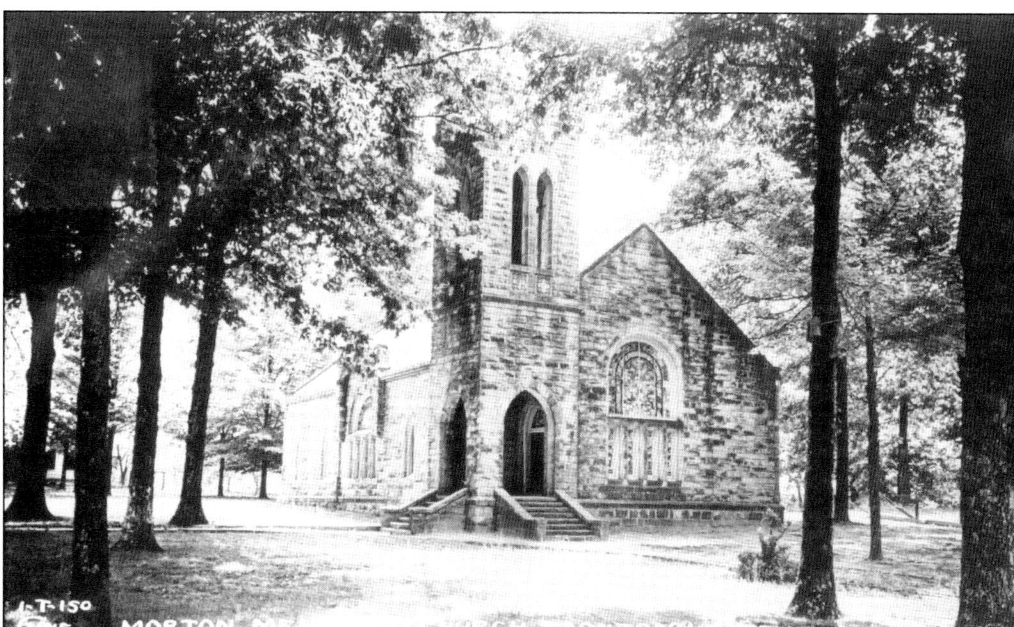

Morton Memorial United Methodist Church is located on Main Street in Monteagle. It is made of mountain stone and was built by a local stonemason, Jim Meeks, who laid the cornerstone in 1897. The church was named in honor of David Morton, who secured funding for the project but died before it was completed.

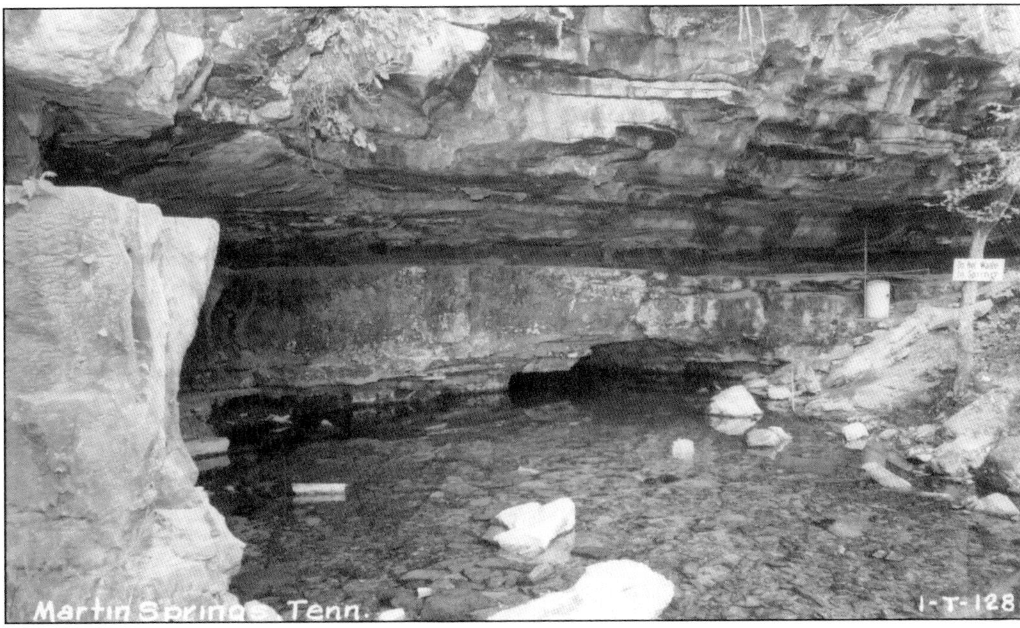

Martin Springs Cave is located on the east side of Battle Creek Valley in Marion County. It has a large opening from which a spring emerges, and there are several water-filled passages inside. Martin Springs Cave was once a campsite on the Trail of Tears. It was named after Thornton Herbert Martin, postmaster of the Dove post office (renamed the Martin Springs post office in 1932). Martin built tourist cabins and a boardinghouse to take advantage of the cave's crystal-clear water, which supposedly had medicinal properties. Before construction of Interstate 24 and the partial rerouting of US 41 in the early 1960s, the Dixie Highway passed through Battle Creek Valley on a section of US 41 connecting Monteagle to Jasper.

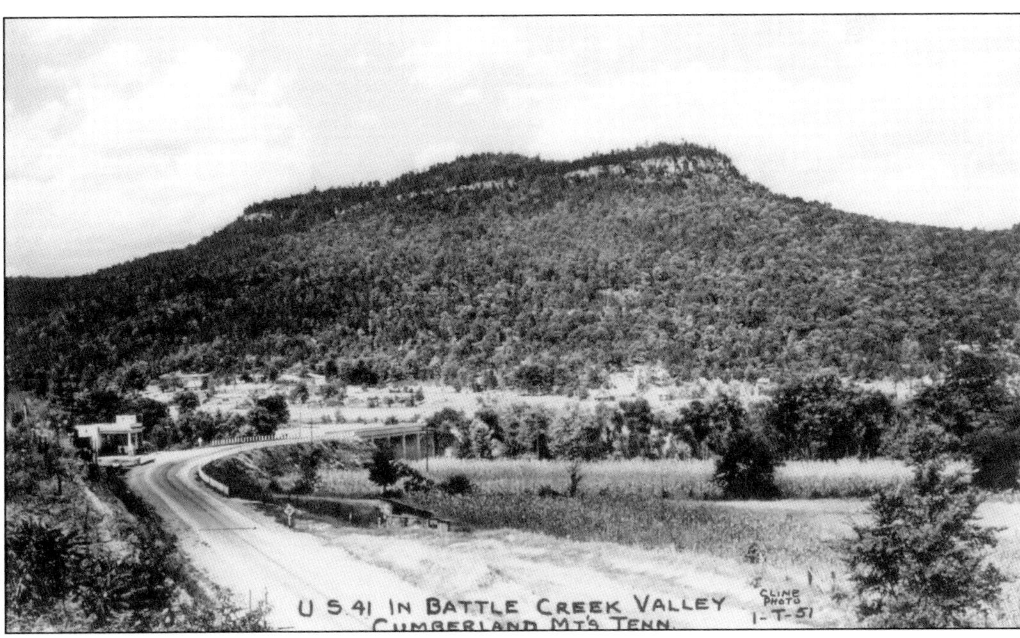

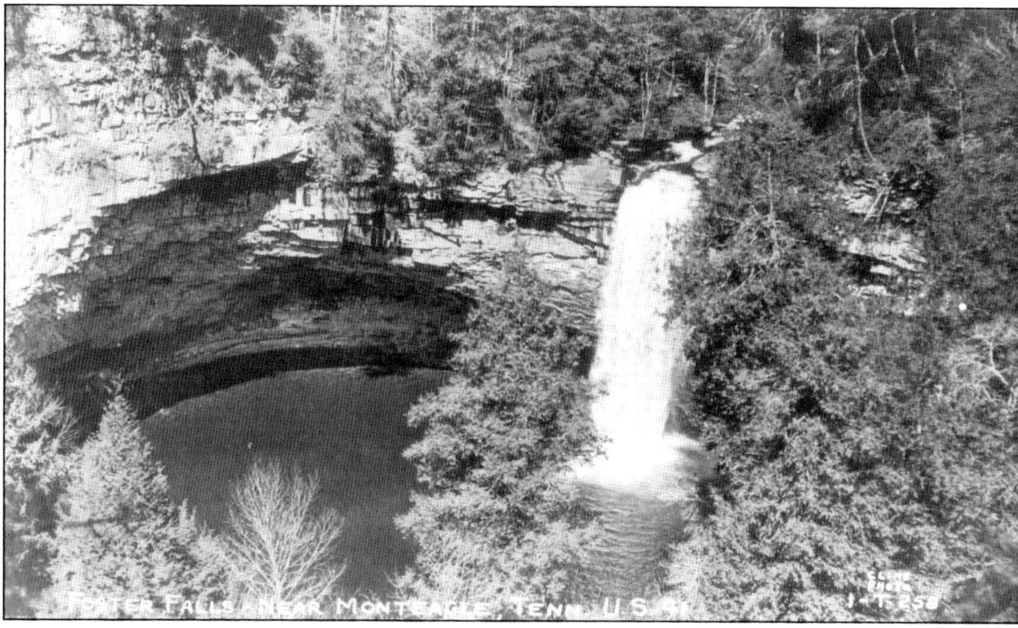

Foster Falls Small Wild Area is jointly managed by the Tennessee Valley Authority and the South Cumberland State Recreation Area. The park is located south of Tracy City on US 41, and the campground is open from mid-spring until mid-fall. A trail from the picnic area offers a scenic view of Little Gizzard Creek cascading 60 feet down into the Foster Falls basin.

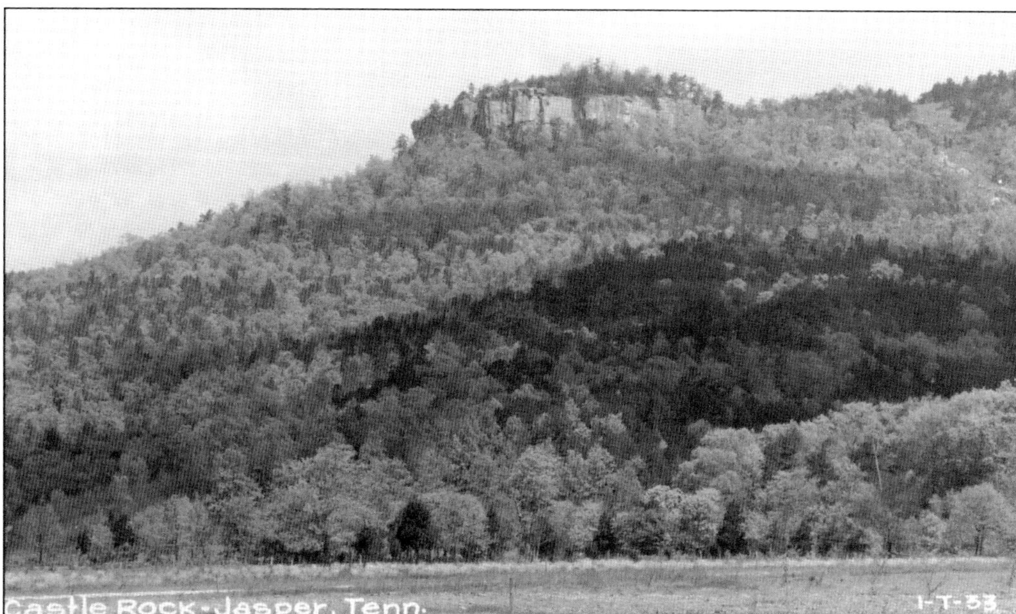

Castle Rock is located about three miles northwest of Jasper, not far from Foster Falls. The rock is over 100 feet high in many places and approximately one half-mile in length. Located on private land, Castle Rock is not open to the public. However, since it is a very popular destination for rock climbers, the Southeastern Climbers Coalition currently leases climbing and hiking access for its members.

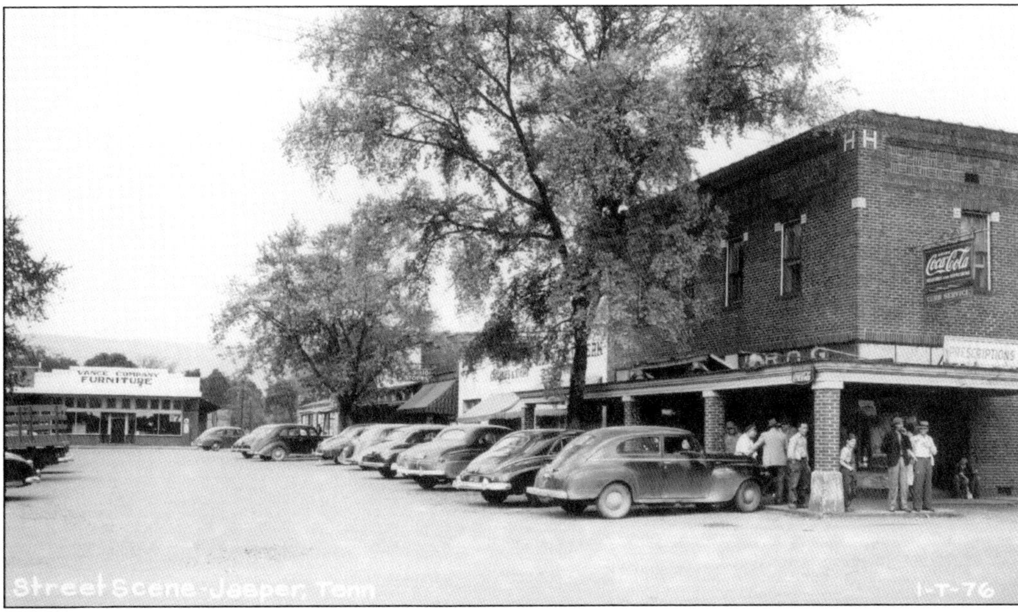

Opened in 1925, Jasper Drug (in the foreground at right) remains on the Courthouse Square as a thriving business today. The Dutch Maid Bakery opened next door in 2008. The original Dutch Maid Bakery was opened in Tracy City in 1902 by John Baggenstoss, a Swiss immigrant. Cynthia Day, the current owner of both locations, still uses recipes brought from Switzerland more than 100 years ago.

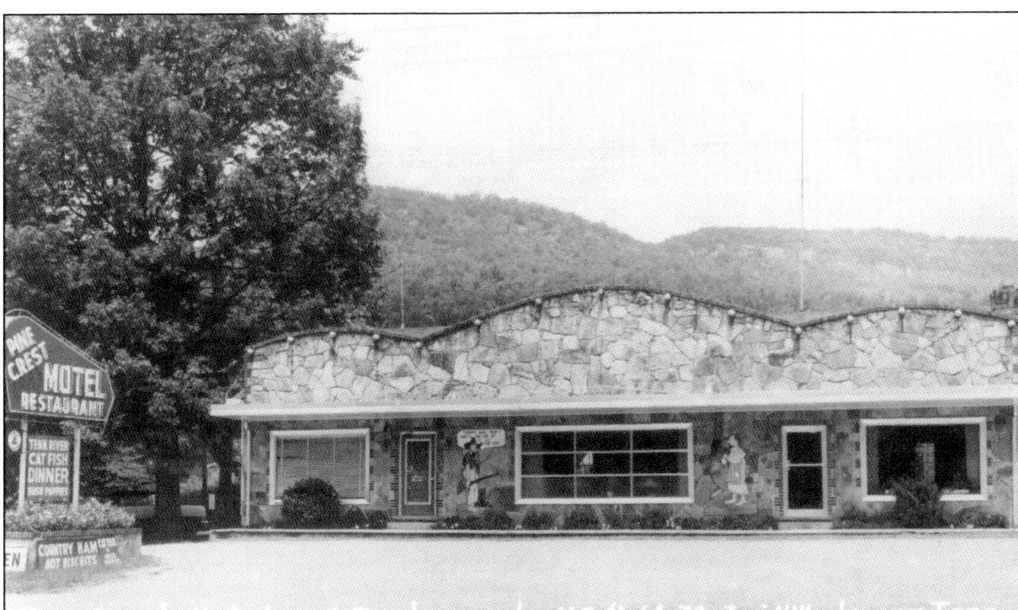

Jasper's Pine Crest Motel and Restaurant provided accommodations for Dixie Highway travelers. Jasper, named after William Jasper, who fought in the Revolutionary War, is the county seat of Marion County, which was also named after a Revolutionary War hero, Francis Marion. Betsy Pack, whose father was a Cherokee chief, donated land to establish the town in 1820.

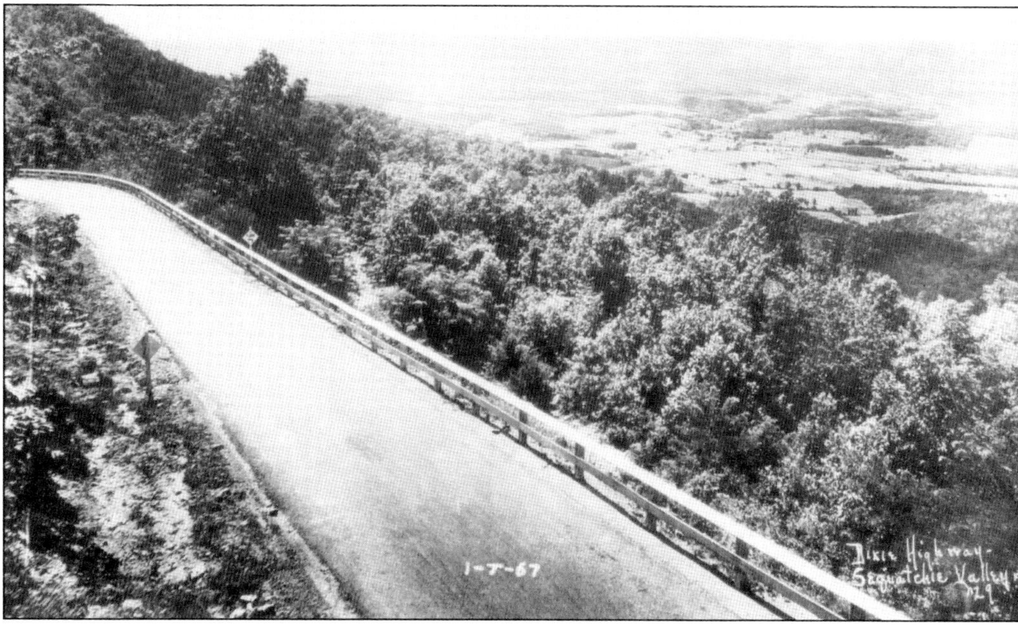

The Tennessee section of the Sequatchie Valley is approximately 75 miles long and five miles wide and travels in a southwest direction through Bledsoe, Sequatchie, and Marion Counties. In 1877, the Nashville, Chattanooga & St. Louis Railway purchased a railroad in the Sequatchie Valley that ran from Bridgeport, Alabama, to Victoria, Tennessee. By 1891, they had extended the track to Pikeville. The railroad was used to transport coal until highways were built, providing cheaper transportation. These postcards show where the Dixie Highway passed through the Sequatchie Valley on US 41 in Marion County, near the town of Jasper.

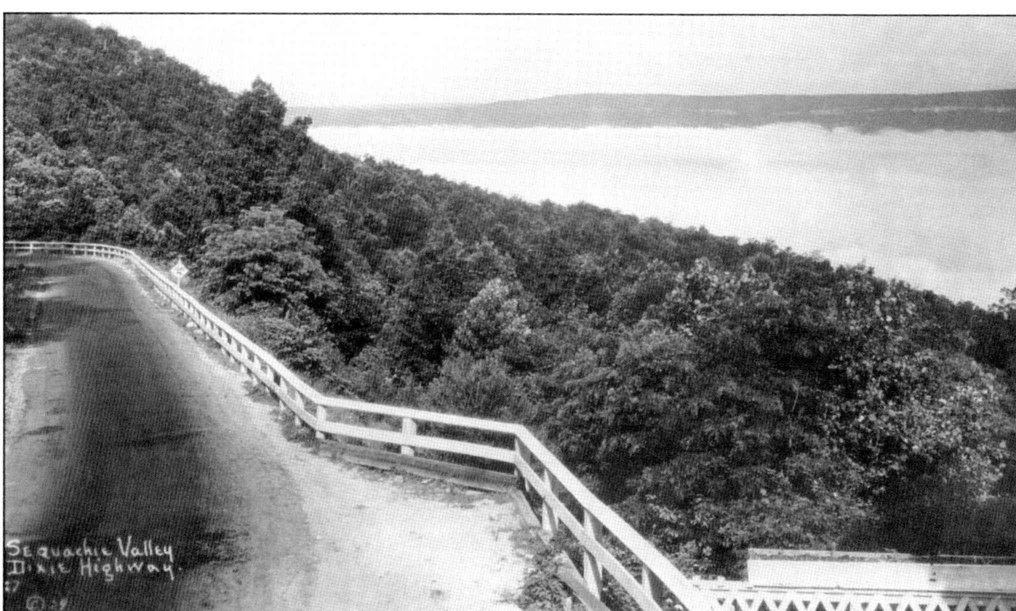

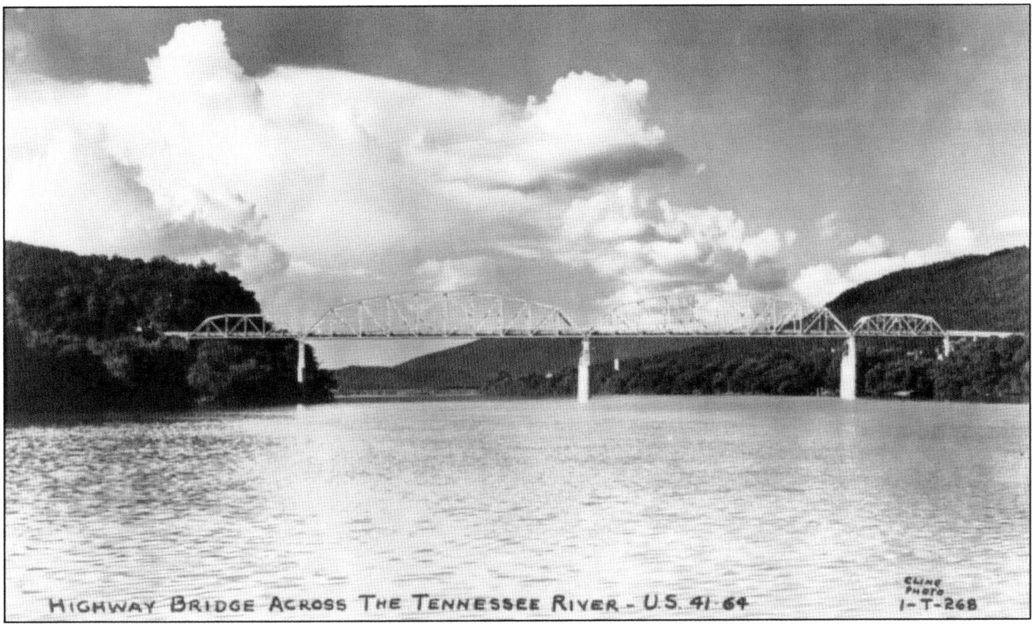

The Hales Bar Power Plant opened on November 13, 1913, at a total construction cost of $10 million. Construction of the dam took more than eight years, partially due to flooding and foundation issues. Upon completion, it was over 60 feet high and nearly a half-mile wide. The Hales Bar project was made possible through capital provided by Anthony N. Brady, a New York businessman who died prior to its completion. As a result of a US Supreme Court decision (*Tennessee Electric Power Company v. TVA*), the Tennessee Valley Authority was able to purchase the dam in 1939. Due to foundation problems, Hales Bar was replaced by Nickajack Dam in 1967.

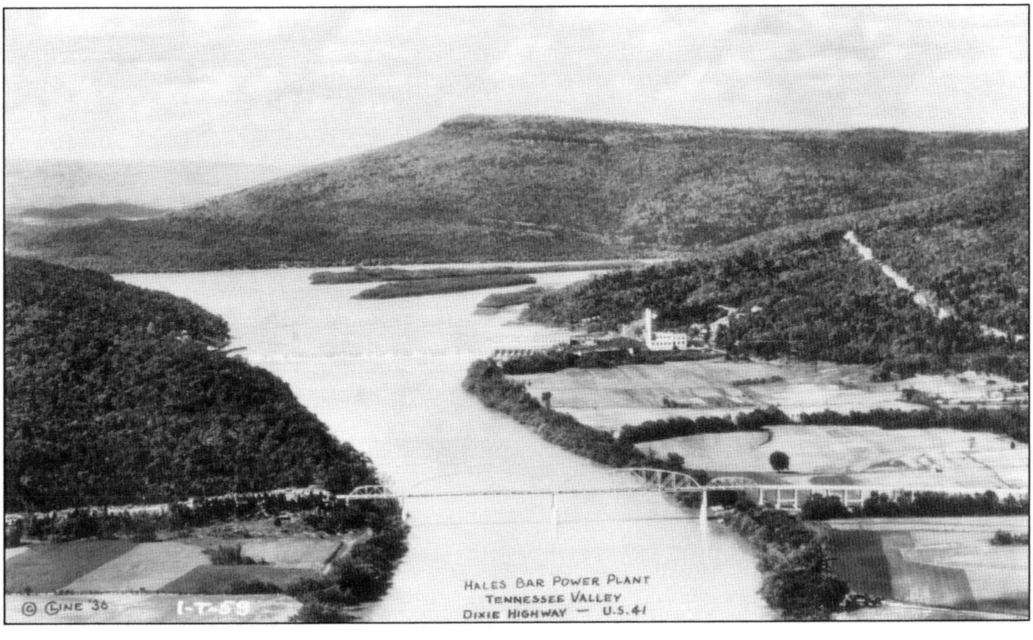

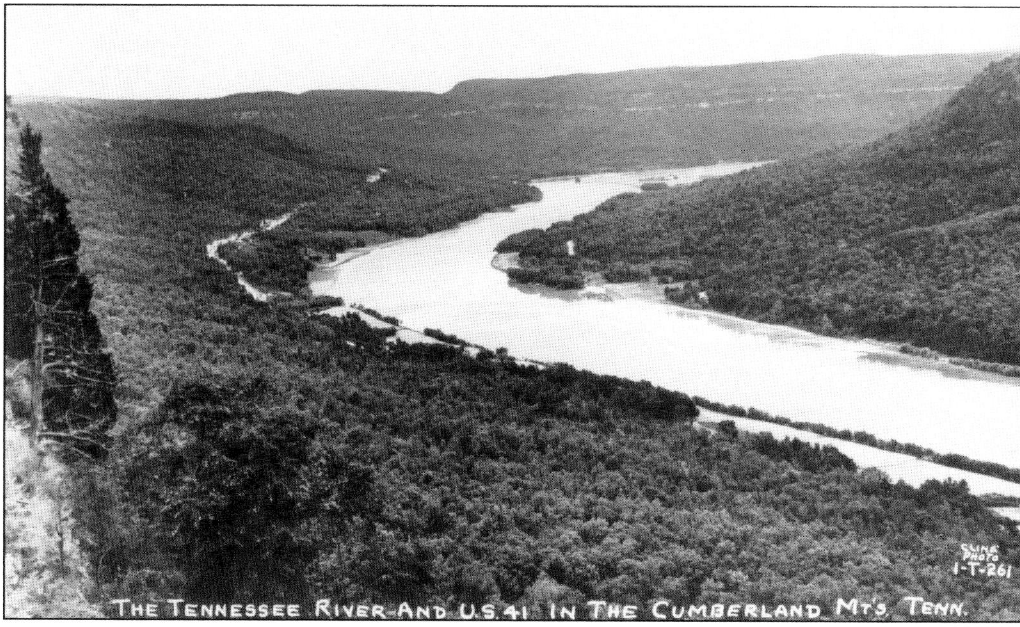

The Tennessee River is about 650 miles long and is the largest tributary of the Ohio River. It flows in a southern direction in eastern Tennessee and in a northern direction in western Tennessee. The *Str. Gordon C. Greene* (shown below) was built in 1923 and originally named *Cape Girardeau.* It was sold to Greene Line Steamers in 1935 and renamed in honor of Capt. Tom Greene's father, Gordon. A popular tourist boat for several years, it was sold in 1952. For the next several years, it traveled to various cities and was used as a hotel, museum, restaurant, and even a theater and bar in New Orleans. The steamboat appeared in several movies, including *Gone with the Wind.* After a long and prestigious career, it sank in St. Louis on December 3, 1967.

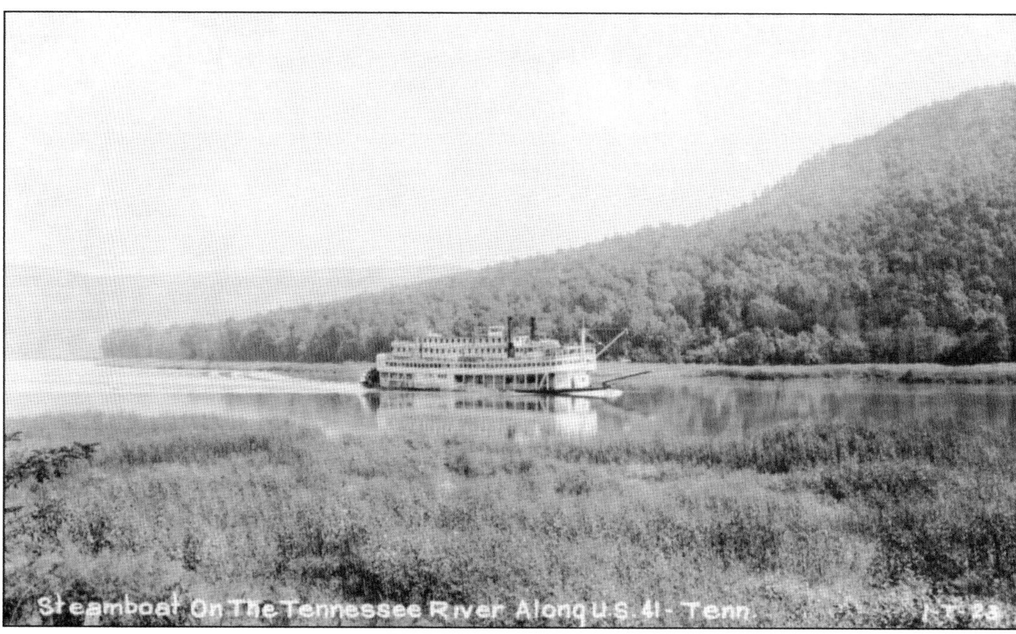

Two

Chattanooga and Lookout Mountain

Chattanooga, the southern terminus of both of the Dixie Highway routes in Tennessee, was home to the Dixie Highway Association and was the community embraced by the Cline family. The city was appropriately central to the north-south highway plan and was an obvious choice for the DHA headquarters. Both Clines, father and son, actively worked to promote the area. Their photographs were used in local tourism promotions and by attractions like Rock City, Ruby Falls, and the Incline. Though Rock City is actually in the state of Georgia, it has always been a considerable draw for those traveling to or through Chattanooga.

This chapter begins at Lookout Mountain, exploring the Incline and Point Park, detours to the Lookout Mountain Hotel (now Covenant College) and Garnet Carter's Fairyland, and spends considerable time at the ever-popular Rock City. Directly across the street, the charming Chanticleer Inn has been a pleasant lodging establishment since 1930. Ruby Falls, another venerable destination, opened a few years before Rock City. A Cline Studios photographer, possibly Cline himself, is reported to have been among the first to see the great underground falls. Continuing into Chattanooga, Cline Sr.'s interest in Civil War history continues to be evident in his photographs of the Chattanooga National Cemetery, the locomotive known as the *General*, and Civil War veteran reunions. In 1905, shortly after moving to Tennessee, he wrote an article about the Chickamauga and Chattanooga National Military Park for his hometown paper, the *Cambridge Jeffersonian*. A view of Cline Studios is the highlight of this section, allowing a rare glimpse directly into the Cline family business. Rounding out the chapter are postcards of downtown Chattanooga, the Chickamauga Dam, and the Tennessee River Gorge—along with Williams Island and Signal Mountain. Traveling north toward Dayton along Walden Ridge, the final photographs are of Montlake, sometimes referred to as "nature's masterpiece."

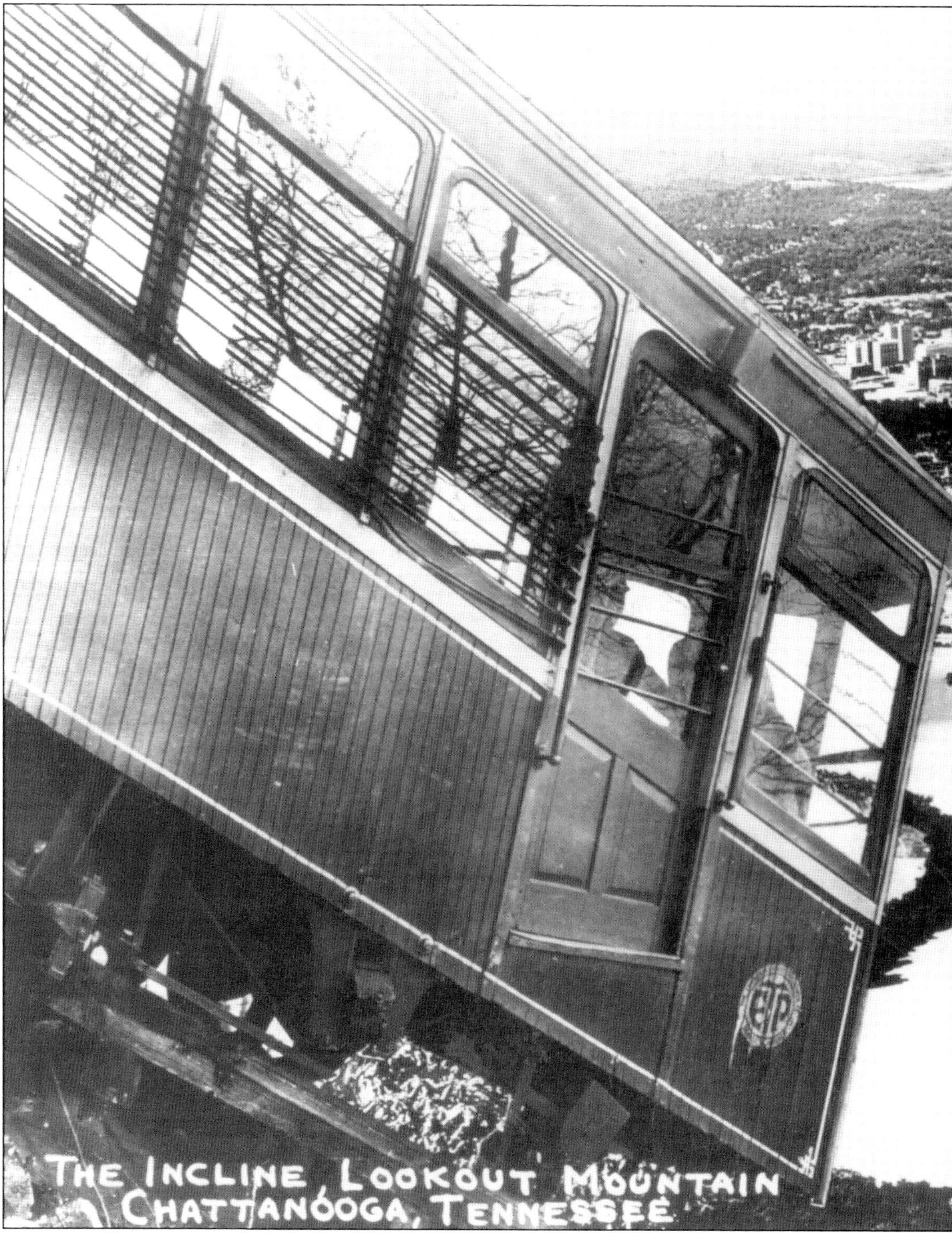

The Lookout Mountain Incline Railway is the steepest passenger railway in the world. It is listed in the National Register of Historic Places and was the 100th National Historic Mechanical Engineering Landmark to be designated. Known as "America's most amazing mile," the track extends up the mountain for nine-tenths of a mile. The cars are pulled by motor-driven cables,

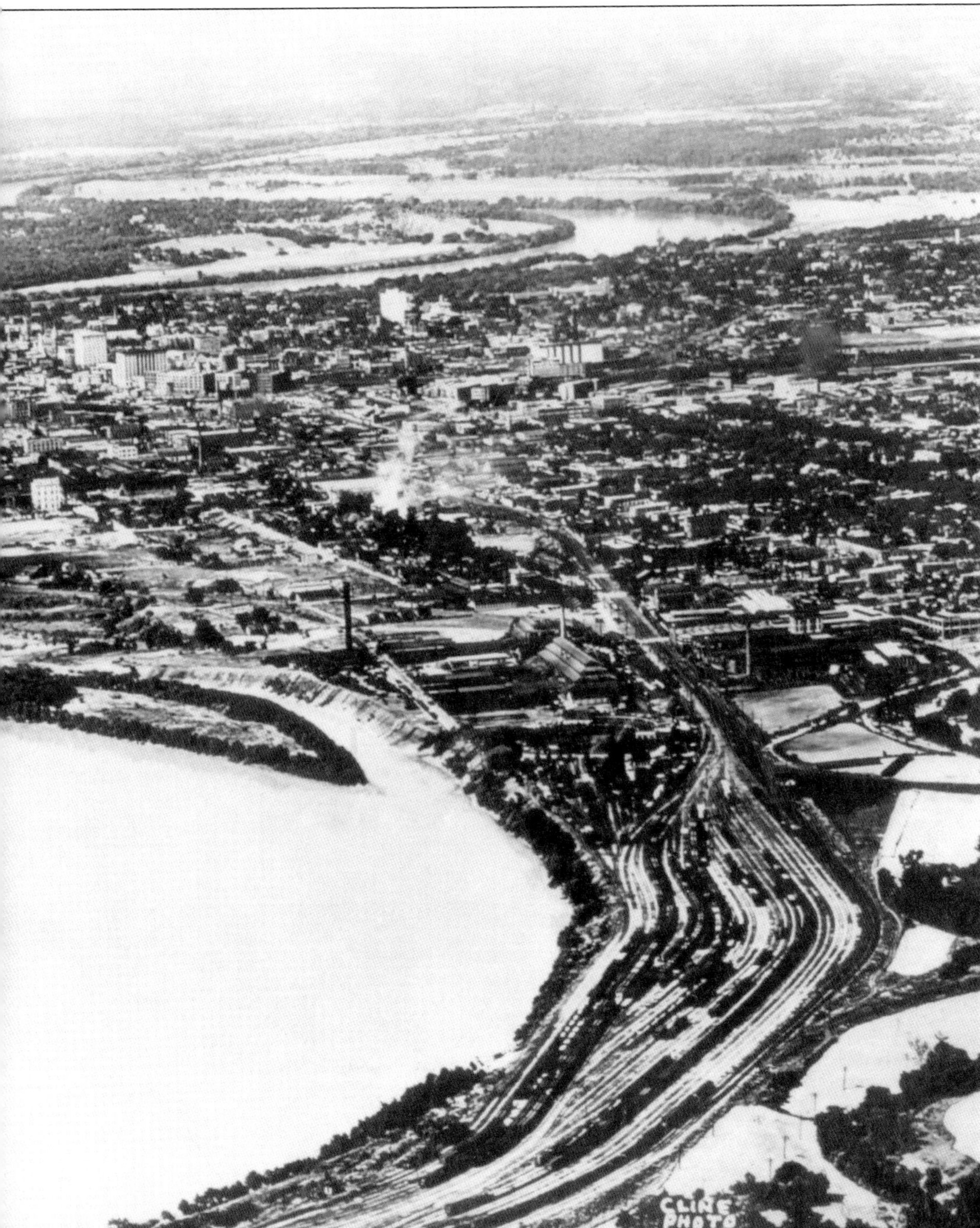

and with numerous safety devices, there have never been any passenger fatalities. It has been operated by the Chattanooga Area Regional Transportation Authority (CARTA) since 1978. Millions of tourists have enjoyed the breathtaking view from the train's windows and the Incline's observation tower, the highest overlook on Lookout Mountain.

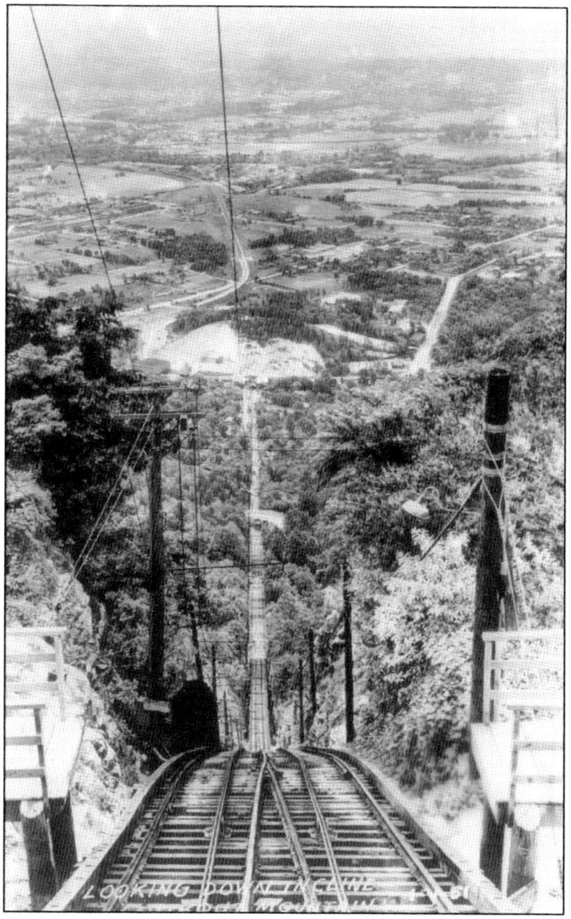

The Incline was built in 1895 on the steepest part of Lookout Mountain by John T. Crass and a small group of investors. Designed by Josephus Conn Guild, it has a 72.7 percent grade near the mountaintop. The cables, capable of pulling over 12 times the weight of the cars when fully loaded, were purchased from the same company that built the Brooklyn Bridge, the John A. Roebling Company. An incline with a less direct route and a maximum grade of only 33 percent was constructed on the mountain eight years earlier, but the company ceased operations in 1899 after Crass purchased it in order to eliminate other railway competition.

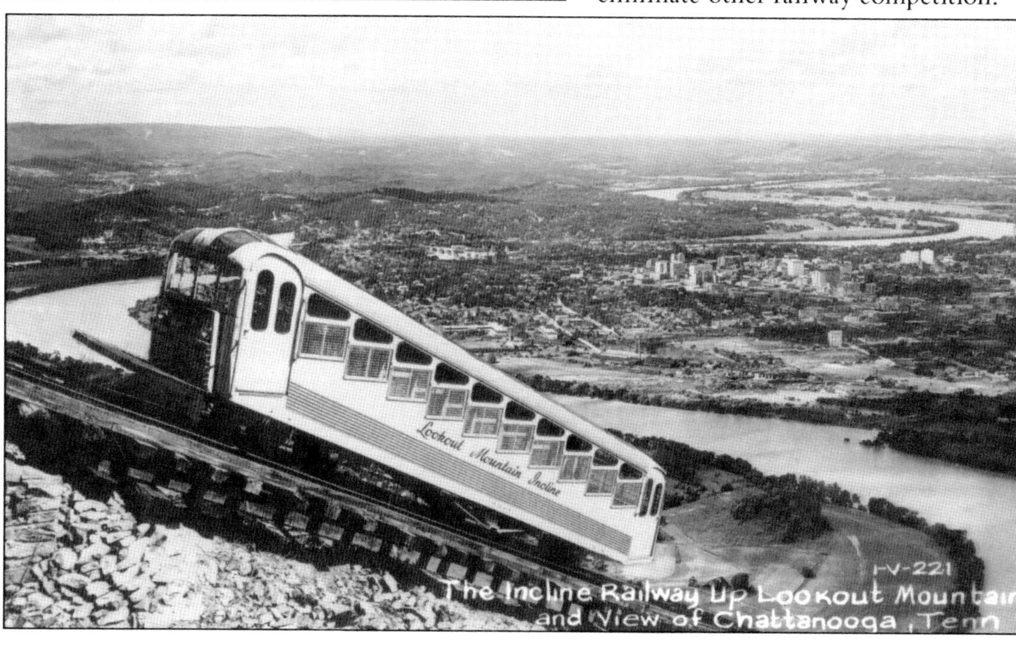

Each of the Incline's two railway cars can hold up to 42 passengers. The cars travel at a speed of less than 10 miles per hour, allowing passengers ample time to enjoy the amazing view. The station at the bottom of Lookout Mountain is located in St. Elmo, where passengers can visit unique shops featuring items such as handblown glass and homemade candles and can go on a brewery tour. The station at the top of the mountain has an observation deck and gift shop and is just a few blocks from Civil War attractions such as historic Point Park and the Battles for Chattanooga Electric Map and Museum.

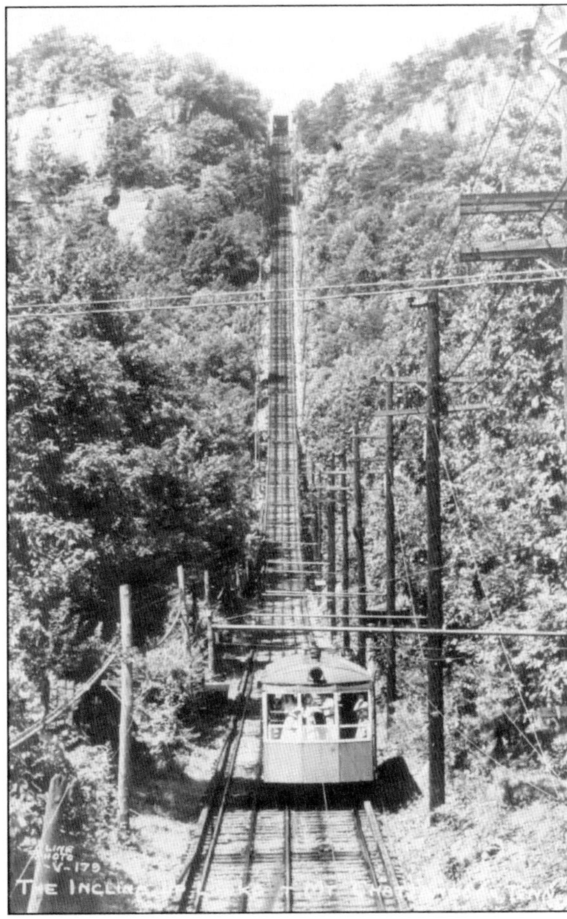

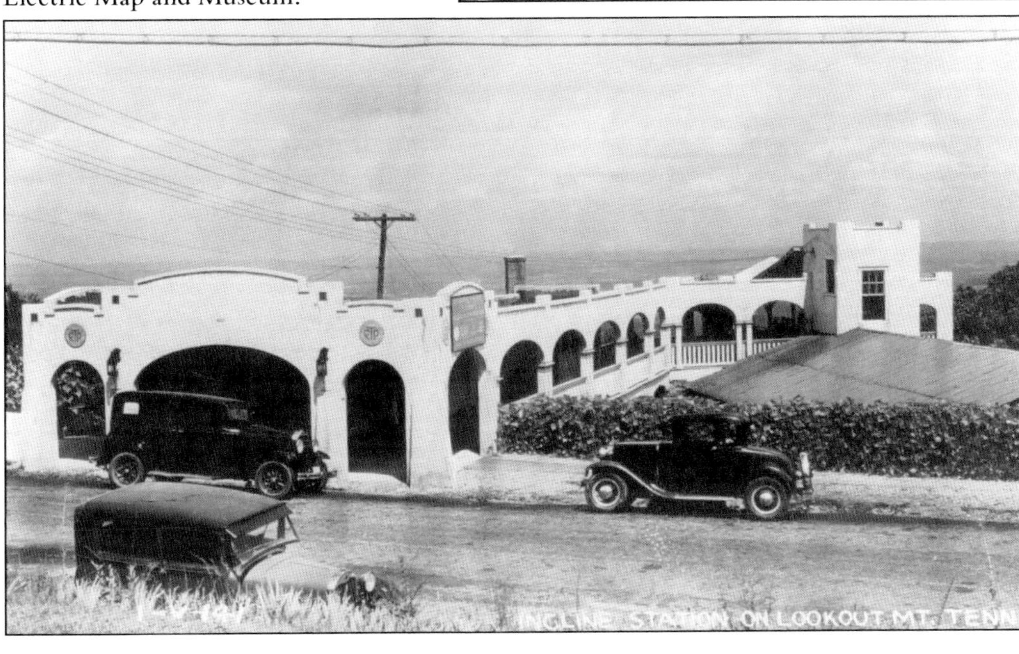

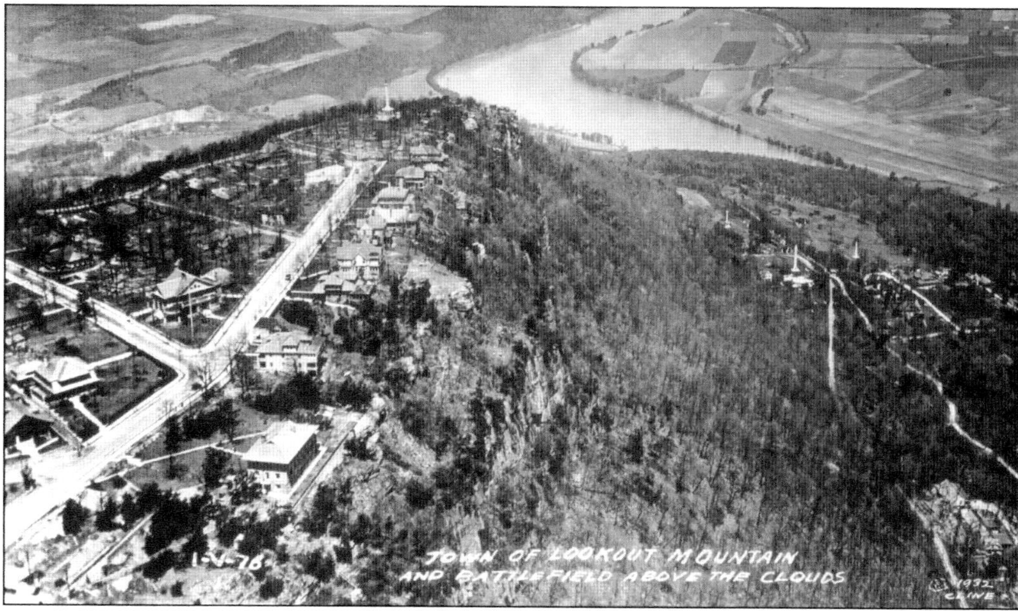

The Battle of Chattanooga, also known as the "Battle Above the Clouds," took place on November 24, 1863, when, after nearly two months of being held inside the boundaries of Chattanooga, Union general Joseph Hooker commanded his men to climb the face of Lookout Mountain toward the summit. Unexpectedly, haze obscured their ascent, and they were able to force the Confederates to flee. In 1890, Pres. Benjamin Harrison signed into law an act that would create the Chickamauga and Chattanooga National Military Park to preserve the surrounding battlefields. A park commission was created to oversee the work, and by 1893, Lookout Mountain Battlefield had been created. The commission successfully obtained the land at the northern edge of the mountain in 1899. By 1905, the entrance to Point Park (shown below) had been built to resemble the US Army Corps of Engineers insignia.

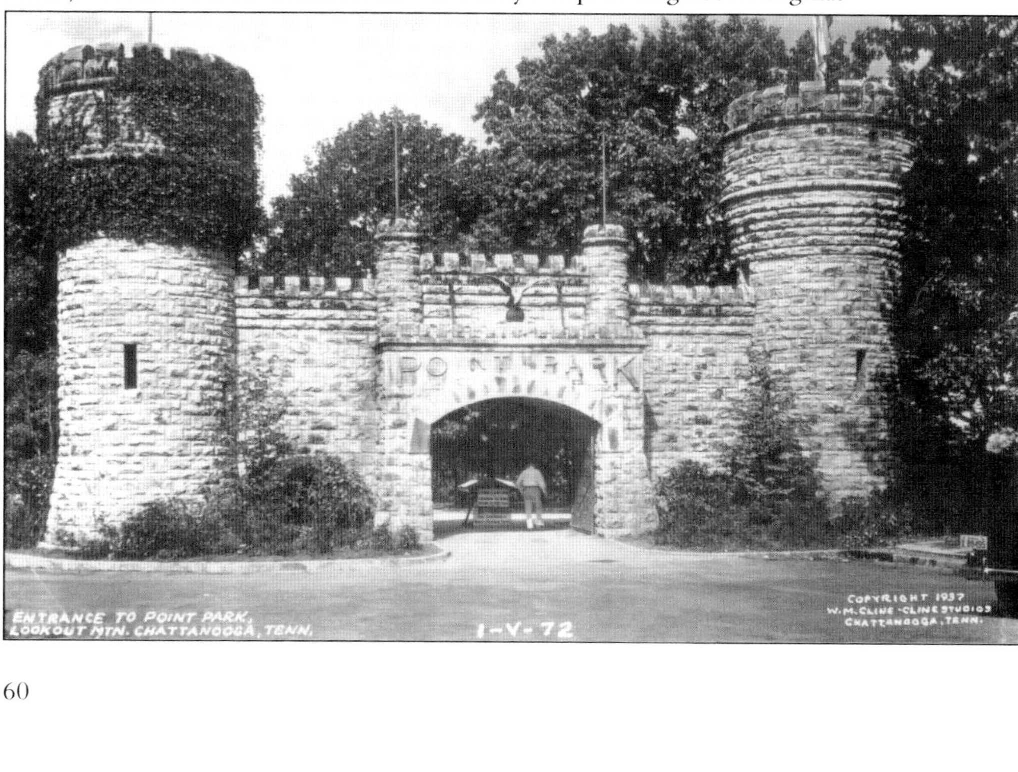

The New York Peace Monument, standing 95 feet high with a 50-foot base, serves as the central focus of Point Park. It was constructed of Tennessee marble and pink Massachusetts granite. Erected in 1907 at a cost of about $80,000, the memorial was dedicated in 1910 with an elaborate ceremony that cost upwards of $20,000. The bronze Confederate and Union soldiers on top are shown shaking hands to represent reconciliation. Using federal stimulus funds, it received much needed repairs in time for the centennial celebration in 2010. Nearby, three cannons are aimed toward Chattanooga as a small representation of the line of defense that existed during the Battle Above the Clouds. Cast-iron tablets throughout the park provide the details of the battle.

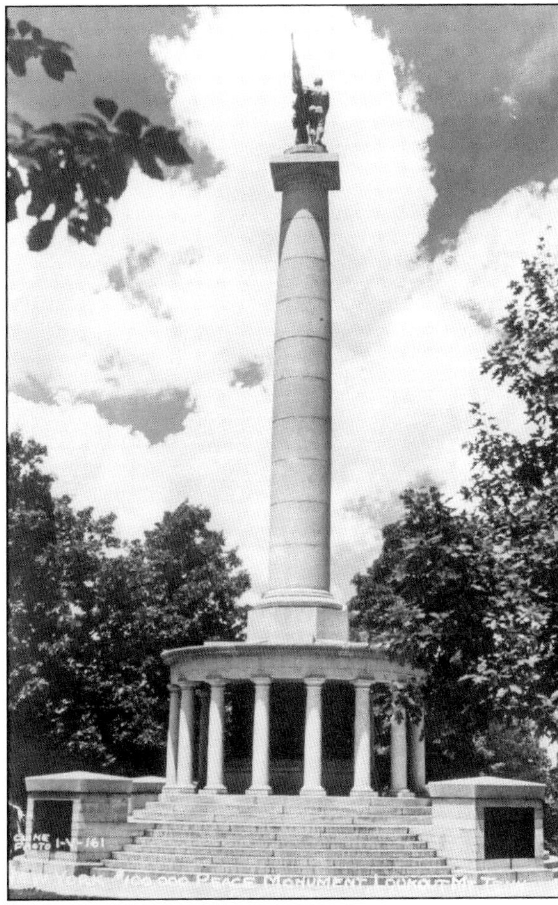

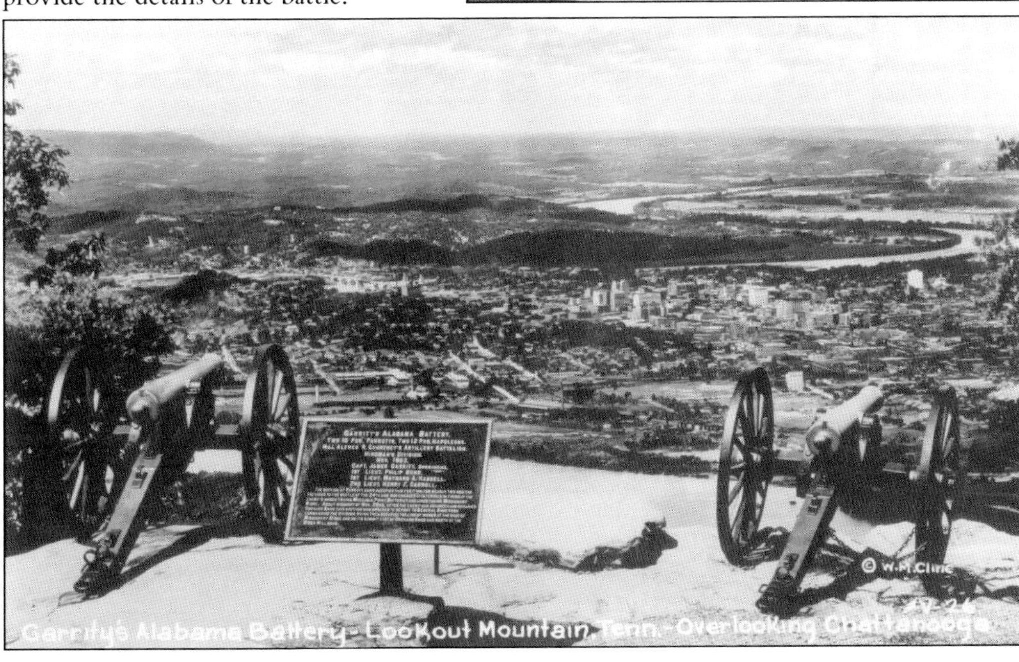

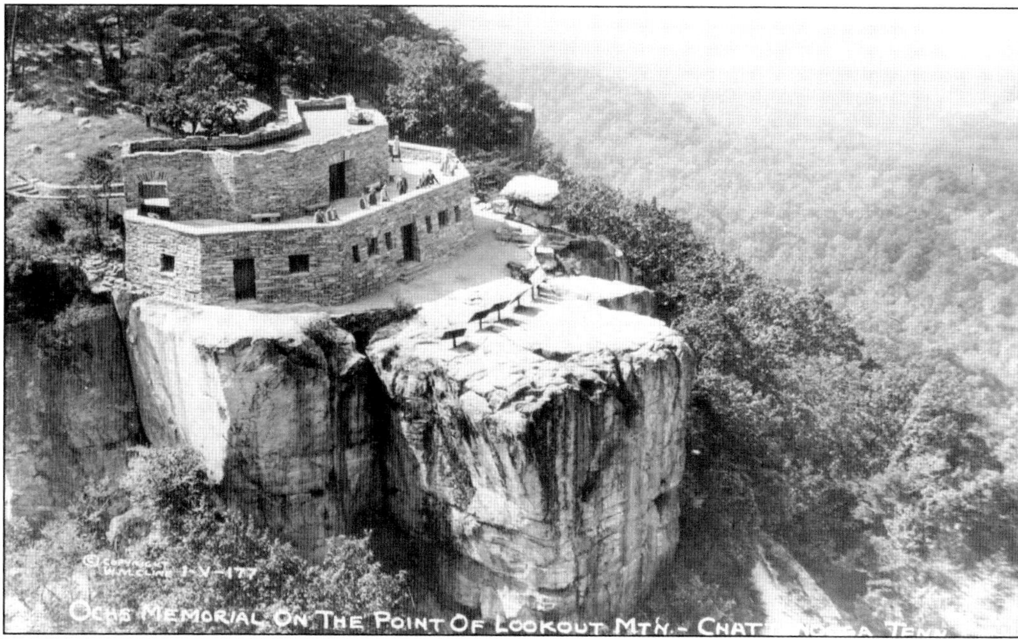

The Ochs Memorial Museum and Observatory at Point Park is named for Adolph S. Ochs. He was a newspaper publisher and conservationist and was influential in the preservation of the battlefield areas around Lookout Mountain. At one time, he owned both the *Chattanooga Times* and the *New York Times*. Ochs led the movement to protect the 2,700 wooded acres below the point and independently contributed more than $230,000 for the acquisition and enhancement of battlefield property. The museum was constructed in 1939, primarily by the Civilian Conservation Corps (CCC), utilizing local stone that allowed it to blend with the natural surroundings. It was dedicated on November 12, 1940.

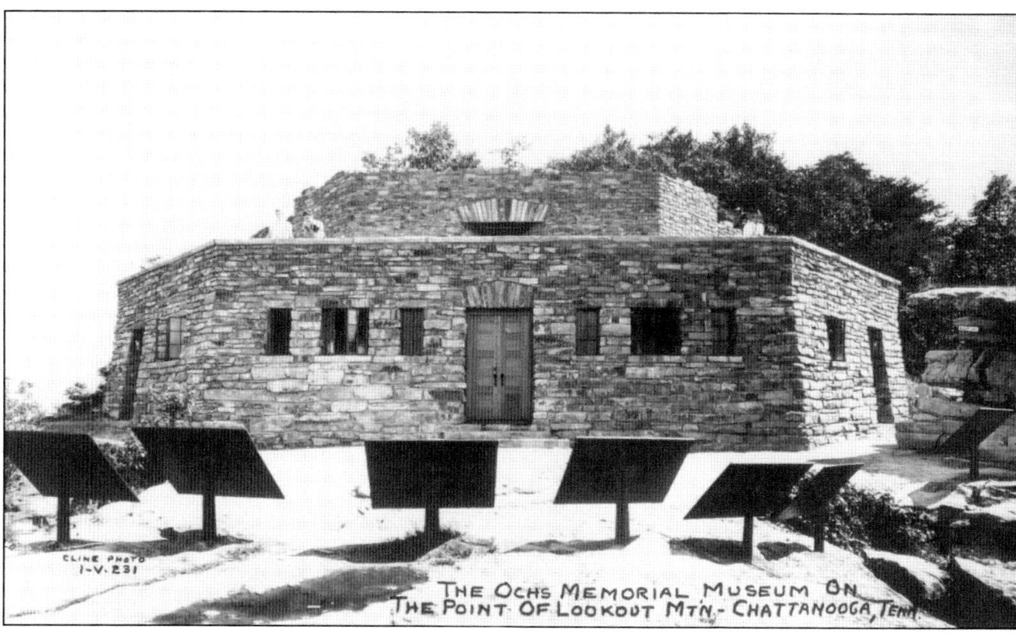

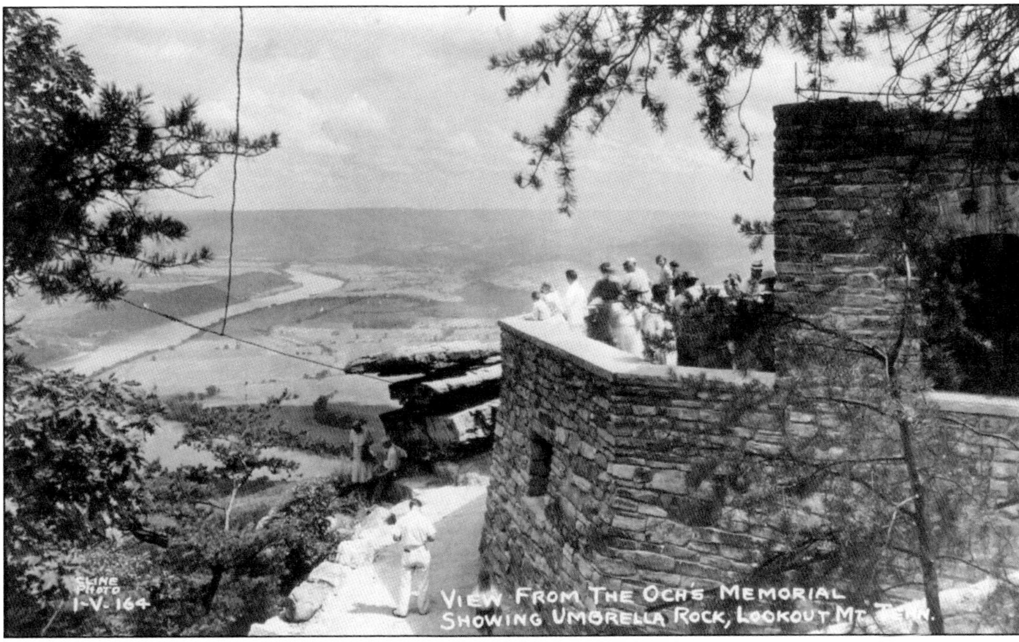

Below the Ochs Memorial is a rock formation that has been known for many years as Umbrella Rock. Since the time of the Civil War, people have often sat on or by this rock to take spectacular photographs with Moccasin Bend and the Tennessee River in the background. Ochs Memorial was built on the previous site of the Linn photographic studio, owned by brothers Robert and James Linn. They operated the business between 1863 and 1886. George Linn, Robert's son, took over after the studio was rented for several years. He worked there from 1900 until the memorial was constructed in 1939. For safety reasons, a chain-link fence now blocks access to the rock, and the explanatory tablets that once lined the edge of the cliff have been relocated.

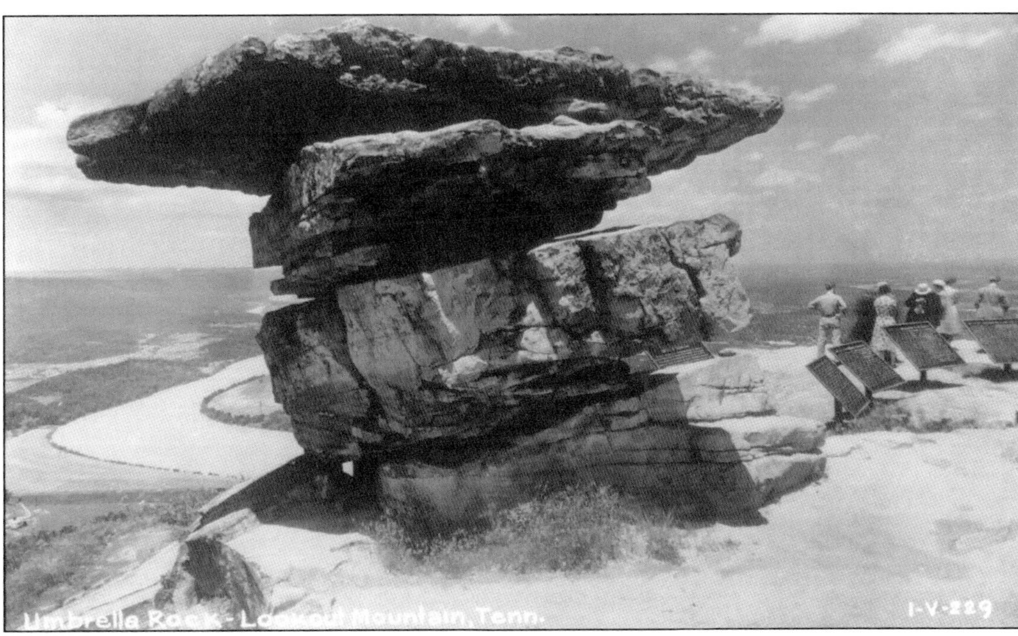

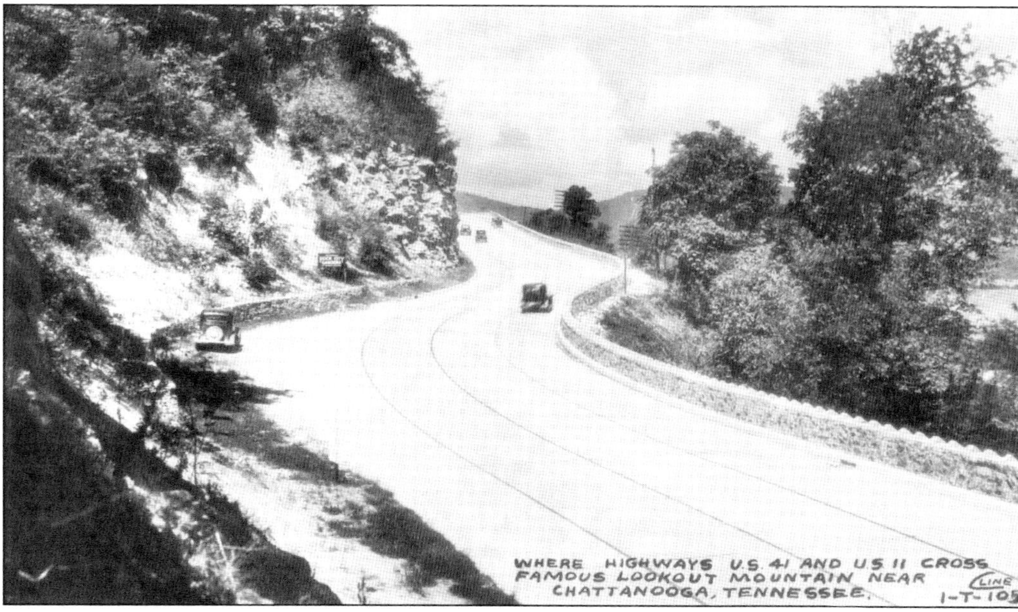

The highway pictured above was named for William Cummings, a Hamilton County judge who was a member of the Dixie Highway Association and an activist for the Good Roads Movement. Designated as the Will Cummings Highway in 1931, the 24-mile section was part of Old Wauhatchie Pike (US 41, the Dixie Highway), the first federally funded road in Tennessee. Beginning in Chattanooga, the Cummings Highway winds around the base of Lookout Mountain and continues to the town of Jasper. The Scenic Highway extends from the Cummings Highway to the top of Lookout Mountain. This thoroughfare, along with the Ochs Highway, provided drivers in the 1930s with toll-free access up the mountain, increasing tourism for the growing number of attractions.

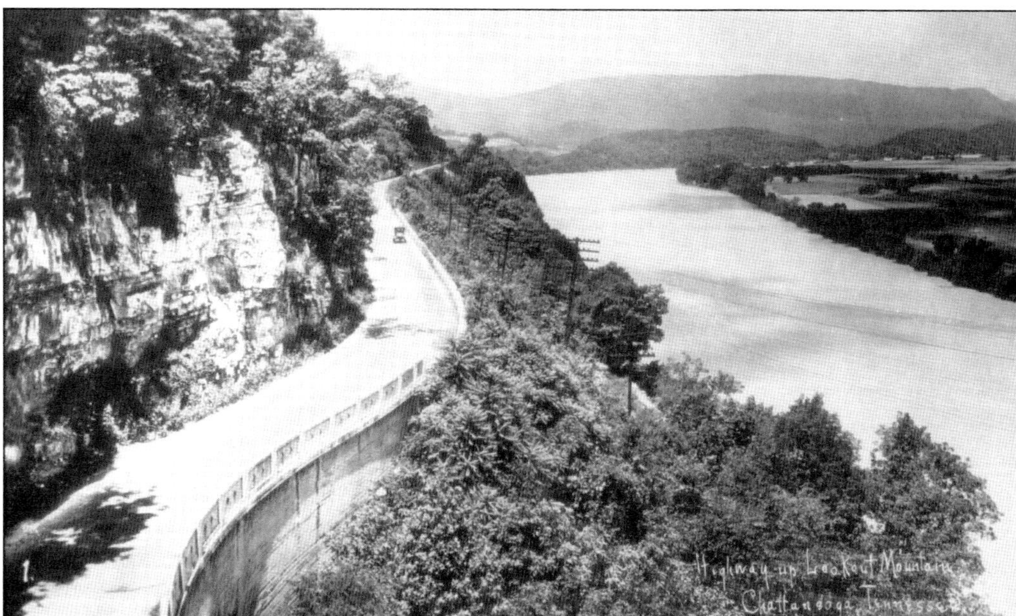

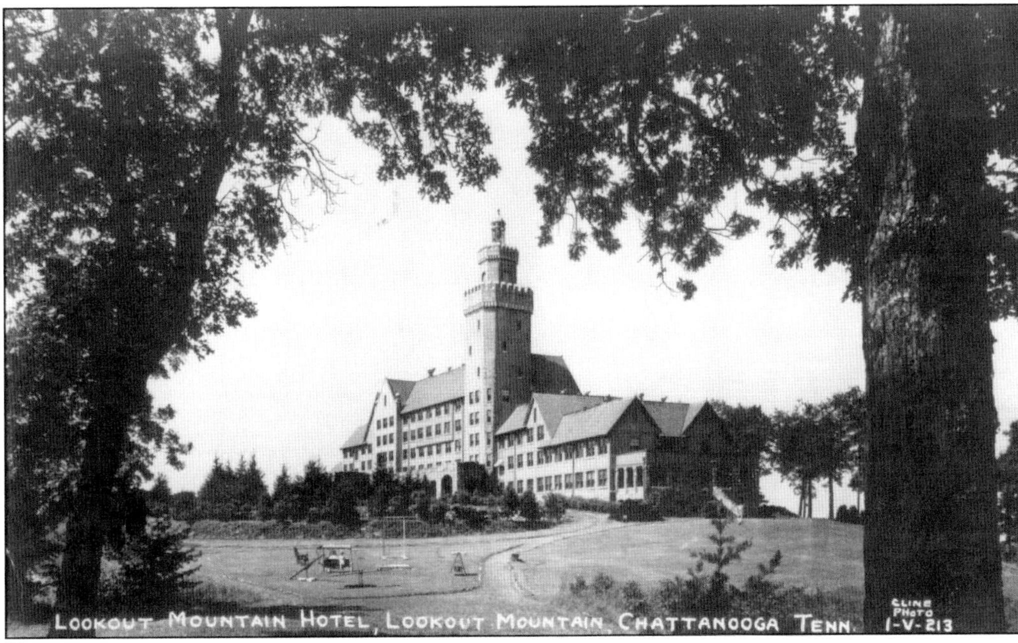

Due to increased tourism on Lookout Mountain, the Atlanta-based Dinkler Hotel Corporation decided to build a luxury hotel there and chose Paul Carter, younger brother of Garnet Carter, to manage it. The ground-breaking for Lookout Mountain Hotel, known as the "Castle in the Clouds," was held on June 14, 1927. Due to bad weather, the ceremonies had to be held a few miles away in the ballroom of Garnet Carter's Fairyland Inn. Constructed for a cost of nearly $1.5 million, Lookout Mountain Hotel—which opened in 1928—had 200 rooms and the largest ballroom in the South. The structure was purchased by Covenant College, which moved into the hotel in 1964.

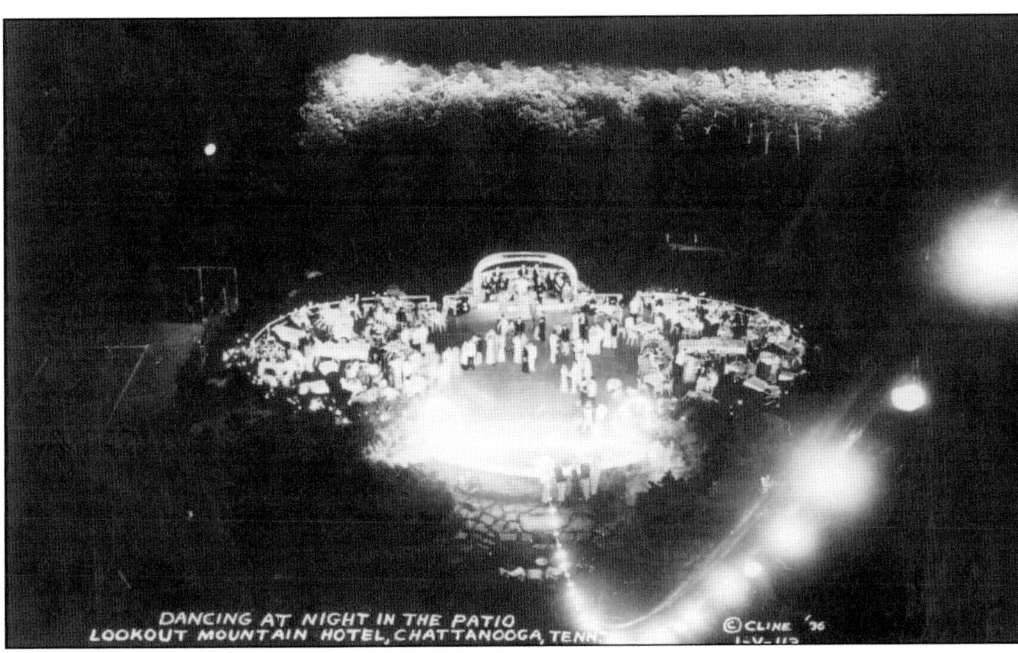

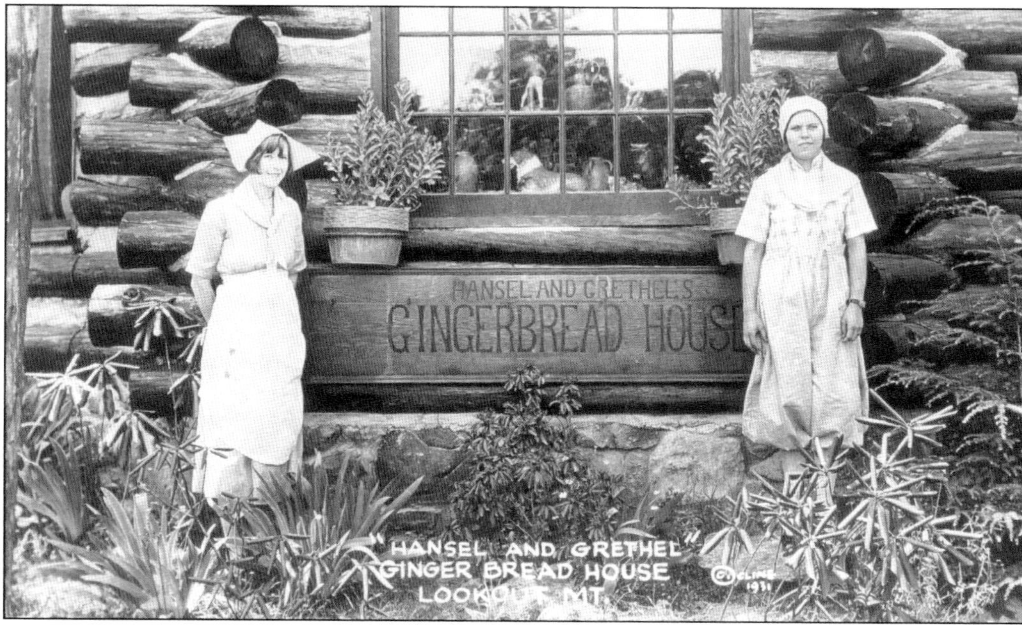

Garnet Carter and Oliver Andrews purchased land on top of Lookout Mountain and began selling lots in late 1924. Carter called his residential section Fairyland because Frieda, his wife, loved classic fairy tales. Possessing natural architectural abilities, Frieda designed a gas station and several houses in Fairyland. She also designed Hansel and Grethel's Gingerbread House, a souvenir shop that sold homemade gingerbread, ice cream, and other refreshments. She decorated the neighborhood with colorful statues of elves and gnomes imported from Germany. Statues of geese and an intricate wrought-iron sign adorned the entrance to her Mother Goose Village. Years later, these were moved to Fairyland Caverns in Rock City Gardens and repainted in fluorescent colors.

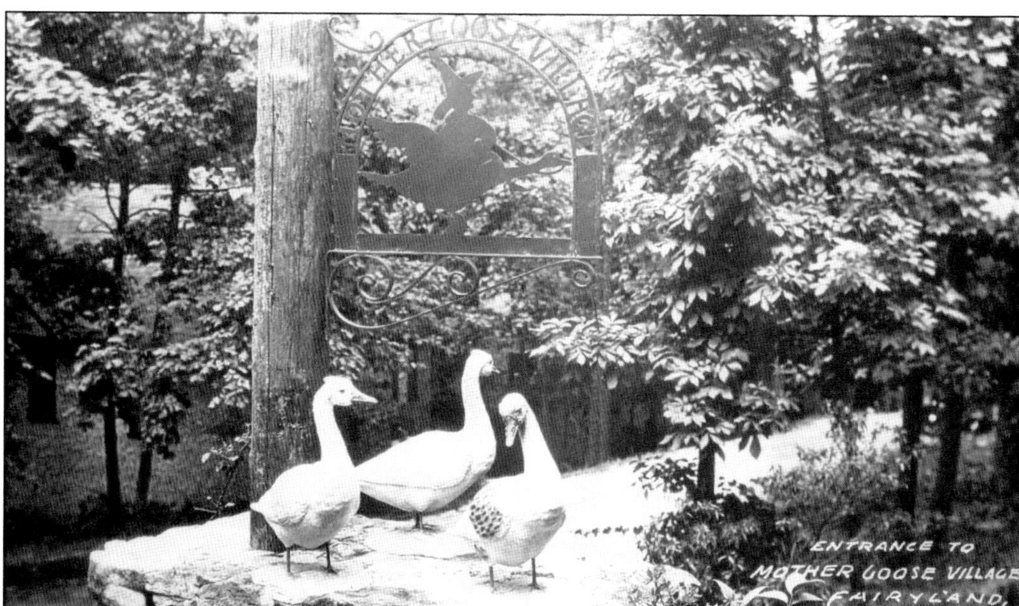

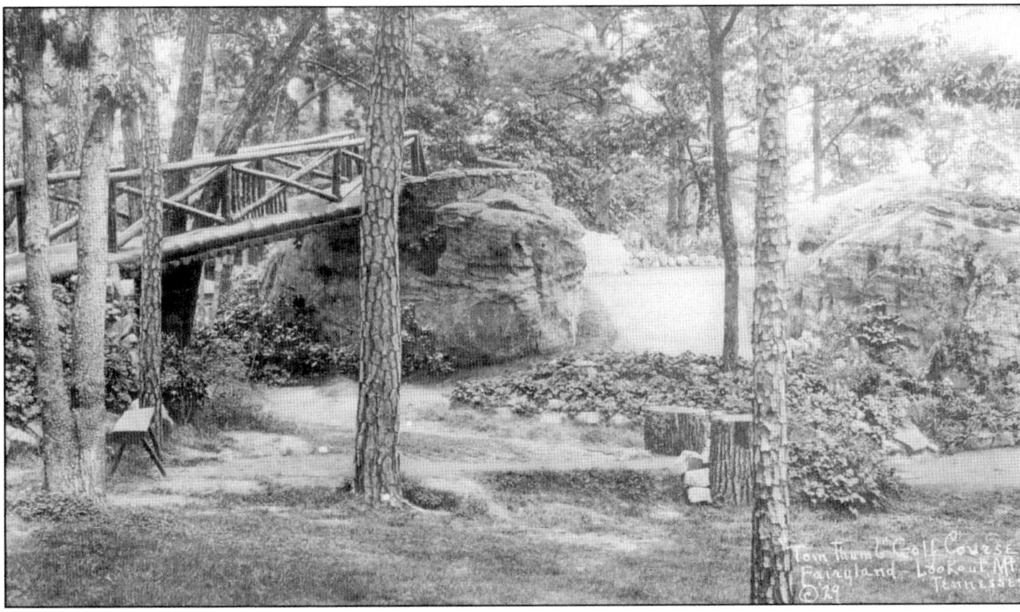

Designed in 1929 by Garnet Carter, Tom Thumb Golf was the world's first miniature golf course. Carter designed the course as a temporary amusement for his guests in Fairyland while a full-scale golf course was being completed on Lookout Mountain. It had 18 holes with a par of two or three on each section, depending on the level of difficulty. Various obstacles were in place, as well as the characteristic Fairyland elves and gnomes. The putting green consisted of cottonseed hulls mixed with oil and dye. The game became so popular that he patented it and sold franchises. Approximately 50,000 miniature golf courses were constructed across the country during the 1930s. The original Tom Thumb golf course was demolished in 1958.

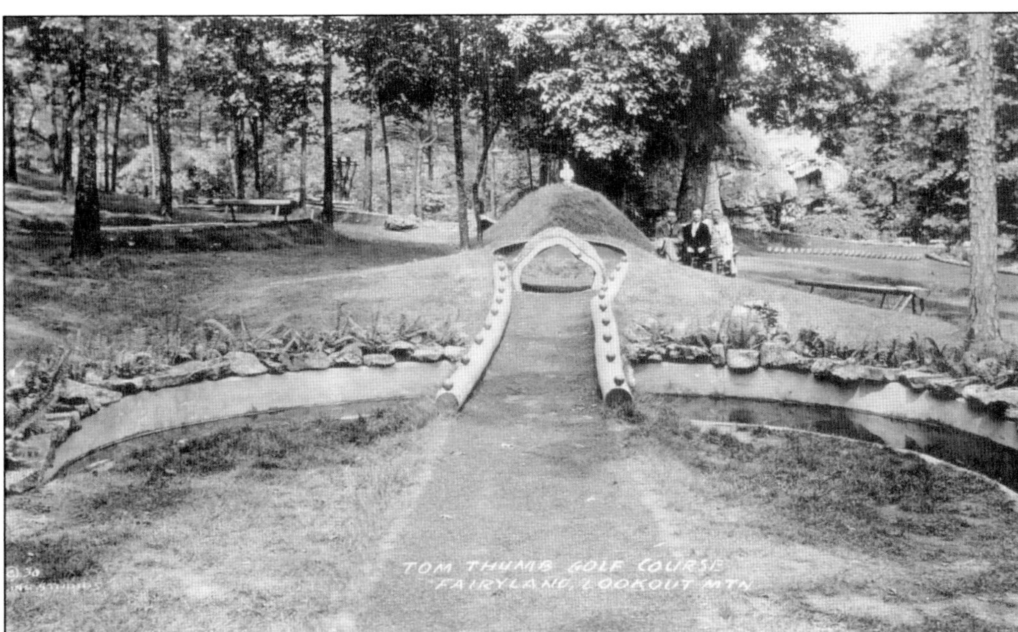

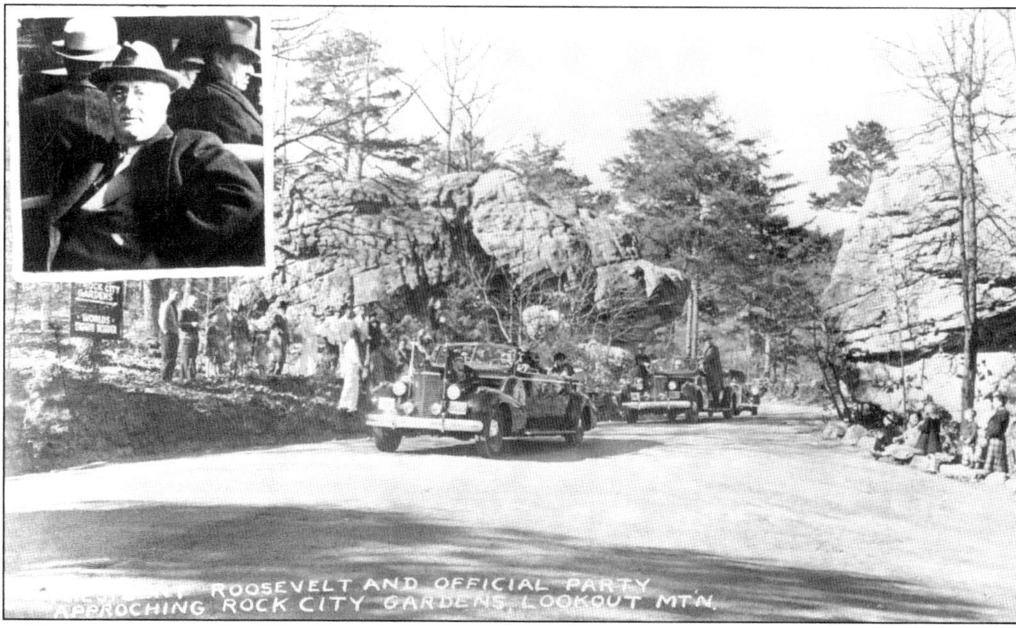

During his visit to Tennessee to dedicate the Chickamauga Dam, Franklin D. Roosevelt and his wife, Eleanor, took a tour of Lookout Mountain on September 2, 1940. They drove to Point Park, where Eleanor walked to the ledge to enjoy the panoramic view of Chattanooga. The delegation continued around the mountain and through Fairyland before driving down Ochs Highway to St. Elmo.

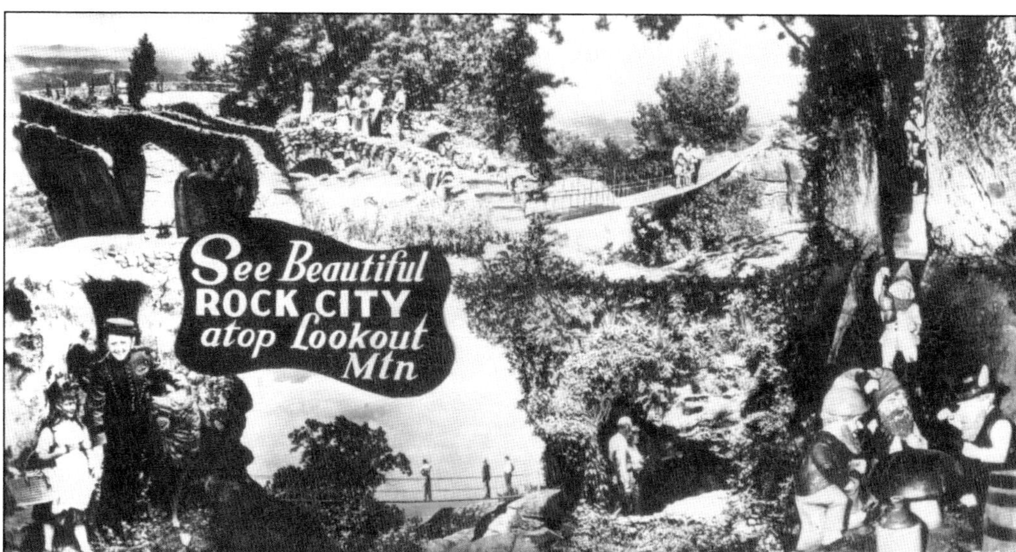

Garnet and Frieda Carter suffered severe financial losses in the stock market crash of 1929. Fairyland Inn closed in 1930 due to poor attendance, and they needed a profitable business venture. Recognizing the beauty and revenue potential of the natural rock formations on their Lookout Mountain property, the Carters opened Rock City Gardens on May 21, 1932.

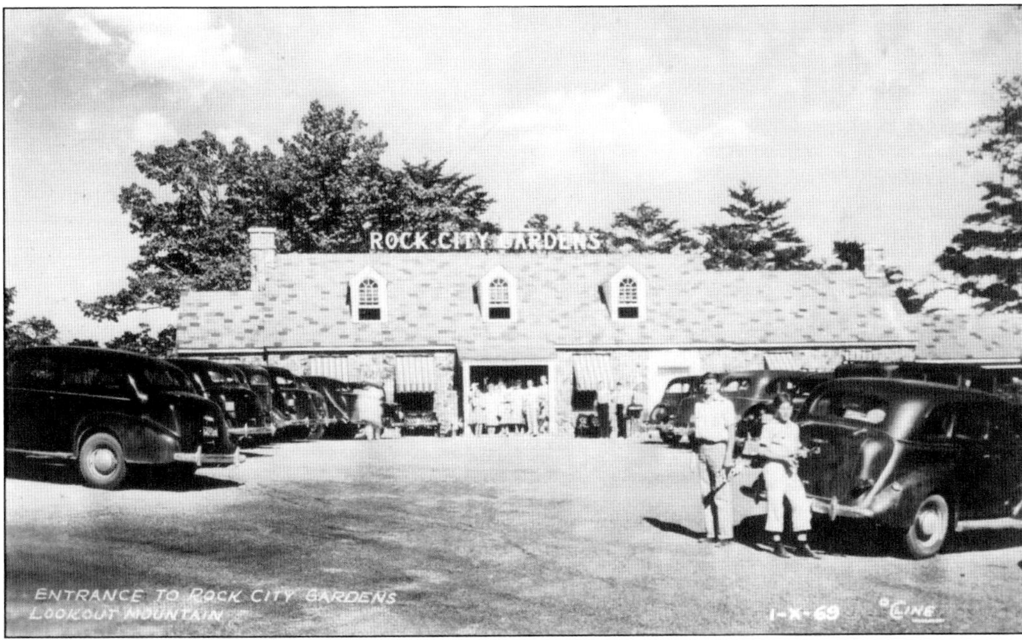

Designed by Frieda Carter, the building shown here contained a restaurant, gift shop, restrooms, and offices. Now a large gift shop, it has served as the entrance to the Enchanted Trail since 1937. The original entrance was a small round building with a cone-shaped roof known as the Sugar Loaf Shop; it can still be accessed during the self-guided tour.

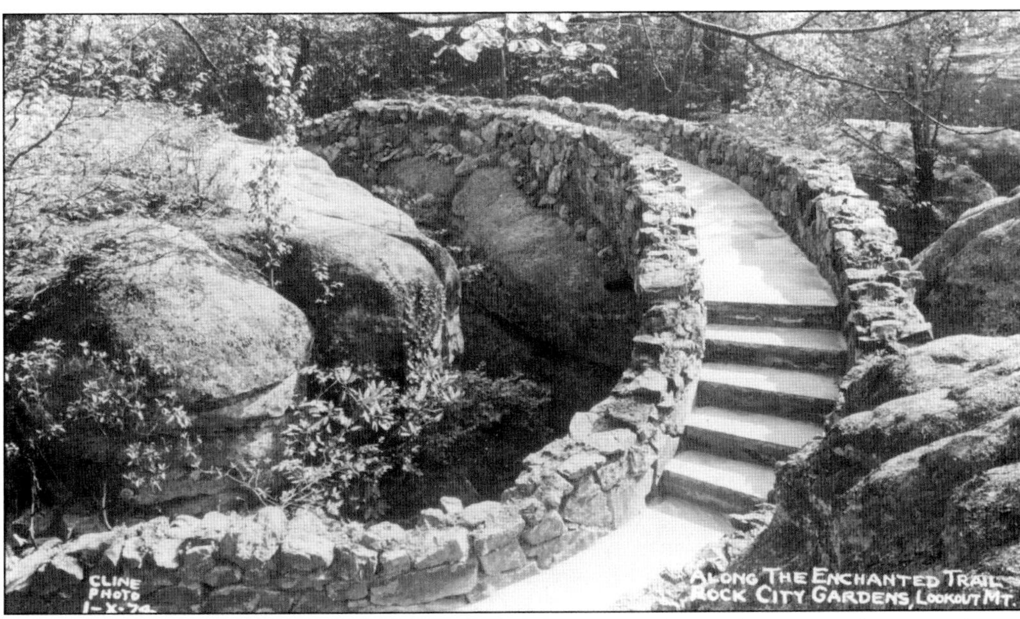

Though many naturally formed pathways already existed in the gardens, several stone stairways were added to the trail in order to improve accessibility and increase safety. New pathways were created when necessary by blasting through solid rock, but for the most part the rock formations were left in their natural states.

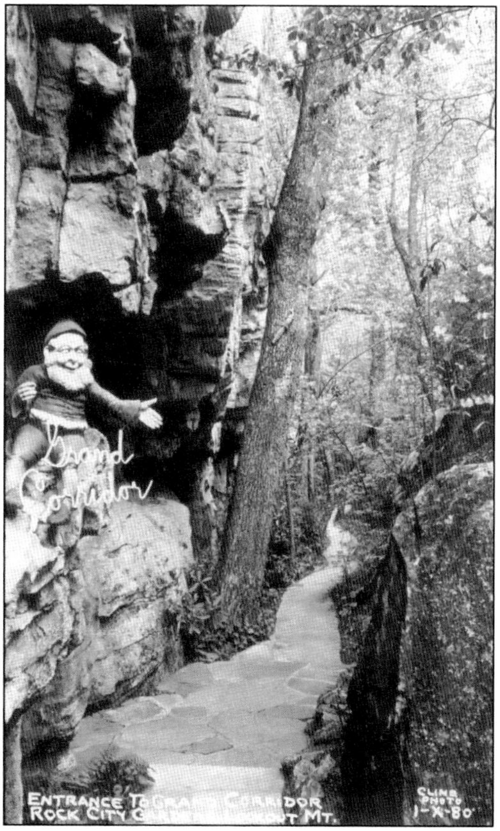

After the opening of Rock City, many of the imported German statues that had decorated the Fairyland subdivision were moved to the new attraction, much to the delight of young visitors. This gnome welcomes guests as they walk through the Grand Corridor. The natural passageway was cut millions of years ago by flowing waters.

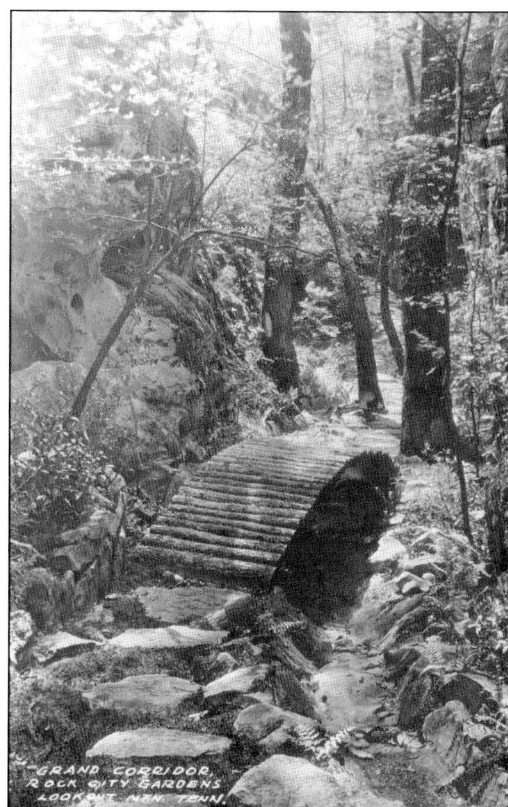

Due to Frieda Carter's hard work and ingenuity, Rock City Gardens possessed a superb collection of wildflowers, shrubs, and trees. This scenic view of the Grand Corridor is one example. Her efforts were rewarded when she received the Horticultural Bronze Medal of Distinction from the Garden Club of America in 1933.

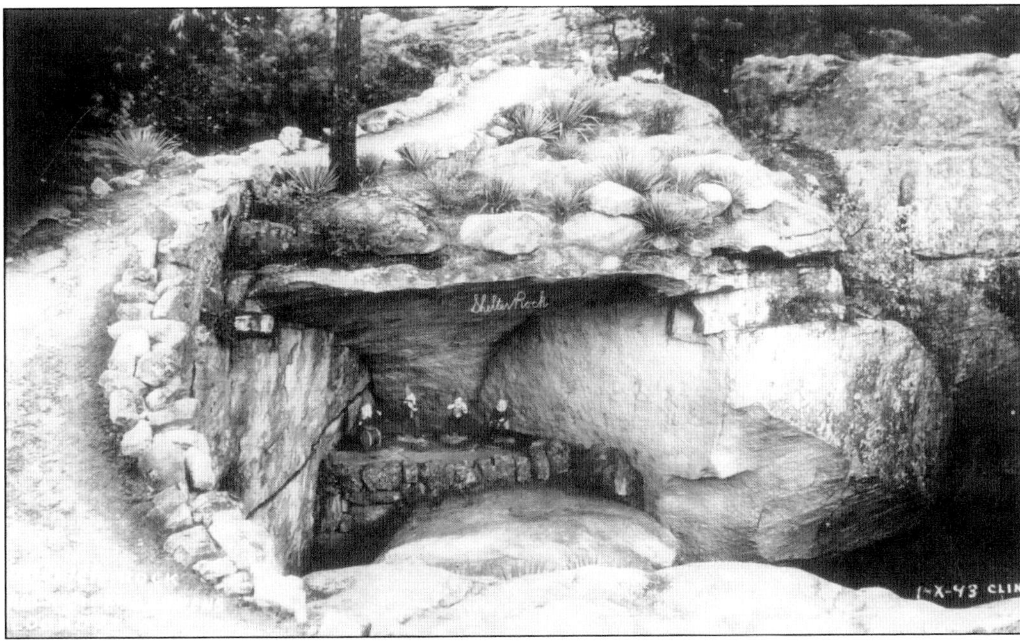

When Shelter Rock was first discovered in the gardens, the back wall was covered with graffiti from earlier decades. To prepare the structure for tourists, the graffiti was removed and gnomes playing musical instruments were placed inside. Shelter Rock originally contained a crevice, which is visible in the photograph. A solid floor was added for safety.

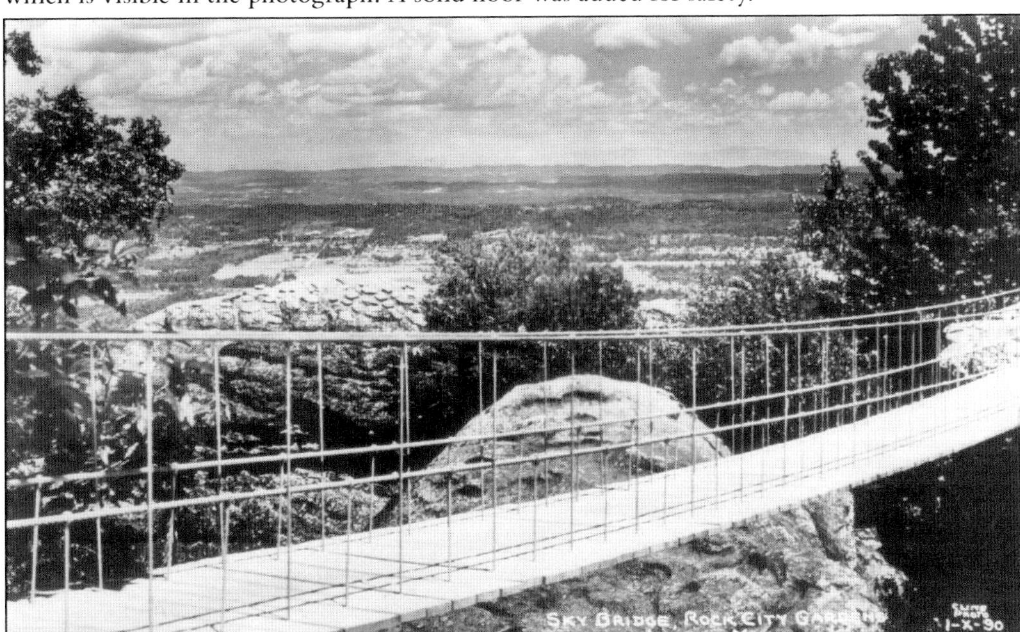

Three swinging bridges were constructed when Rock City first opened. Built with surplus cables from the Incline, the bridges improved accessibility to hard-to-reach areas. As attractions were added in later years and paths were rerouted, Rockaway Bridge and Swing-Along Bridge became obsolete. The original Sky Bridge was later renamed Swing-Along Bridge, and its 180-foot walkway offers today's visitors a spectacular view.

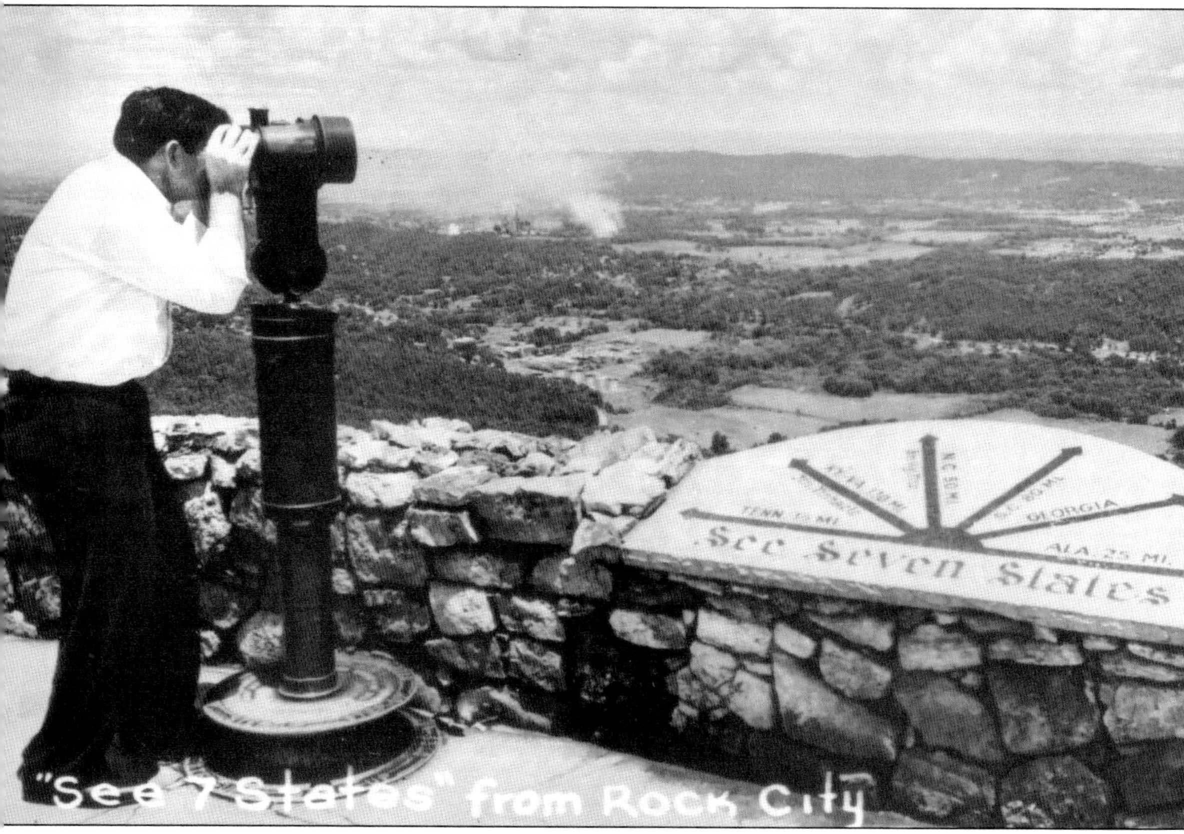

Four years after Rock City opened, Frieda Carter hired Hobby Law to design a house near Lover's Leap. Known as Carter Cliffs, their new home allowed the Carters to enjoy the gardens, visitors, and an incredible panoramic view. When Rock City first opened, advertisements claimed that five states (Tennessee, North Carolina, South Carolina, Alabama, and Georgia) could be seen from Lover's Leap. Ads for Point Park claimed that seven states, including Virginia and Kentucky, could be seen from Umbrella Rock. Rock City soon matched this claim, and "See Seven States from Rock City" became one of the many slogans Clark Byers painted on barns across Tennessee. Byers's barn art, used as an inexpensive way of advertising, made Rock City well known throughout the country. By the 1950s, "See Rock City" and other slogans decorated more than 800 barn roofs, some as far away as Michigan. Laws enacted in the early 1960s forced the end of Byers painting additional barn advertisements.

The folklore of Lover's Leap says that a young Native American named Sautee and a Cherokee maiden named Nacoochee fell in love. Their tribes were engaged in a hostile conflict, so they ran away together. Sautee was captured and thrown from the top of Lover's Leap. Inconsolable, Nacoochee hastily followed, leaping to her own death. Before the rock wall was built around the rim of Lover's Leap, Walter Cline Jr. posed for a photograph near the cliff's edge. Although not visible in either of these postcards, High Falls is a 140-foot waterfall near Lover's Leap. The falls have been a popular attraction since they were built at the end of World War II. During the Shamrock City festival in March, the water runs green in celebration of St. Patrick's Day.

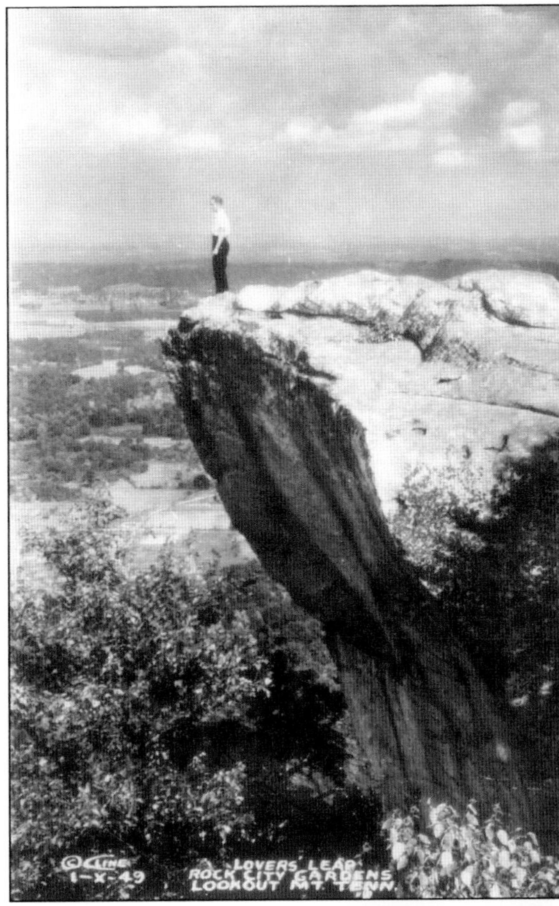

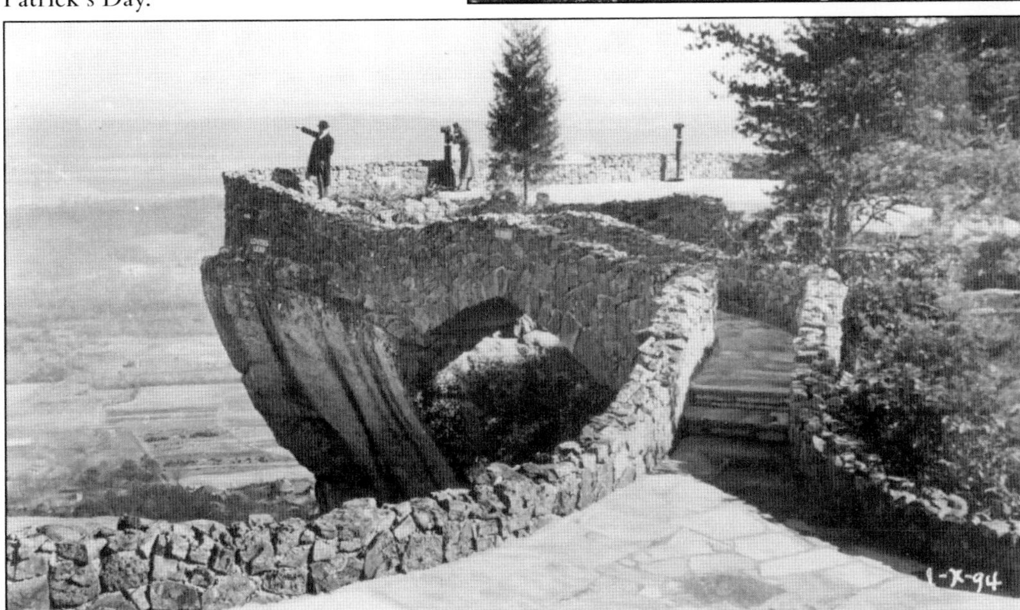

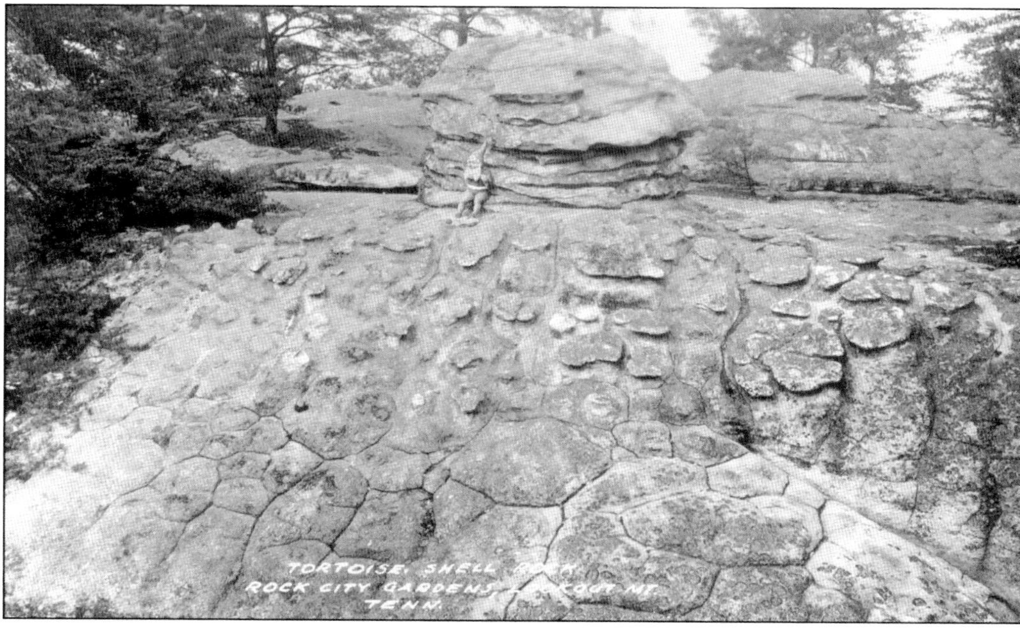

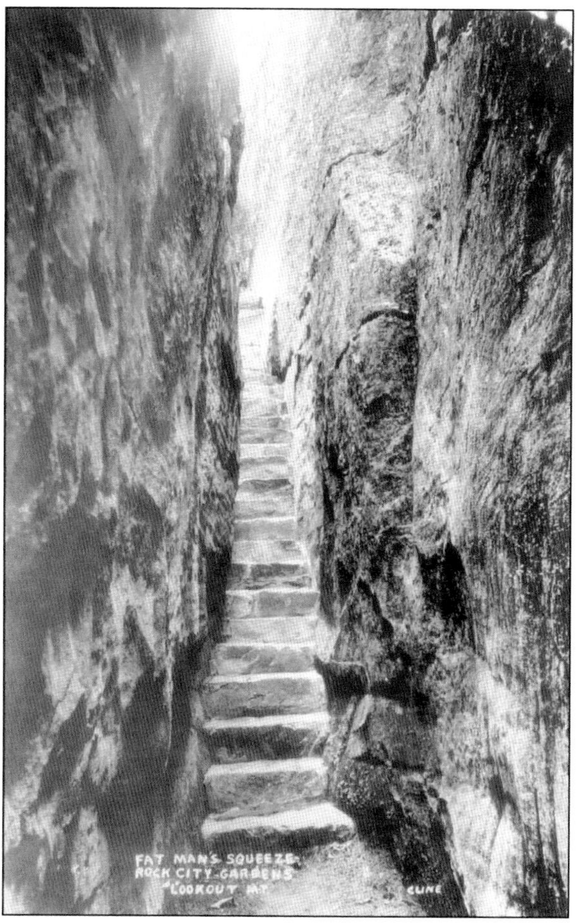

During the winter months, Tortoise Shell Rock undergoes a transformation and becomes Snowman Rock. With large buttons for eyes, a long carrot nose, and a huge red scarf, the giant snowman is just one of more than 30 holiday scenes in the Enchanted Garden of Lights. More than one million colorful lights illuminate the trails from the weekend before Thanksgiving until New Year's Day.

Louis L. Parham wrote about the corridor now known as Fat Man's Squeeze as early as 1876. Parham called it "Fat Man's Misery" in his descriptions of the various sites at Rock City. J. Harris Chappell, reporting secretary of the Southern Educational Association and later president of the Georgia Normal and Industrial College in Milledgeville, referred to the narrow passage using identical terminology on a visit in 1878.

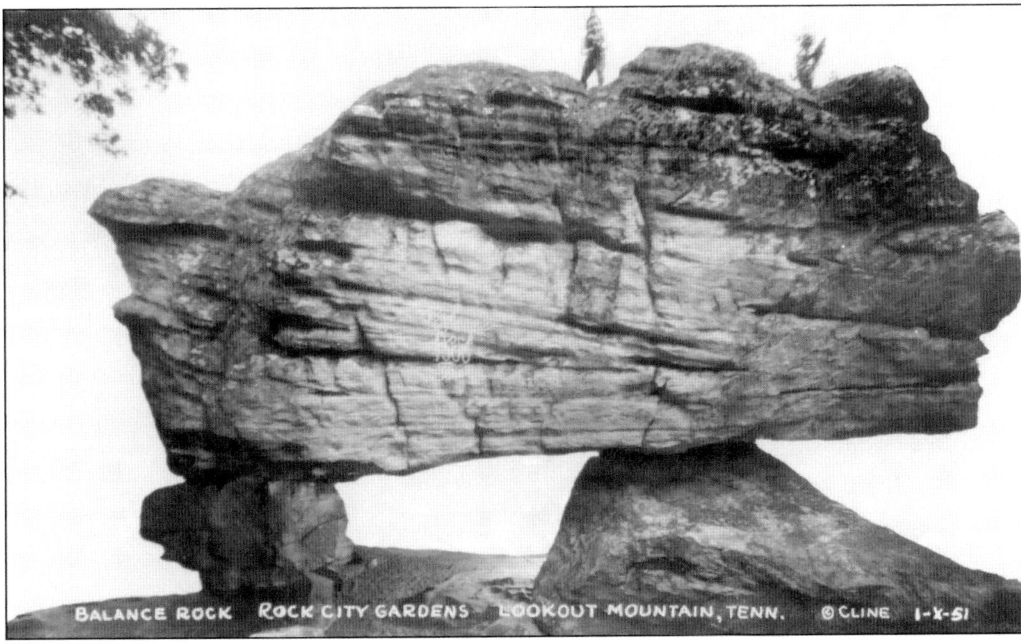

The 1,000-ton Balance Rock was discovered by accident in the mid-1930s. Some workers were digging into the burrow of a groundhog and, during their labors, exposed the now famous rock. The public was not allowed to access the rock for one year in order to ensure it would not fall from the two points upon which it was balanced. A different formation had been called Balance Rock when the gardens first opened, but that name was changed to the more descriptive Mushroom Rock after the discovery. As seen in the two postcards, Balance Rock is safe for both gnomes and humans.

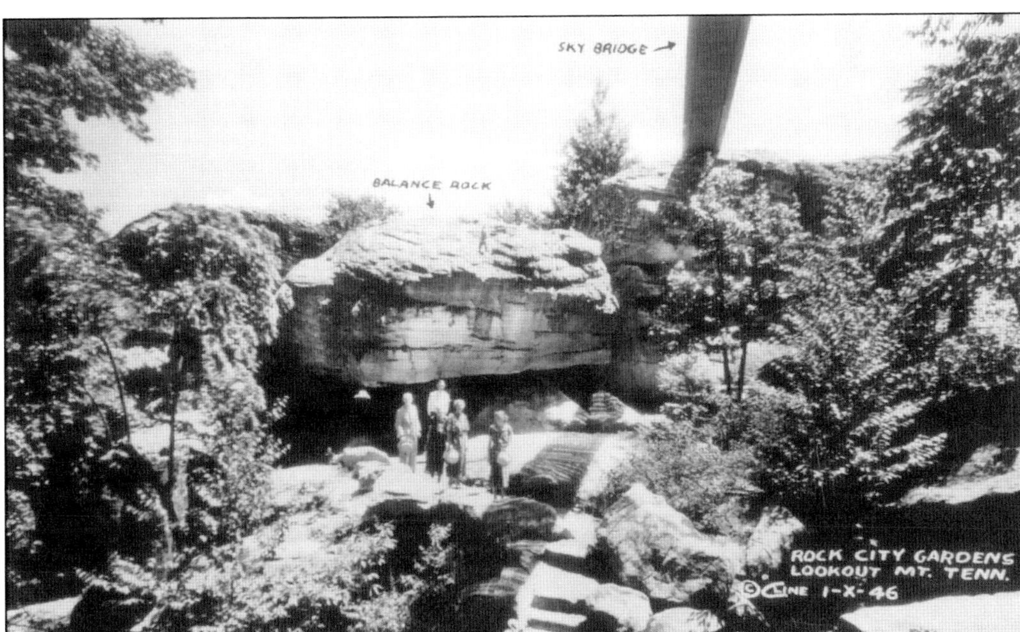

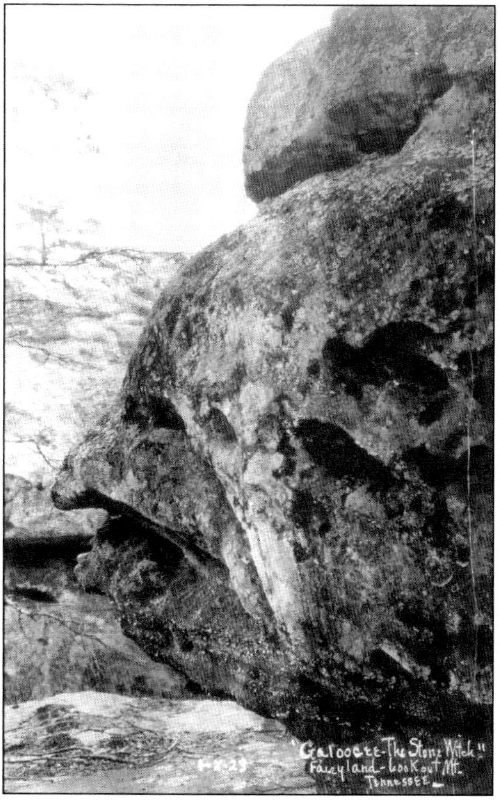

The Stone Witch, known as Galoochee, was a popular sight on the Enchanted Trail until the opening of Fairyland Caverns in 1947. The caverns, created by enlarging an existing crevice, necessitated rerouting the trail, with the new route bypassing the witch and a few other formations. Though no longer accessible on the Enchanted Trail, Galoochee still resides atop Lookout Mountain.

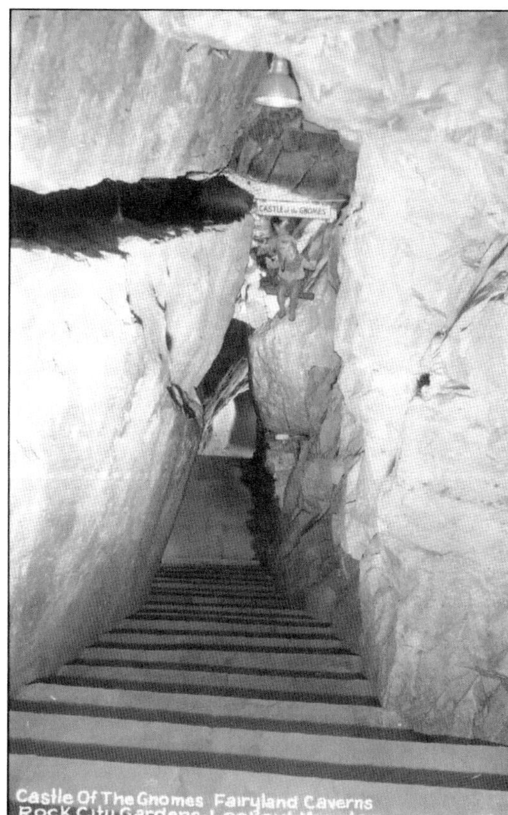

Upon entering the Castle of the Gnomes in Fairyland Caverns, visitors are greeted by elves, gnomes, and other sights. Man-made stalactites have been added and illuminated by black lights to give the area a cave-like appearance. The colorful gnome statues were relocated from the gardens to protect them from weather-related deterioration.

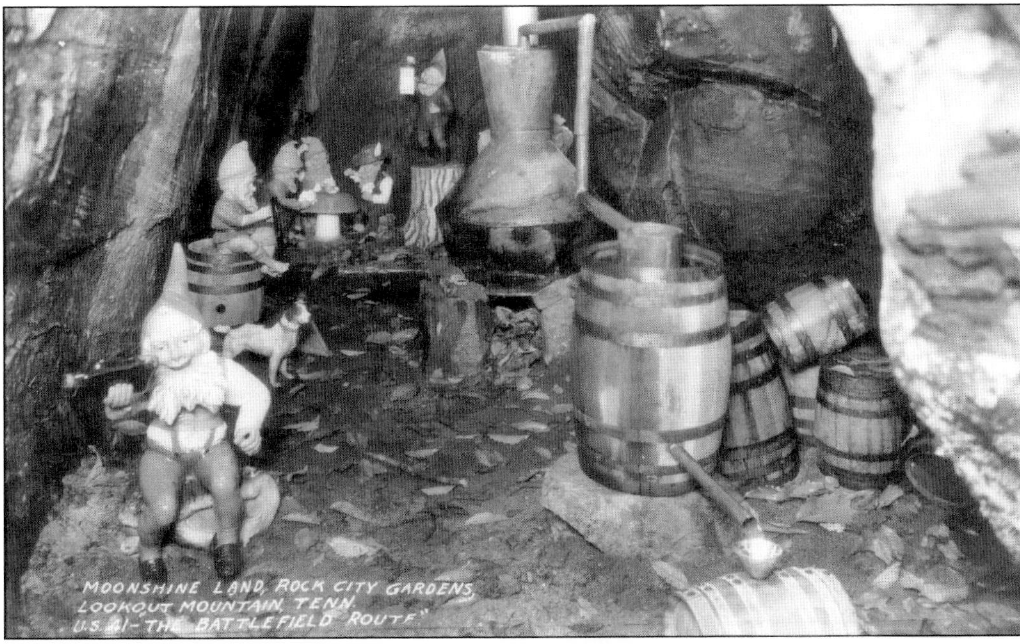

First exhibited in 1933, the moonshine still diorama is on display in Fairyland Caverns today, although with fewer gnomes due to age and wear. A publicity shot was once made of the intoxicated gnomes with bottles of Mountain Dew, playing off of the fact that the product's name was also a slang term for moonshine.

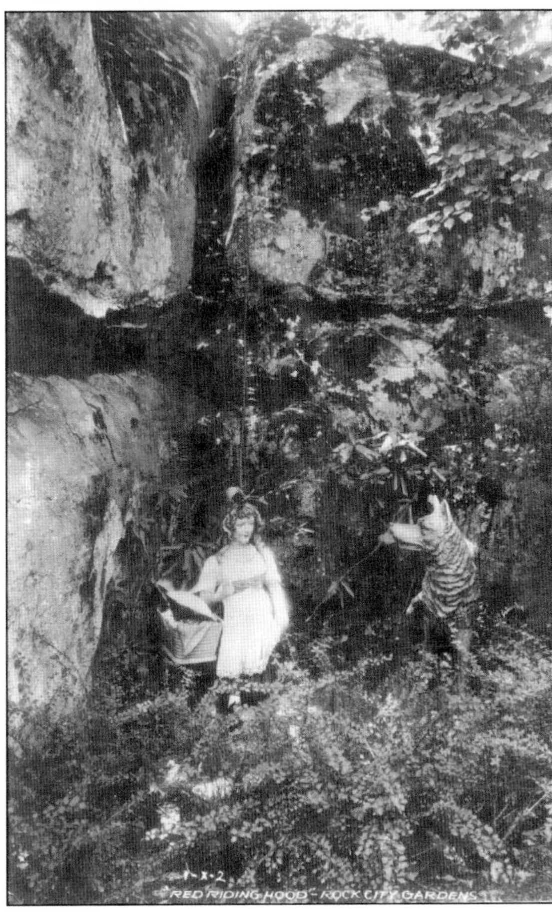

Red Riding Hood first appeared in the Fairyland subdivision, then moved to the Enchanted Trail, and was finally placed in Fairyland Caverns. Continuing with the fairy-tale theme, Mother Goose Village was added to Fairyland Caverns in 1964. Jessie Sanders, an artist from Atlanta, spent years designing the intricate sets, which showcase a variety of popular children's stories.

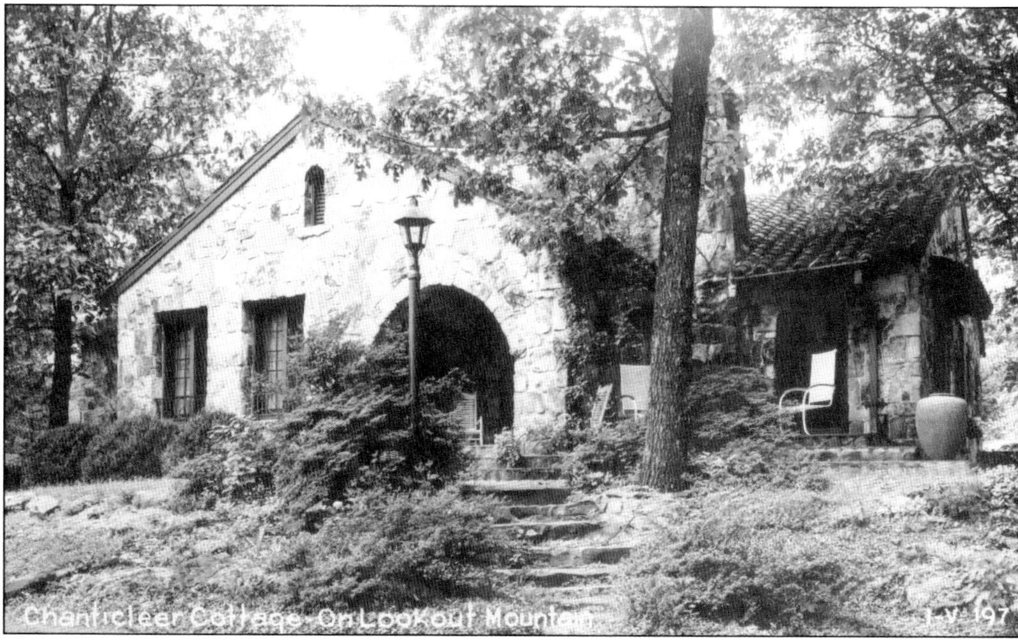

Chanticleer Inn was built in 1927 as a private residence for Richard M. and Annalee Watkins. Richard Watkins spent most of his life on Lookout Mountain, serving as mayor from 1912 to 1914. He also served as deputy clerk for the US District Court from 1898 to 1910.

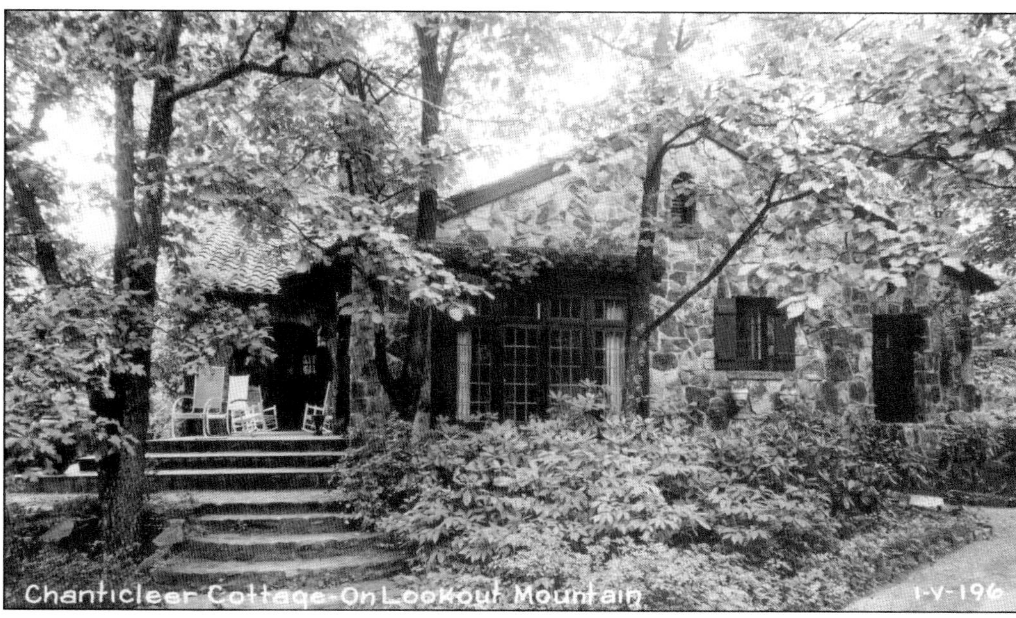

Being located directly across the street from Rock City Gardens definitely had its advantages—as the Fairyland Golf Club and other attractions on Lookout Mountain became more popular, Richard and Annalee Watkins decided to rent out rooms and began operating the Chanticleer as a bed-and-breakfast in 1930. They converted their garage into three additional rooms in 1935 and a few years later built two additional cottages.

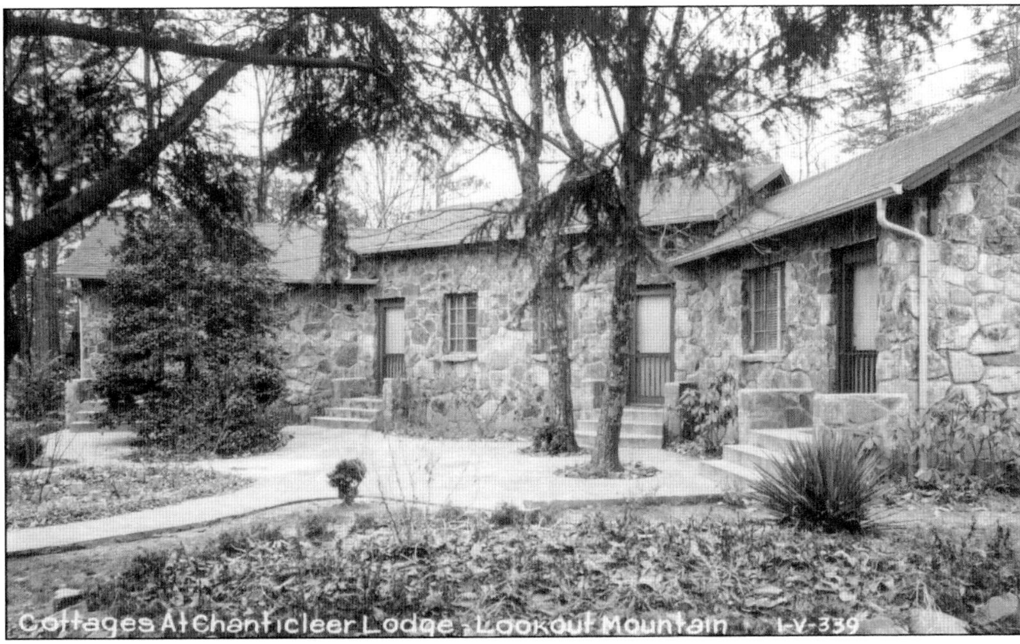

Over the years, other additions were made to the Chanticleer, including a pool in the 1950s. It was extensively renovated in 2002, and the 17 English-cottage-style rooms are now equipped with many modern conveniences, including whirlpool tubs, fireplaces, and private patios. With its beautiful gardens, landscaped areas, and stonework, the inn is a perfect spot for a weekend getaway.

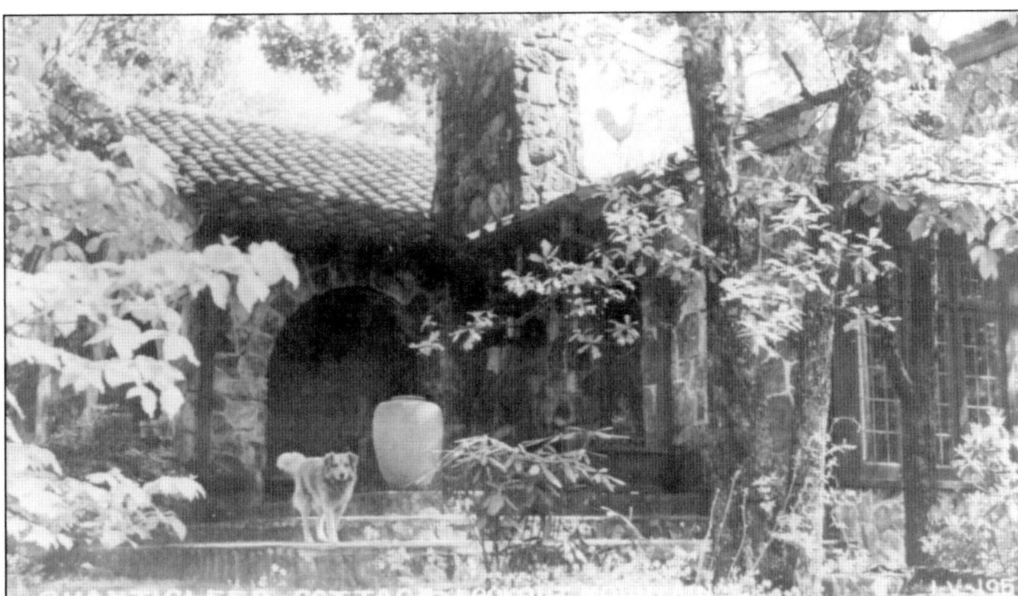

Though the Chanticleer Inn has changed ownership a few times over the years, it has maintained its charm and relaxing atmosphere. The present owners, Robert and Audrey Hart, maintain the grounds and provide homemade breakfasts, but don't let the picture fool you—to accommodate guests with allergies, no pets are allowed.

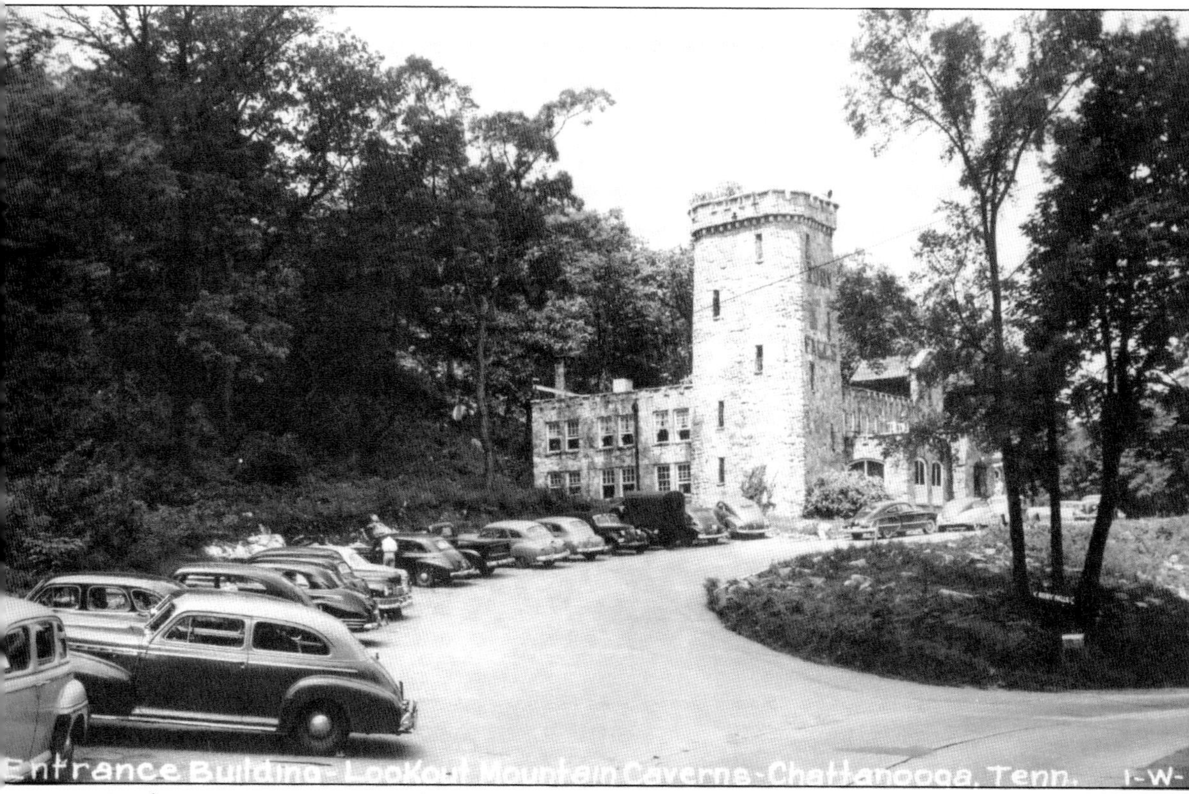

Lookout Mountain Caverns, listed in the National Register of Historic Places, opened in 1929. Leo Lambert, a cave enthusiast, convinced a group of investors to purchase land on the side of Lookout Mountain and drill an elevator shaft to Lookout Mountain Cave in order to open it as a public attraction. During the drilling, a new cavern that had several unusual rock formations and a magnificent underground waterfall was discovered approximately 260 feet down. Lambert named the cavern Ruby Falls after his wife, Ruby. Drilling continued to a depth of 420 feet and reached Lookout Mountain Cave. The elevator shaft was completed in 1929 and Lookout Mountain Caverns was opened for business, although the newly discovered Ruby Falls took an additional year to prepare for the public. An entrance building was constructed from limestone extracted while drilling the elevator shaft. Known as the Cavern Castle, it was designed to look like a 15th-century Irish castle.

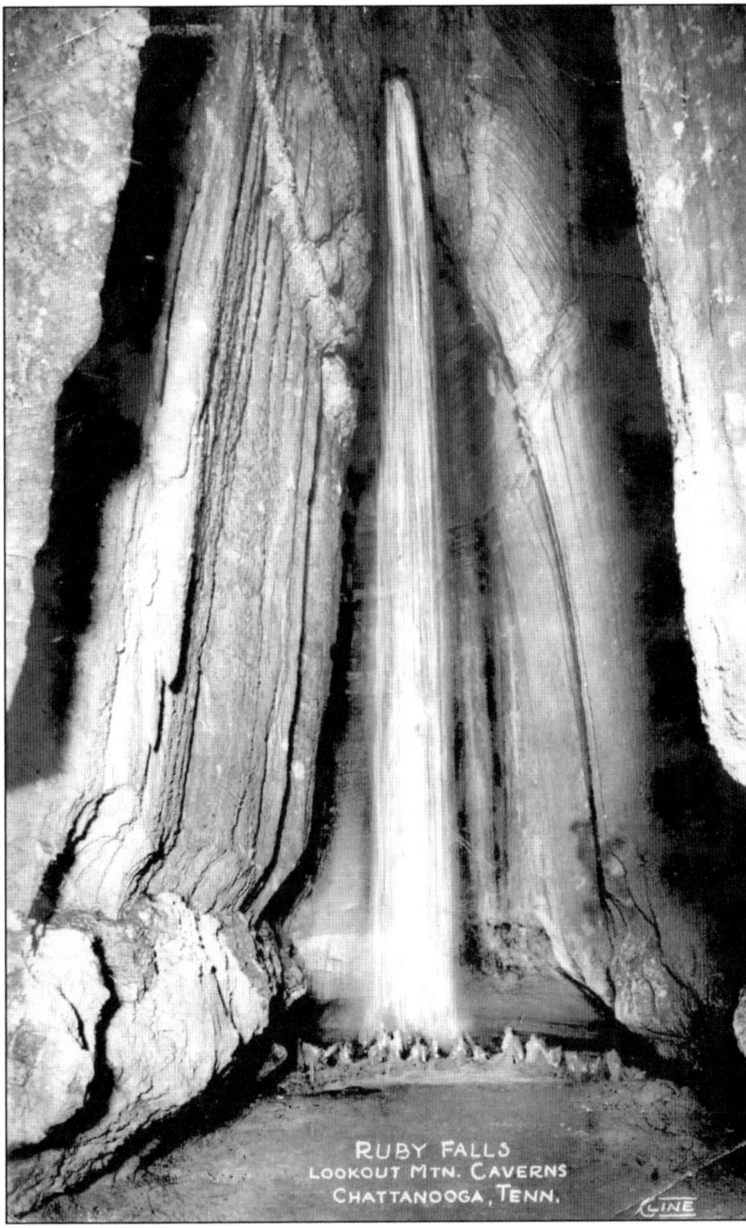

Ruby Falls' existence may never have been revealed had it not been for the fact that Leo Lambert wanted to open Lookout Mountain Cave to the public. Lookout Mountain Cave was discovered centuries ago by Native Americans and had a colorful history, including serving as a hideout for outlaws and a temporary hospital for both Union and Confederate soldiers during the Civil War. Many names had been inscribed on its walls, including that of Andrew Jackson. In 1905, the cave's entrance, located at the foot of Lookout Mountain on the banks of the Tennessee River, was sealed off by the Southern Railroad Company during construction of a tunnel through part of the mountain. This necessitated drilling an elevator shaft, which led to the accidental discovery of the falls. Located more than 1,100 feet underground, Ruby Falls is the tallest underground natural waterfall open to the public. The water cascades a total of 145 feet from the ceiling to the pool.

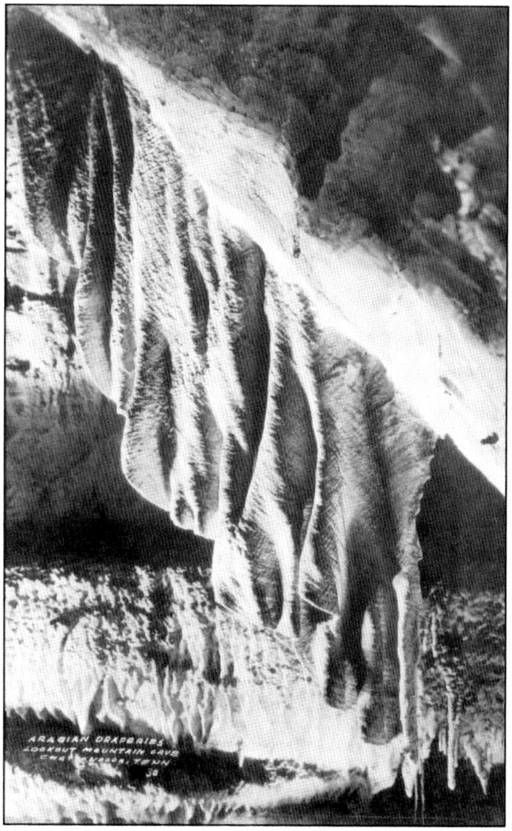

When Ruby Falls opened in 1930, its popularity quickly grew. The cavern was full of amazing geological formations, such as the Arabian Draperies shown here in Cline's postcard. Draperies, also known as curtains, can be formed when water drips down the cave's ceiling and solidifies as a thin sheet of calcite, with air currents forming the shapes of waves.

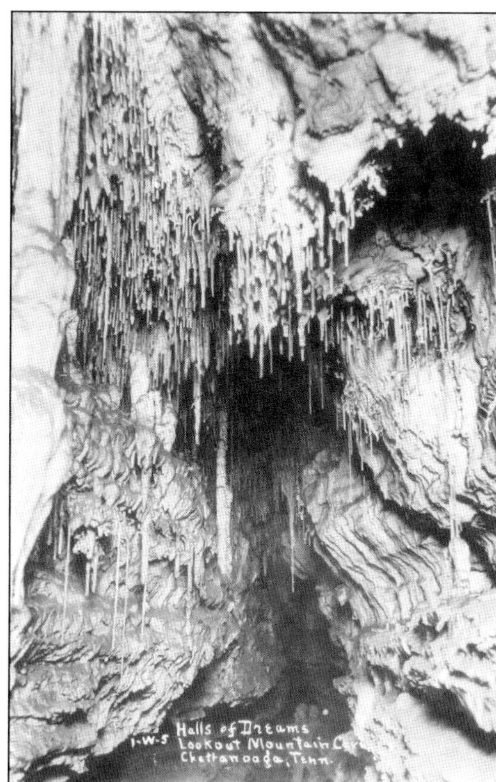

The Hall of Dreams, another natural wonder, is full of various calcite formations such as the delicate soda straws that hang from the ceiling. They were created by water dripping through their centers to form long narrow tubes. Also present in this area are helictites (thin stalactites with twisting, branch-like shapes) and a large stalagmite known as the Leaning Tower of Pisa that is over three million years old.

For six years, visitors were able to tour both Ruby Falls and Lookout Mountain Cave, but the latter closed in 1935 due to poor attendance and the heavy soot from the railroad tunnel that kept it constantly dirty. Also, Ruby Falls had more spectacular formations, such as the Elephant's Tusk, a large stalactite located in the Onyx Jungle.

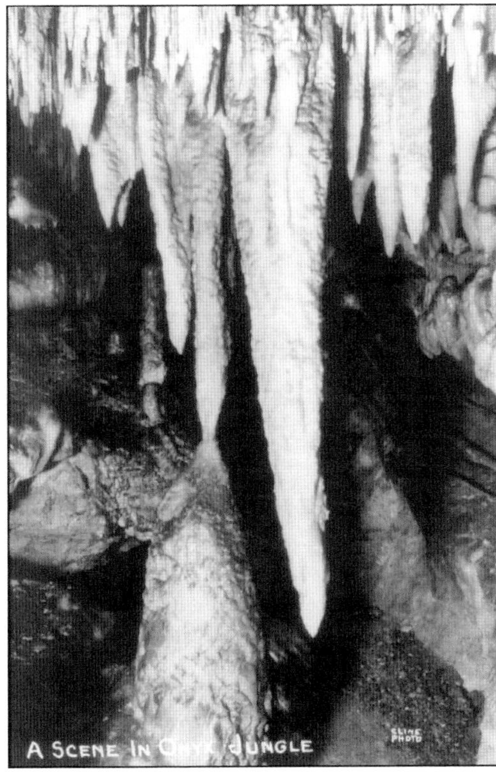

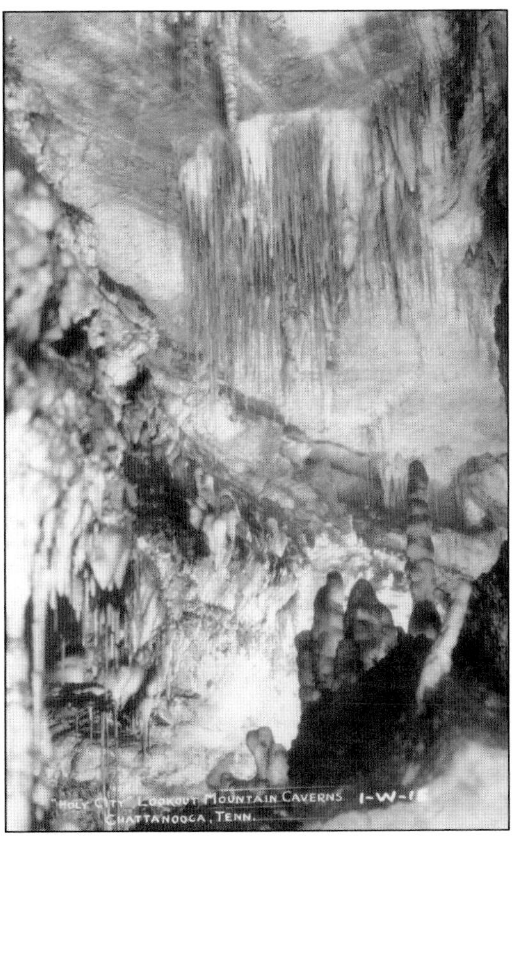

A cubic inch of calcite takes over 100 years to form, which makes areas such as the Holy City even more wondrous. A large cluster of stalactites resembling a crystal chandelier hangs from the ceiling. Beneath it are formations which some say look like Joseph, Mary, and the baby Jesus. With all of these interesting geological structures, including the falls themselves, Ruby Falls continues to be a popular tourist destination.

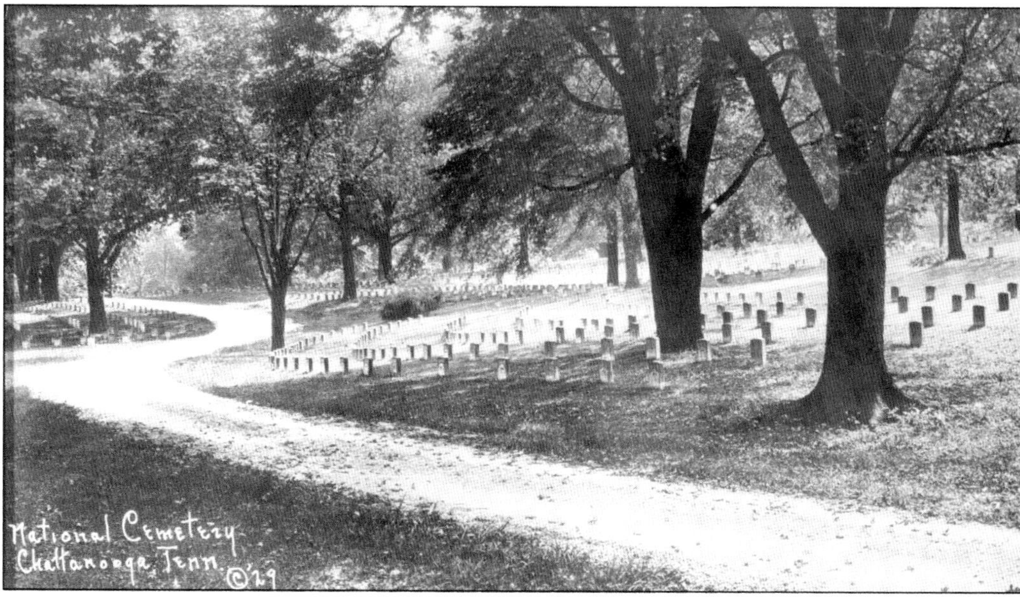

The Chattanooga National Cemetery, which was created in 1863, has three large monuments and thousands of small headstones. The largest among them is the Andrews Raiders Monument, topped by a bronze locomotive replica which commemorates the daring attempt by Union spies to steal the train known as the *General*. Their mission was to destroy telegraph lines and the railroad track between Chattanooga and Atlanta. The attempt was only marginally successful, and most of the men were caught and imprisoned or hanged. Eight of the 24 men involved are buried around the monument, including the leader, James J. Andrews. The *General* was housed in Chattanooga's Union Depot from 1901 to 1961. In 1972, the Louisville & Nashville Railroad (L&N) moved it to the Kennesaw Civil War Museum in Georgia, where it remains.

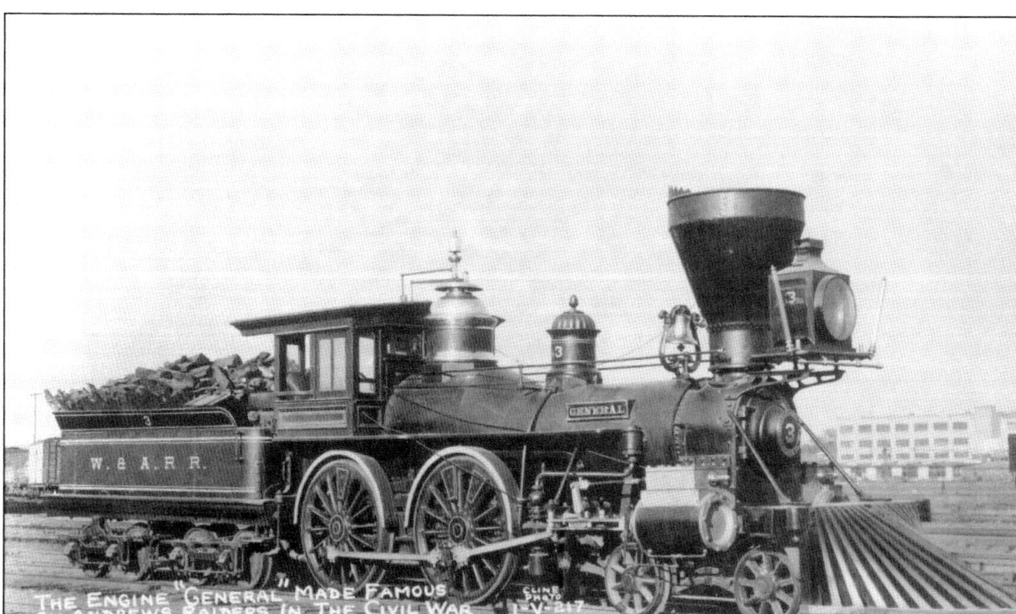

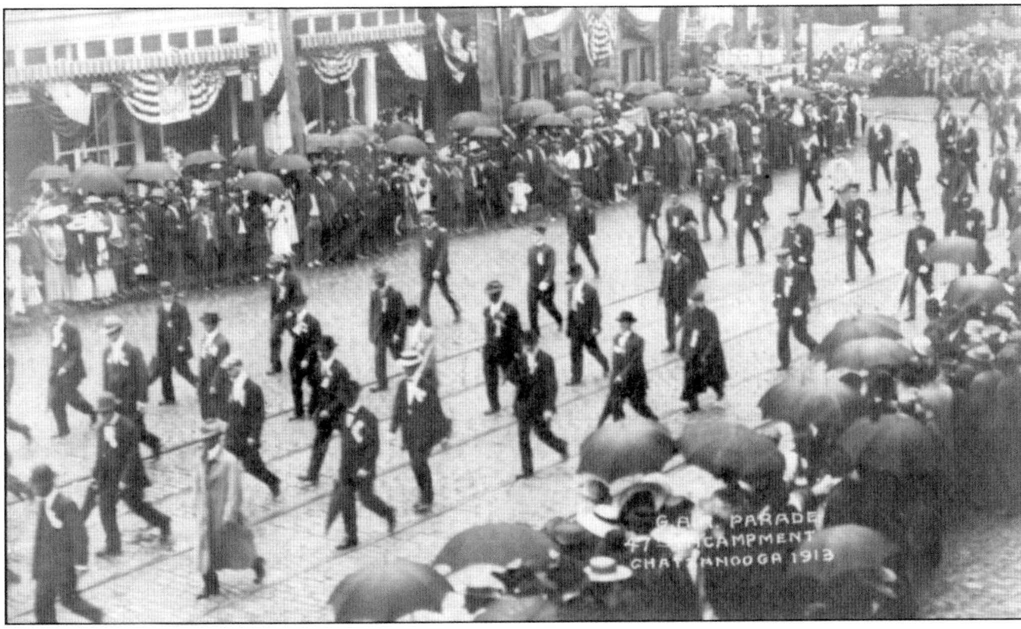

In 1913, during the semicentennial of the Civil War, the Grand Army of the Republic (GAR) and the United Confederate Veterans (UCV) held separate reunions in Chattanooga. The UCV held their 27th National Reunion on May 27–29. The larger event, hosted by the GAR, was held September 15–19 on the anniversary of the Battle of Chickamauga. It was their 47th National Encampment, and the theme was "One People, One Nation, One Flag." Both events were filled with parades, speeches, and special presentations meant to honor the men who died and to unite those who survived. These two photographs are a sample of some of the oldest known postcards taken by Walter M. Cline Sr.

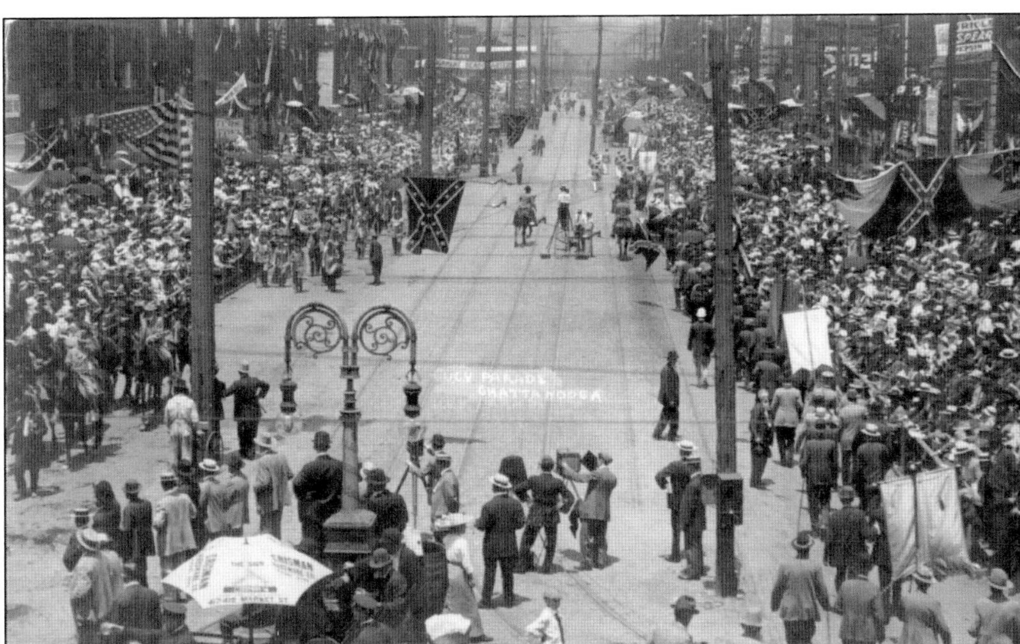

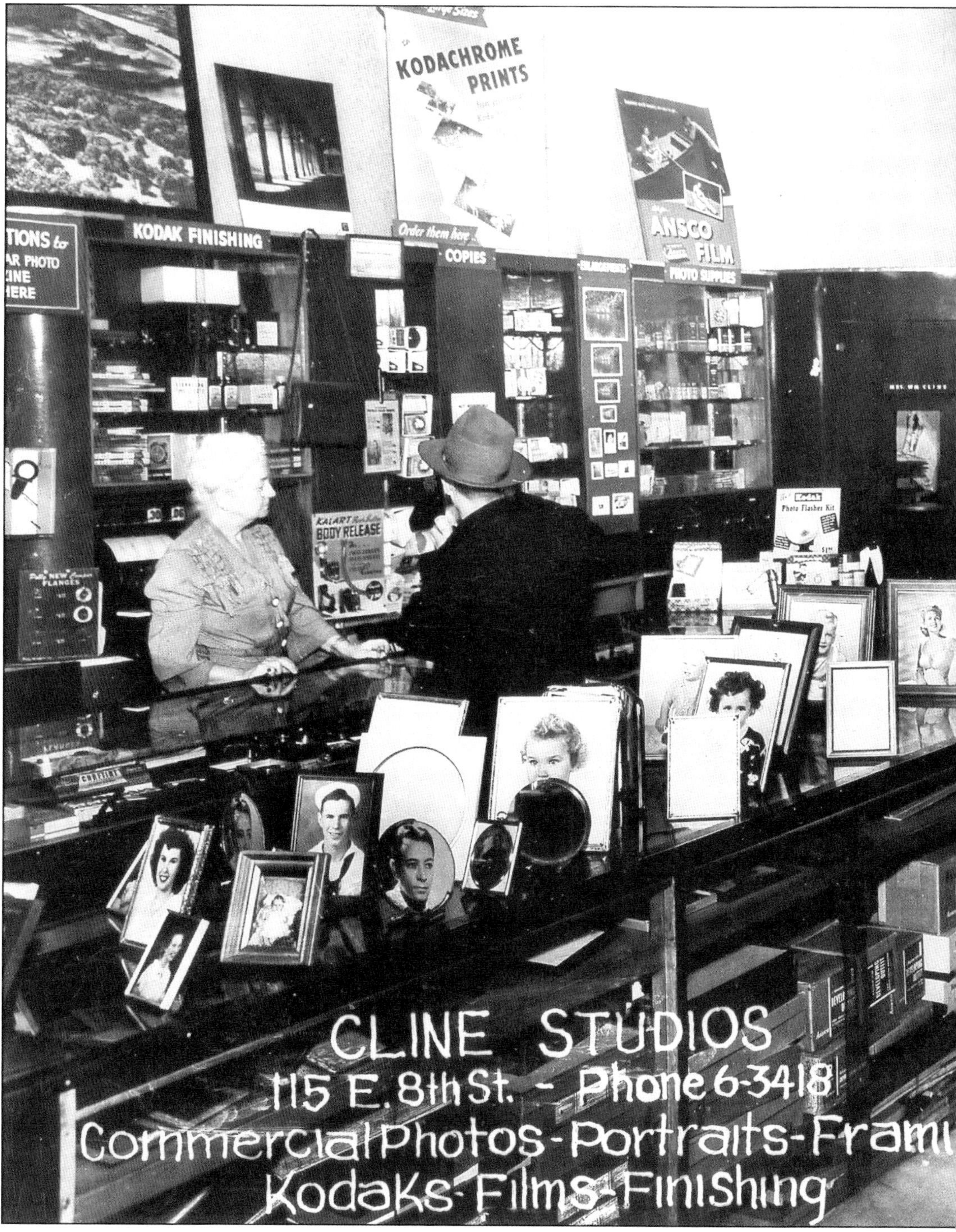

"Personality, versatility, and adaptability are Cline characteristics," wrote Richard K. Wood in an April 1934 *Commercial Photographer* article entitled "Walter M. Cline—Photographer of the South." Cline Studios adapted to the difficulties of the Depression and flourished when similar businesses were lost to bankruptcy. His philosophy was to give the public what it wanted—photographs of familiar places taken with a seasoned photographer's eye for composition. Cline

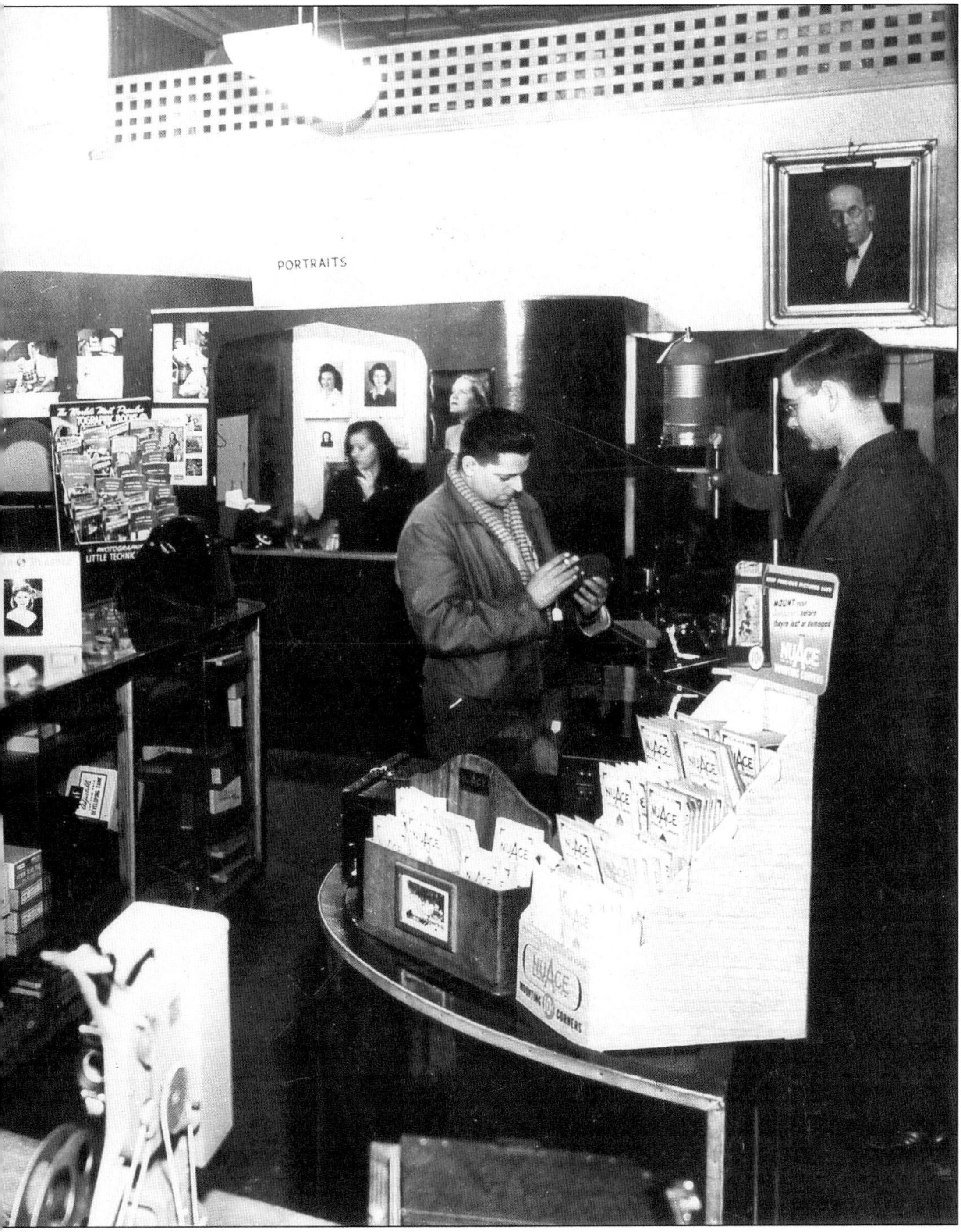

postcards were sold all over the Southeast and beyond. Chattanooga-area attractions like Rock City's Sugar Loaf Shop displayed his work in their gift shops. Located in the top right of the postcard is a portrait of Walter Cline Sr.; the man just below the photograph is Herman Lamb, who worked for the Clines from the time he was 17 until retirement. (Courtesy of Chattanooga–Hamilton County Bicentennial Library.)

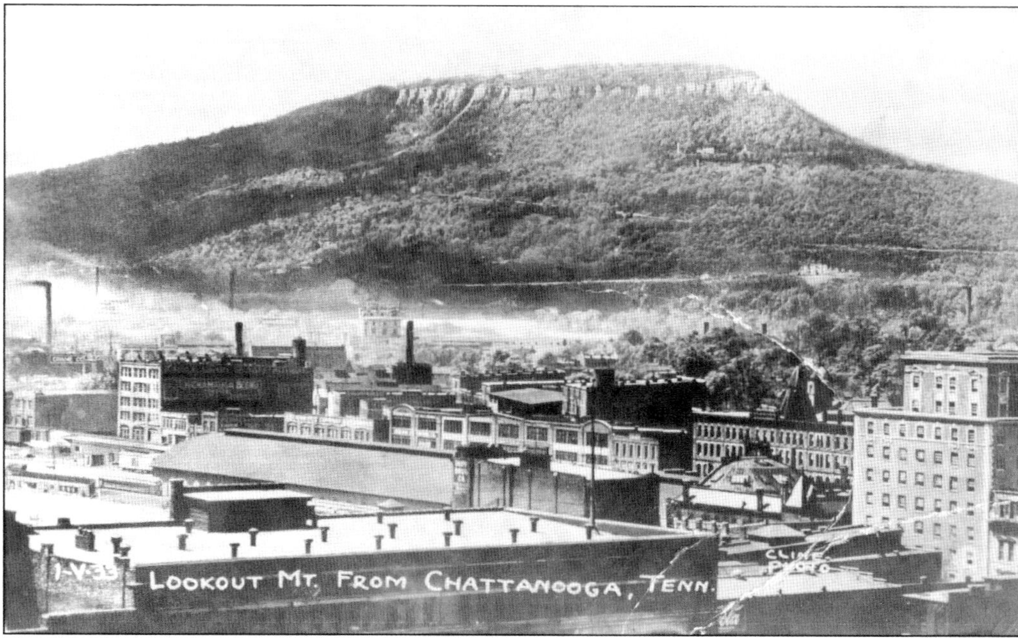

Incorporated in 1839, Chattanooga is located on the Tennessee-Georgia border. It has many tourist attractions, including the Tennessee Aquarium and the Chattanooga Choo Choo, and numerous historical areas, many of which relate to the Civil War. The town served as headquarters for the Dixie Highway Association during its years of operation from 1915 to 1927.

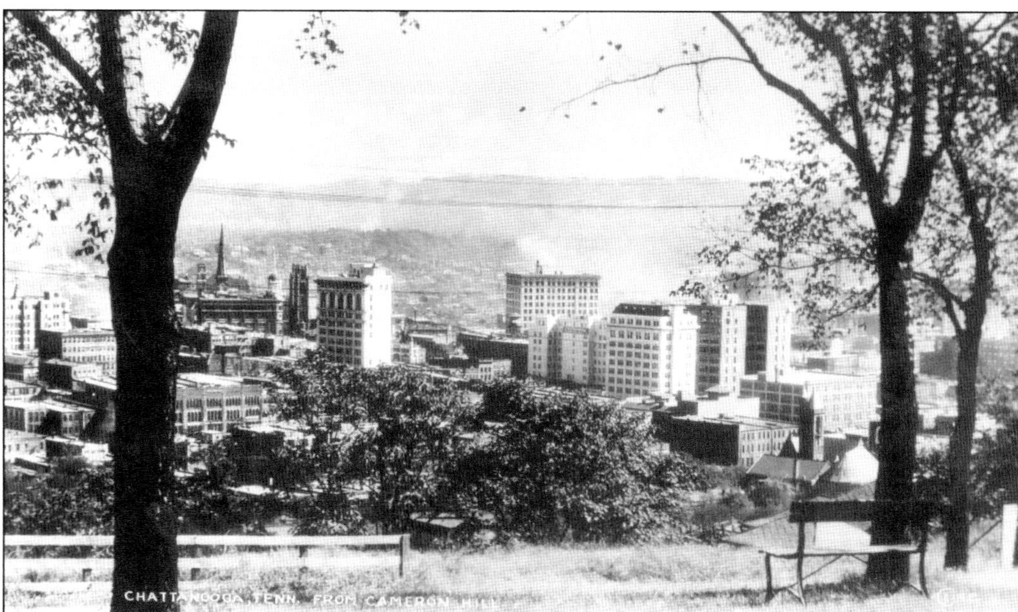

Cameron Hill, which overlooked downtown Chattanooga, was a strategic position utilized during the Civil War. It was named for artist James Cameron, who lived in the city until after the Civil War began. Despite its historic significance, Cameron Hill was decapitated in the 1960s when the Golden Gateway Redevelopment Project called for the removal of dirt from the peak of the hill to be used in building a new highway.

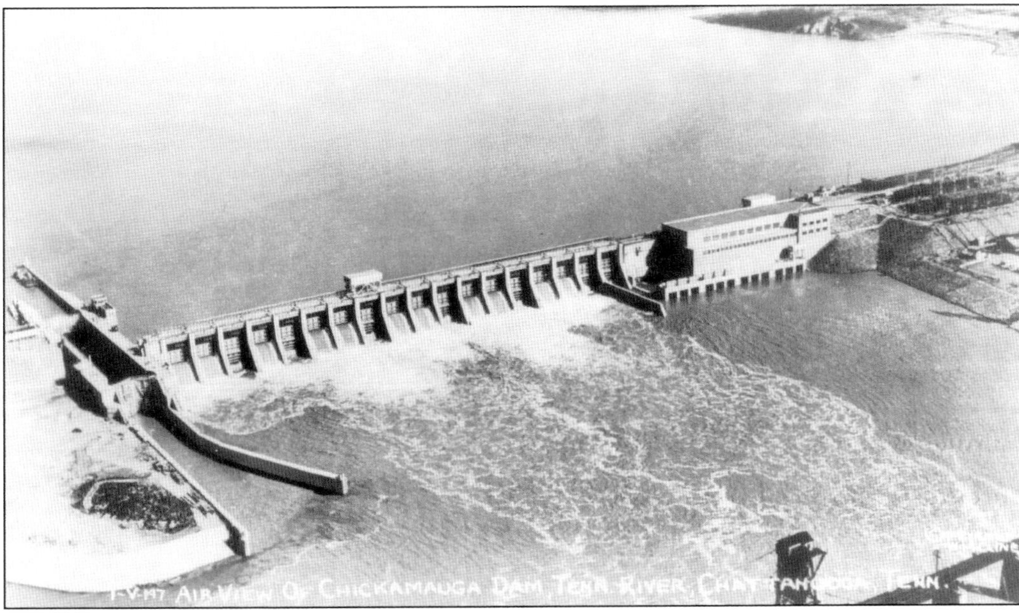

The Tennessee Valley Authority (TVA) began building the Chickamauga Dam, just north of Chattanooga on the Tennessee River, in 1936, and construction was completed in 1940. Prior to the creation of this dam and others above Chattanooga, the city had one of the worst flooding problems in the country.

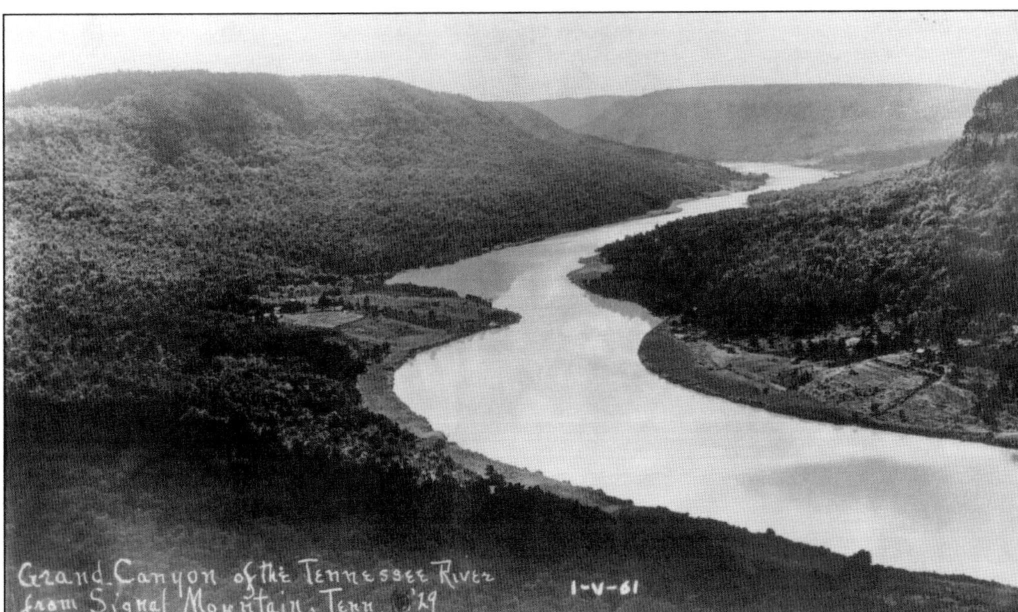

Known as "Tennessee's Grand Canyon," the Tennessee River Gorge is the fourth largest river canyon east of the Mississippi River. A wide variety of plant and animal life can be observed on the Tennessee Aquarium's *River Gorge Explorer.* The two-hour cruise begins near the aquarium and travels downstream past Lookout Mountain, Williams Island, and Signal Mountain on Walden Ridge.

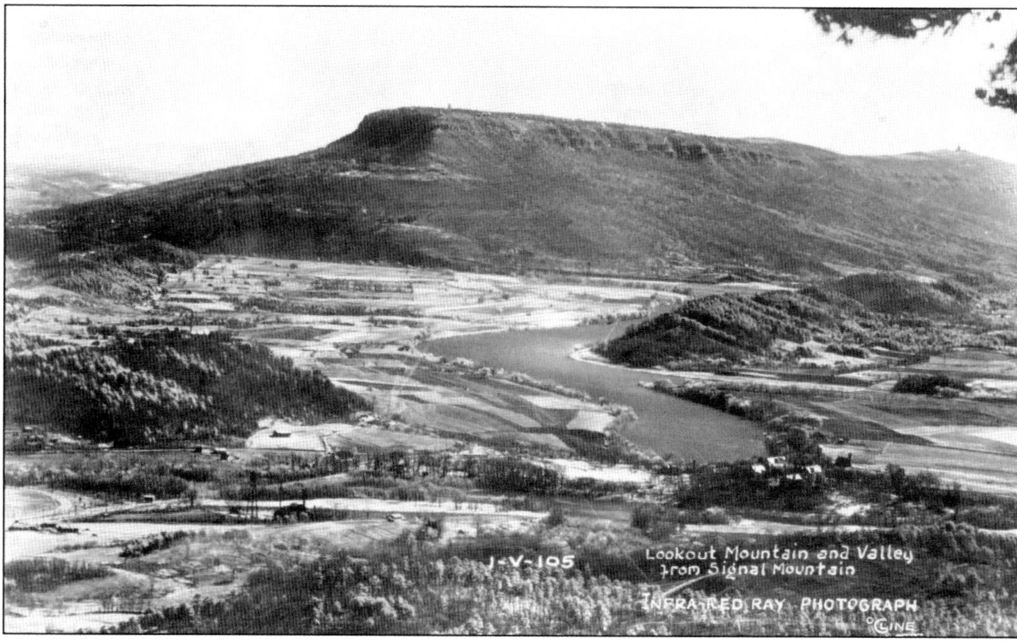

Both Union and Confederate armies used the Tennessee River for transportation during the Civil War. The river section winding around the base of Lookout Mountain is known as Moccasin Bend. During the Battle Above the Clouds, Union soldiers began their assault on Confederate troops from this area before fighting their way up the mountain.

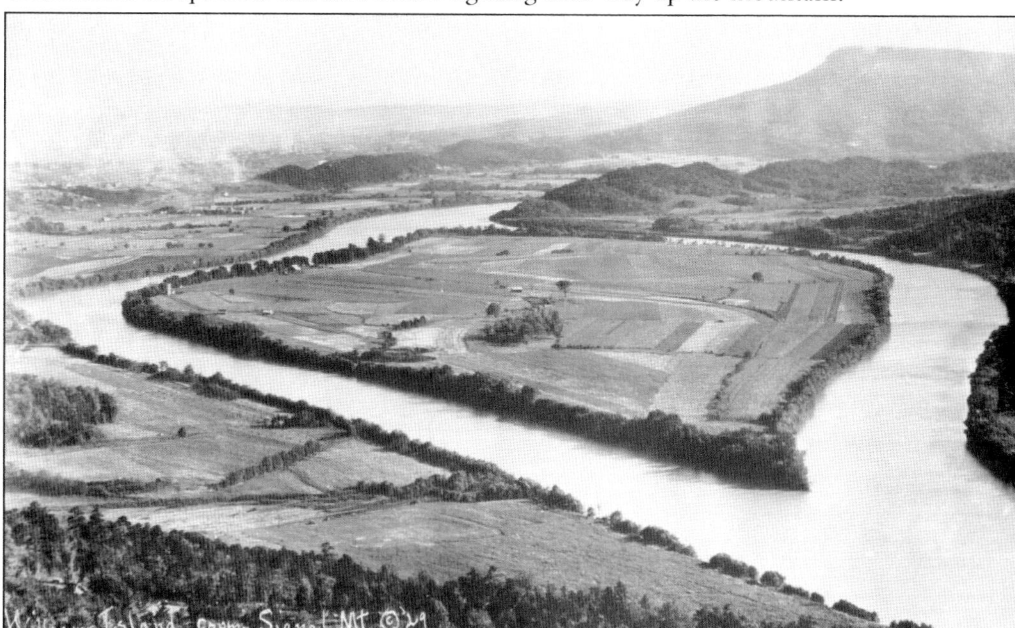

Williams Island is approximately two miles long and covers a 450-acre area. Located downstream from Moccasin Bend, it is owned by the Division of Archaeology of the State of Tennessee and is currently managed by the Tennessee River Gorge Trust. During the Civil War, one of the Union soldiers who had stolen the *General*, a Southern train, escaped and was recaptured on Williams Island.

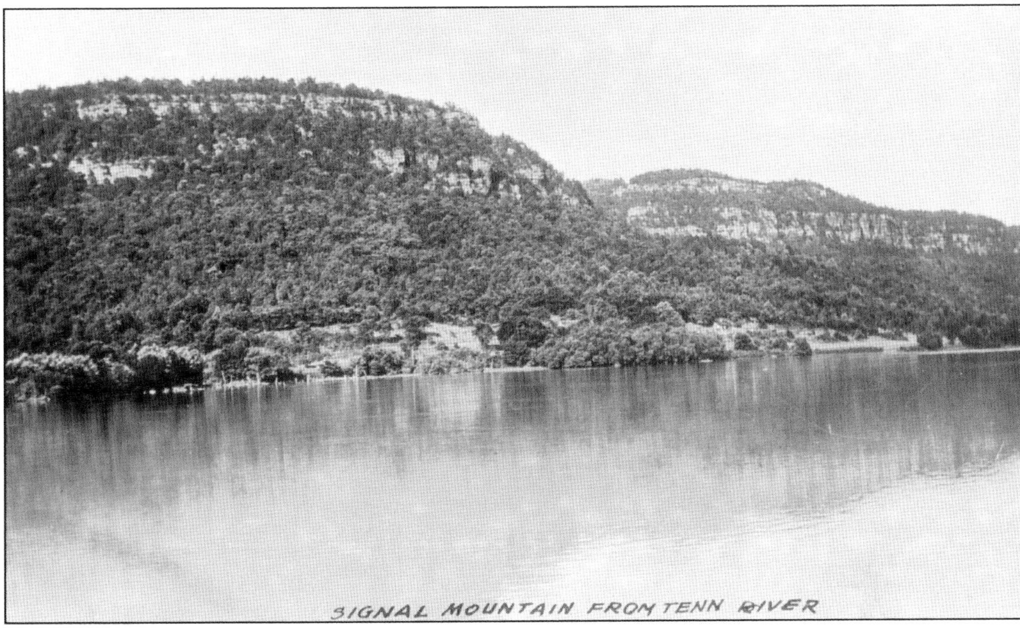

Incorporated in 1919, the town of Signal Mountain is located in the Signal Point area on Walden Ridge. Signal Point served as an important overlook for the Union army as it monitored Confederate troop movement and sent communications to Cameron Hill and other locations. The area offers numerous hiking opportunities, including access to the Cumberland Trail.

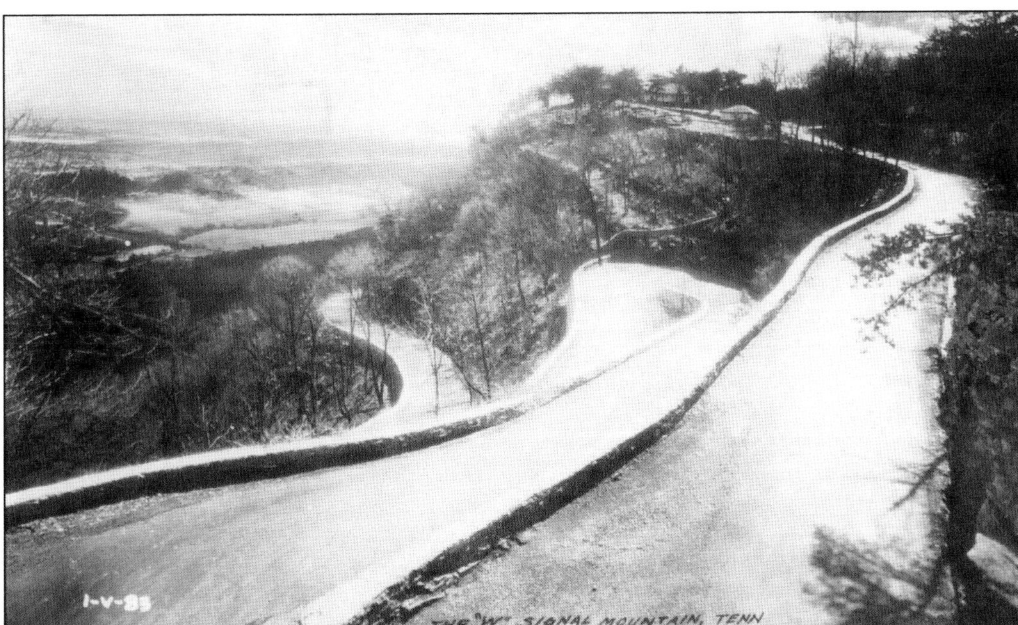

Local landowner Josiah Anderson built a toll road across Walden Ridge in the early 1860s to provide access to Chattanooga for residents in Sequatchie Valley. For several years, tolls for the Anderson Road, also known as the W Road, were collected at the Conner Toll House. Constructed in 1858 by Hamilton County's first sheriff, James C. Conner, the house is listed in the National Register of Historic Places.

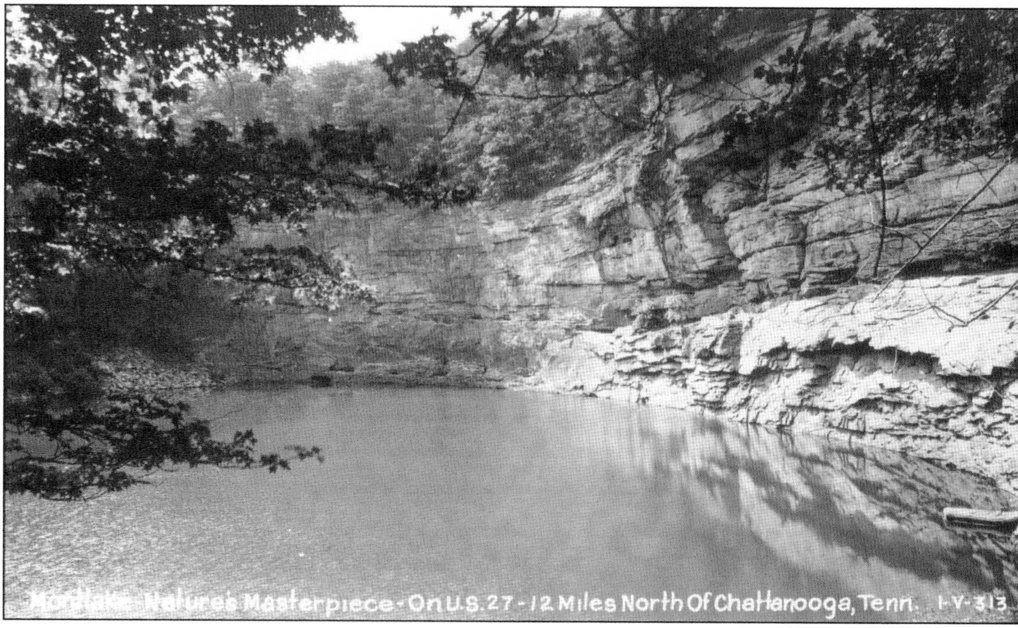

According to local legend, Montlake was formed by the New Madrid earthquake of 1812. However, in a 1936 article in the *Journal of Geology*, Paris B. Stockdale of the Ohio State University stated that the lake was not located on a fault and was actually a large sinkhole, likely formed by a slow collapse of rock layers into an underground cavern. Due to information provided by satellite photographs and other sources, Robert L. Wilson disputed the sinkhole theory at an annual meeting of the Geological Society of America, Southeastern Section, in 1984. Though its origin is still open to debate, Walter Cline's reference to Montlake as "an amazing freak of nature" is difficult to dispute. Once a popular tourist destination, the lake property on Walden Ridge is privately owned and no longer accessible to the public.

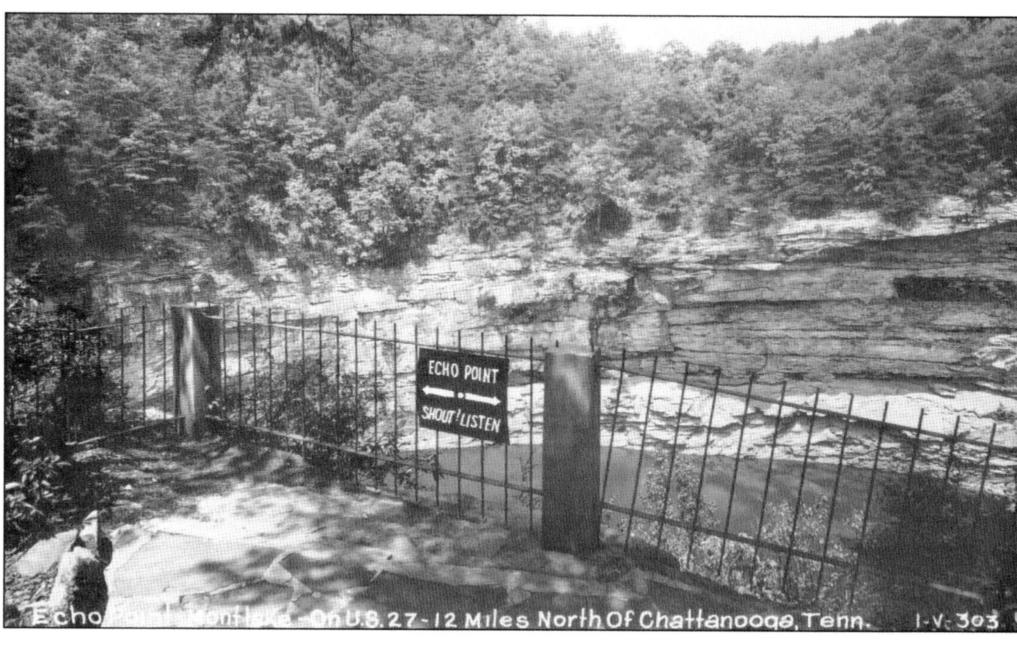

Three

From Chattanooga to Jellico

Traveling north from the Chattanooga area, the eastern section of the Dixie Highway in Tennessee goes along today's US 27 to Dayton, Rockwood, and Harriman. After Harriman's appeal to be added to the highway was successful in 1916, the route went from there through Kingston and Knoxville by present-day State Route 1. Originally, the highway left Knoxville and went along the current State Route 33 through Maynardsville, Tazewell, and Cumberland Gap. When road improvements were not completed on time, the Dixie Highway Association rescinded their inclusion and changed the course to go through Clinton, Coal Creek (now Lake City), Jacksboro, LaFollette, and Jellico along what is now US 25W.

This chapter follows that eastern Dixie Highway route north through the state, starting in Dayton. The town will most likely always be best known as the location of the famous Scopes Monkey Trial, and the creation of Bryan College can be seen as a direct result of the trial. Traveling from there to the Rockwood, Harriman, and Kingston areas, the tourism created after the construction of the Watts Bar Dam is evident. Cline's work frequently focused on small towns and well-liked travel sites, such as the motor courts and lake regions viewed along the road through Lake City, Caryville, and Jacksboro. The Norris Dam State Park, housing Norris Lake and a gristmill, is still a popular area to visit today, along with Cove Lake State Park, just off US 25W. Cline seemed to be captivated with the LaFollette and Jellico areas, creating dozens of postcards along the thoroughfare and throughout the towns.

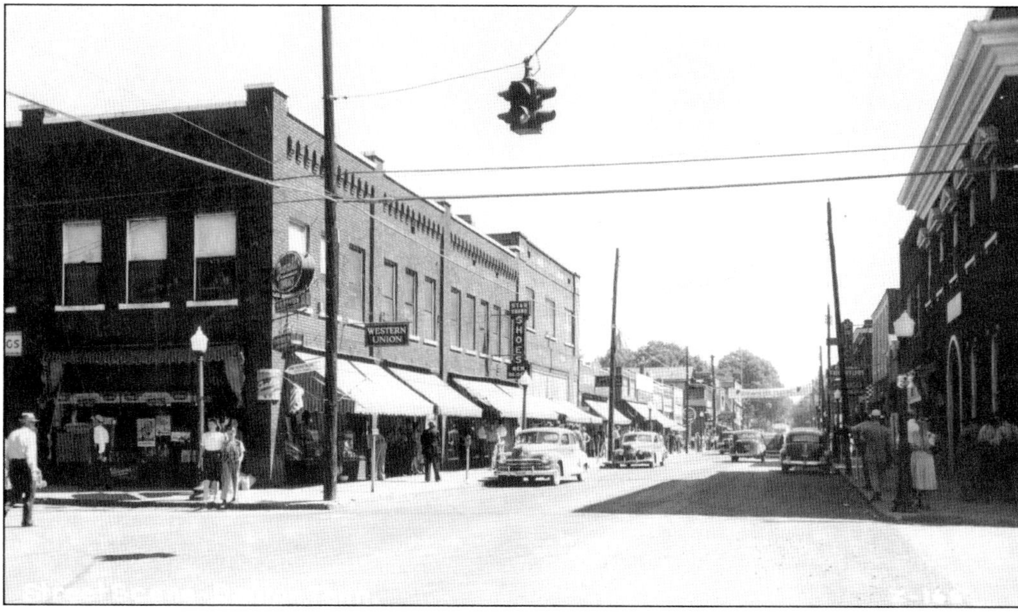

Rhea County was once known as the Strawberry Capital of the World, and Dayton has been the location for the annual strawberry festival (see banner in postcard above) since 1947. The town of Dayton is also known for the Scopes trial, which took place in 1925. A few townspeople convinced a biology teacher named John T. Scopes to challenge a Tennessee statute that prohibited the teaching of evolution in public schools, thinking the publicity would boost the town's economy. William Jennings Bryan, who believed in fundamentalism and actively opposed teaching evolution in schools, was one of the prosecuting attorneys. Scopes was represented by Clarence Darrow, who called Bryan as a witness and sharply questioned him on his literal interpretation of the Bible. Scopes was convicted but later released on a technicality. Bryan died a few days after the trial.

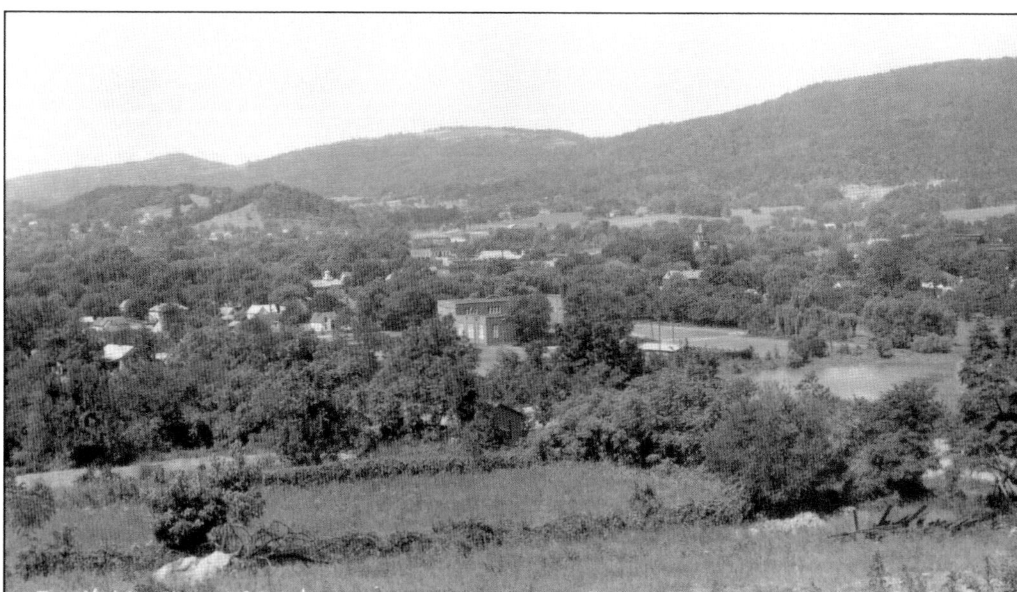

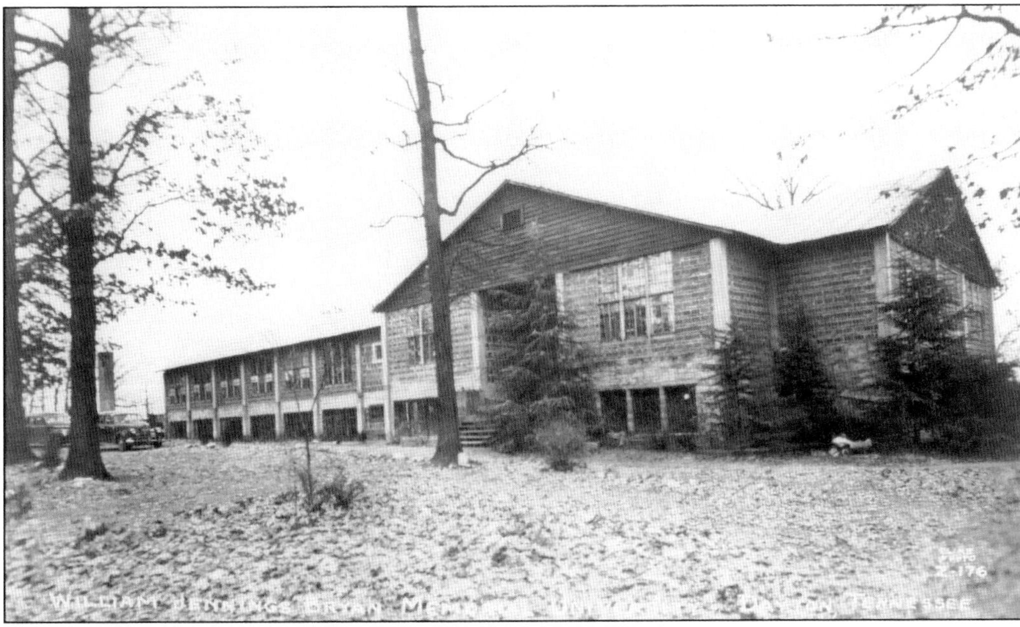

Bryan College, named in honor of William Jennings Bryan, was founded in 1930 with the stated purpose of providing "for the higher education of men and women under auspices distinctly Christian and spiritual." Accredited by the Southern Association of Colleges and Schools Commission on Colleges, the 125-acre campus is located on a hilltop in Dayton.

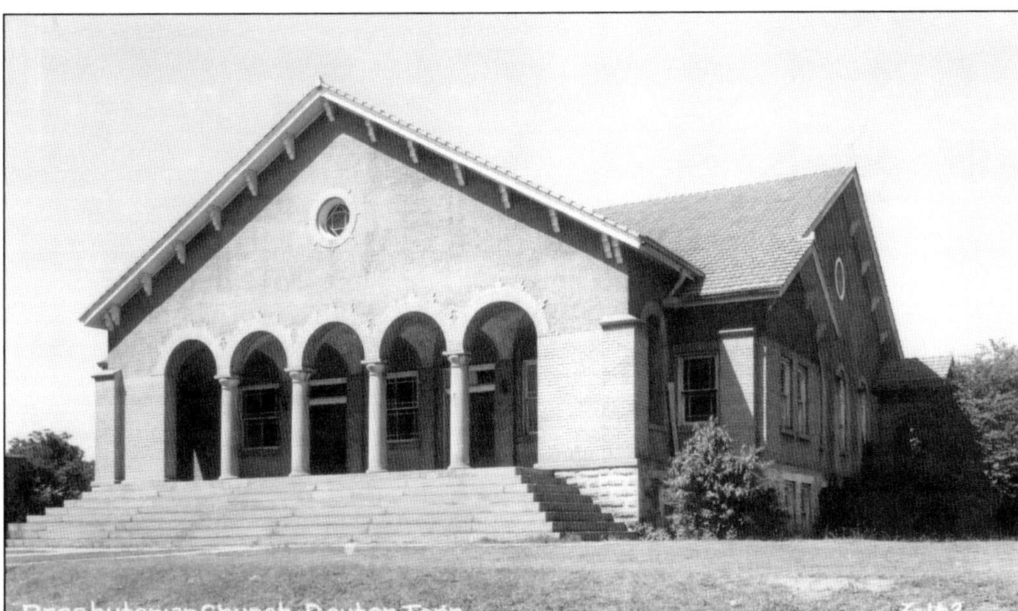

The Cumberland Presbyterian Church was located on Main Street in Dayton, just off the Dixie Highway. The Dayton Revival Center, a nondenominational church, is now located here. The church was built a few years after the Scopes trial, and upon seeing it, Clarence Darrow stated, "I guess I didn't do much good here after all!"

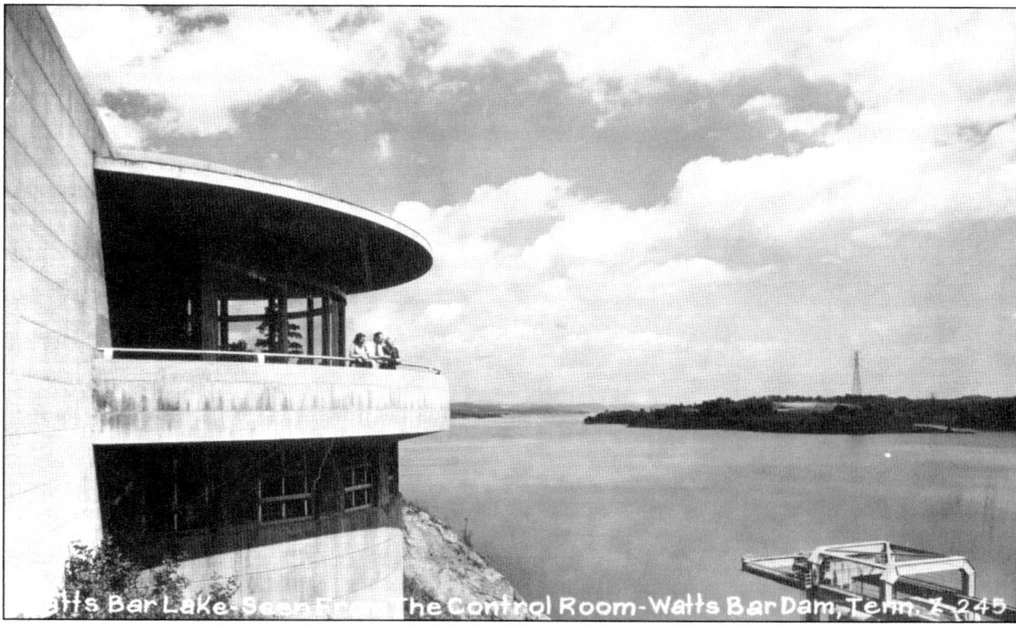

Completed in 1942, Watts Bar Dam is located between Knoxville and Chattanooga on the Tennessee River. The structure is 112 feet high and nearly 3,000 feet across. The reservoir covers about 39,000 acres, and the water is 70 feet deep in some areas near the dam. The Tennessee Valley Authority has nine dams on the Tennessee River. They were built to control flooding and to produce electricity. The reservoirs created by these dams have also brought revenue to lakeside communities, as tourists visiting the Roane County towns of Rockwood, Harriman, and Kingston enjoy year-round activities at Watts Bar Lake.

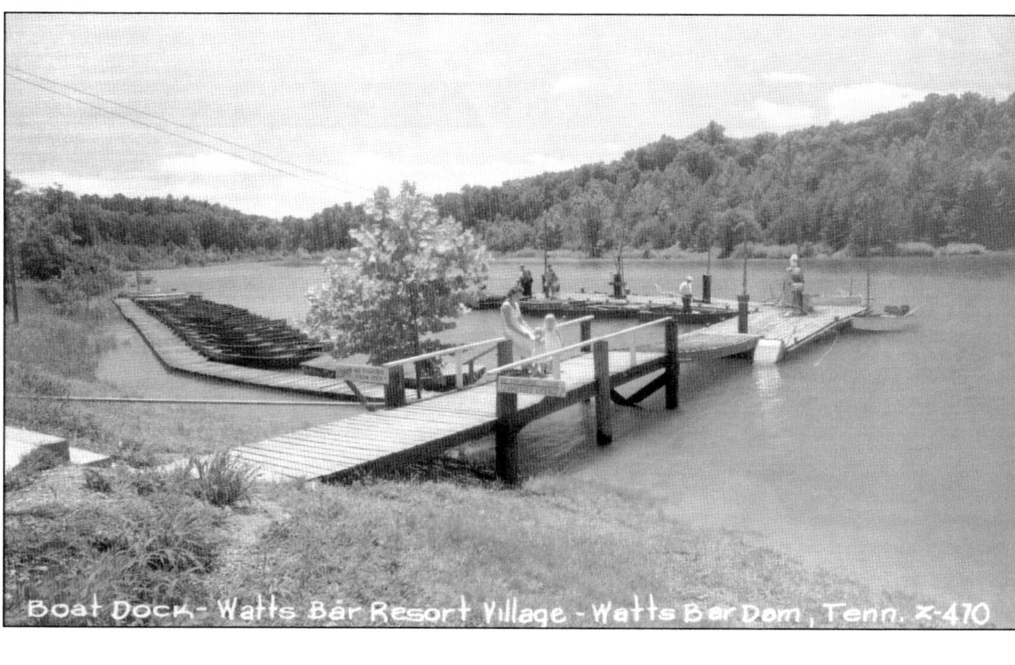

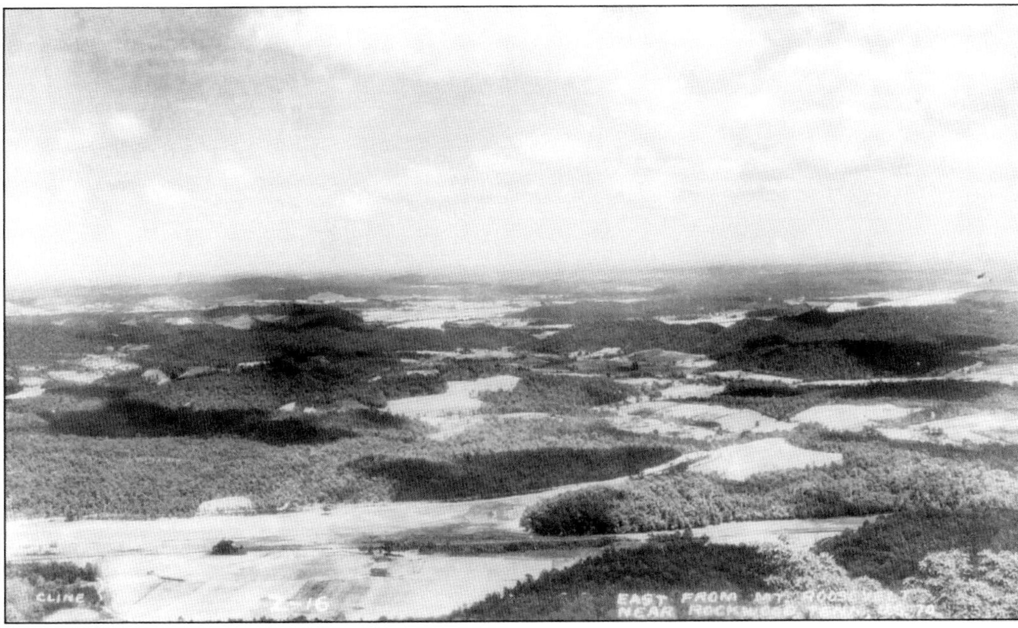

Roosevelt Mountain is located near Rockwood in Roane County. With an elevation of over 2,000 feet, it offers a splendid view of the Tennessee Valley and Rockwood community. The Mount Roosevelt Wildlife Management Area, managed by the Tennessee Wildlife Resources Agency, covers about 11,000 acres and provides a scenic overlook, a connector trail to Walden Ridge Trail, picnic tables, and a small parking lot. Besides viewing breathtaking landscapes, visitors can also enjoy seeing the migration of birds and butterflies during the fall. The overlook is located at the end of Tower Road off US 70 near Rockwood.

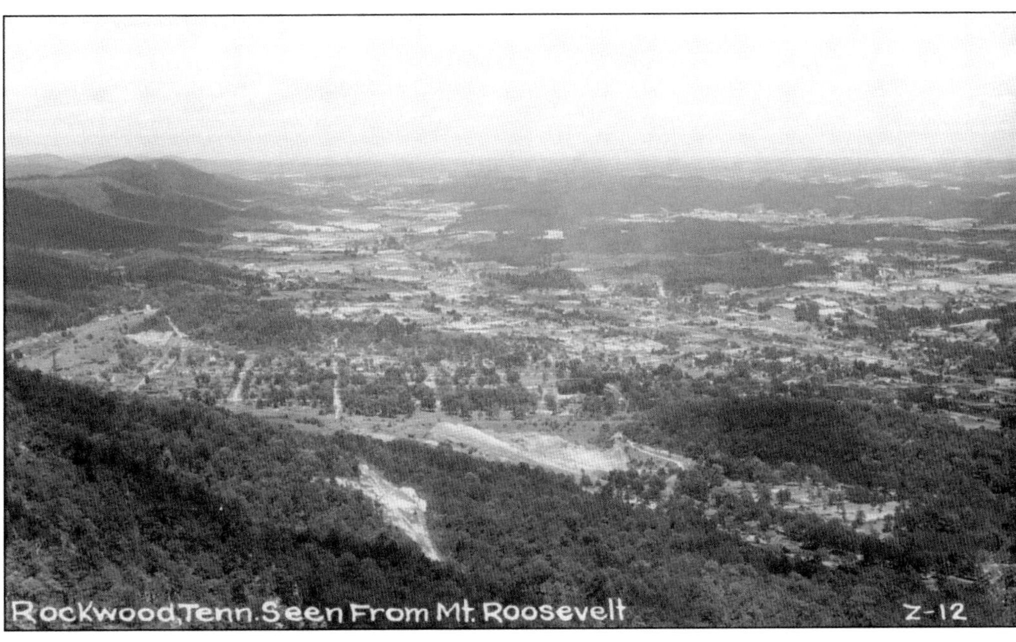

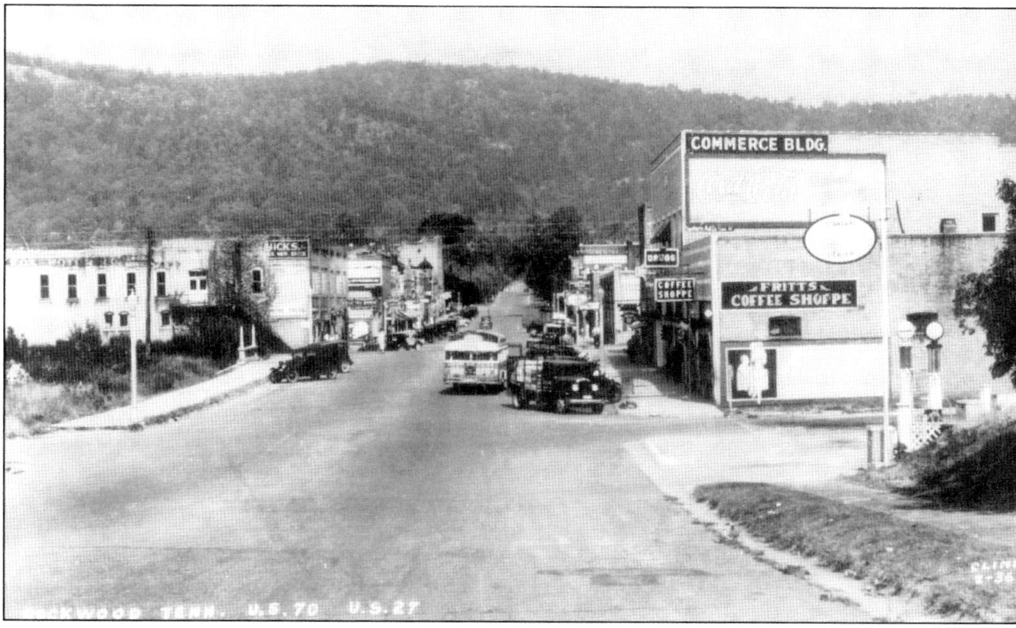

Rockwood was originally a mining town formed by the Roane Iron Company in 1868. Located in Roane County, it was named after William O. Rockwood, a major in the Union army and president of the iron company. The town's rich history and close proximity to Watts Bar Lake make it a popular tourist attraction. Downtown Rockwood has many antique and specialty shops and an old-fashioned ice cream soda fountain that dates back to the 1890s. Also downtown is the century-old Peterman Building, a common venue for traditional bluegrass. Several historical homes are located on Kingston Avenue, which was once part of the Dixie Highway.

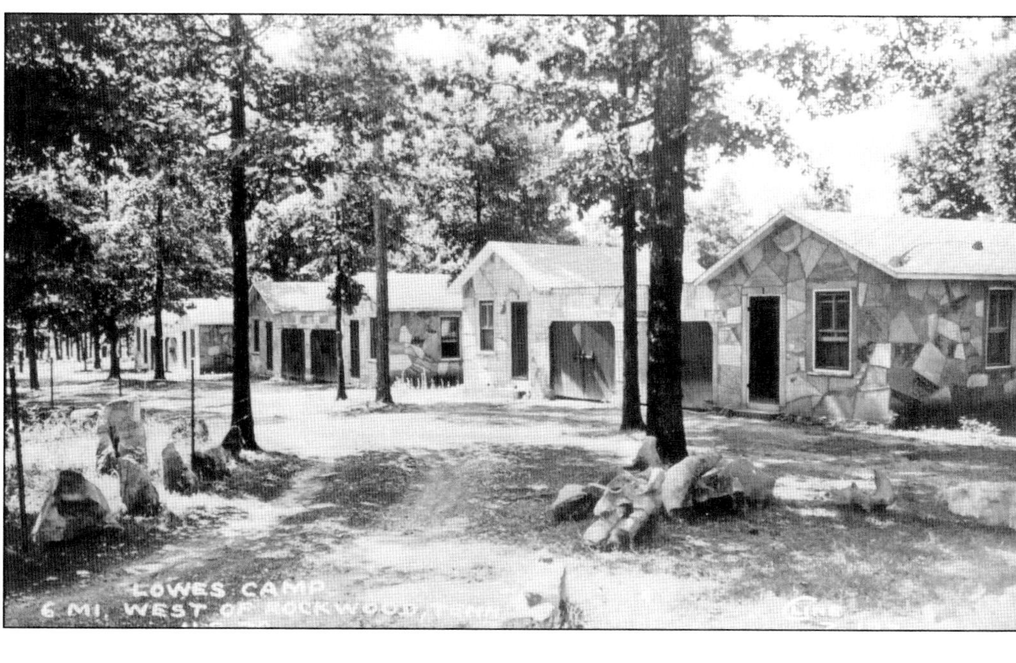

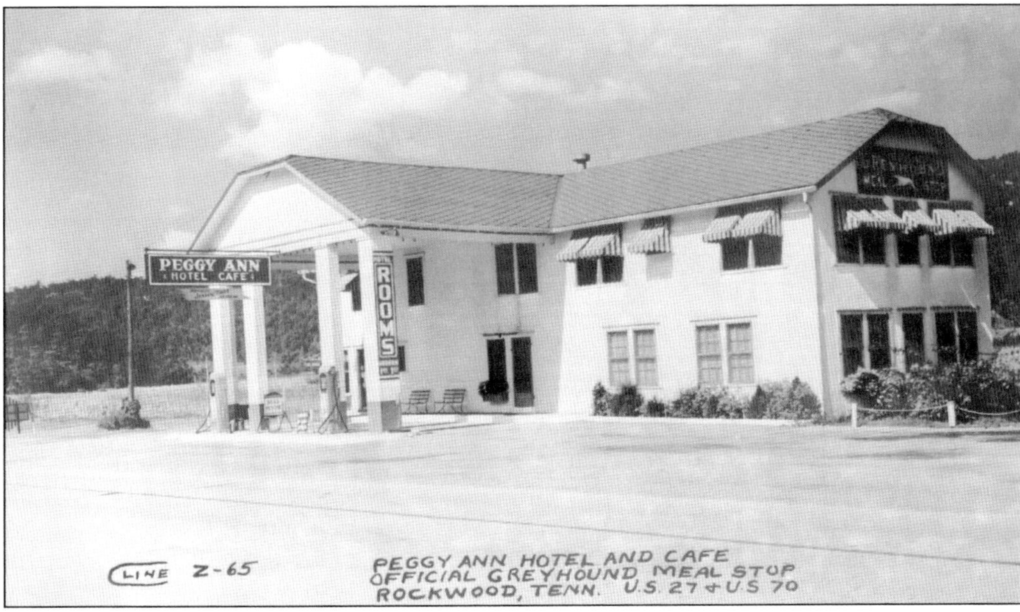

The Dixie Highway on US 27 converged with US 70 for a short distance in the area of Rockwood and was a prime location for auto courts and hotels such as the Peggy Ann Hotel. The hotel and café was an official Greyhound bus stop. In Richard D. Smith's book *Can't You Hear Me Callin': The Life of Bill Monroe, Father of Bluegrass*, the author writes that Peggy Ann's Café in Rockwood was one of Bill Monroe's favorite destinations for hamburgers and coffee while on tour.

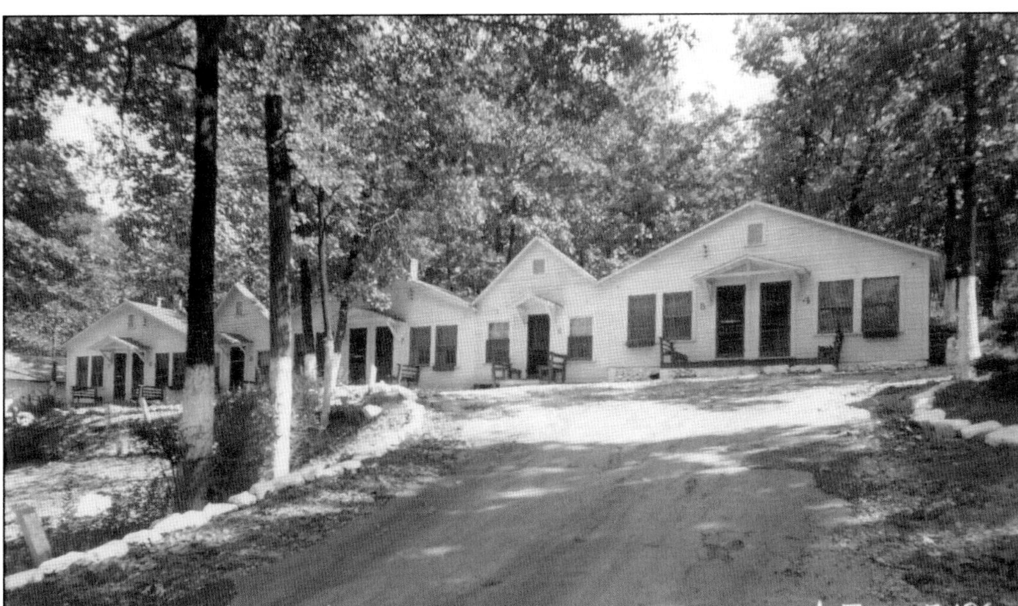

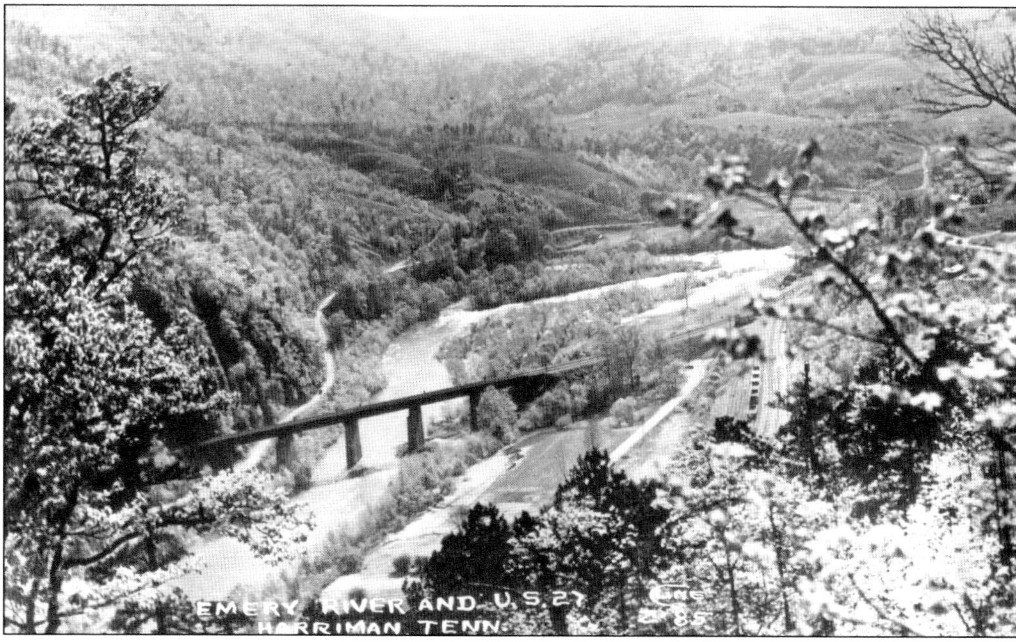

Harriman was founded in 1891 and was known as "the town that temperance built," with no manufacturing or sales of liquor allowed. The Emory River, pictured here, flooded in 1929, causing great damage to the town. Harriman has more than 100 buildings listed in the National Register of Historic Places, and historic home tours are available in the Cornstalk Heights district.

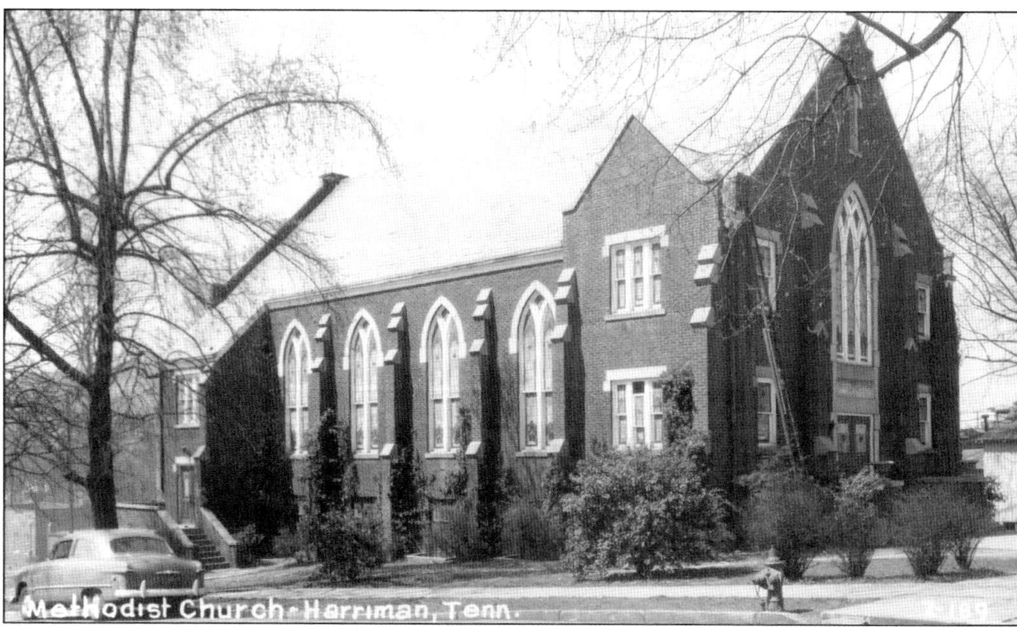

The Methodist Episcopal Church, South, organized in 1890, held its first service in this Gothic-style building on September 25, 1927. First Methodist Episcopal Church, also organized in 1890, merged with the congregation in 1942 to form the Harriman Methodist Church. Located on Queen Street, services are still held there today.

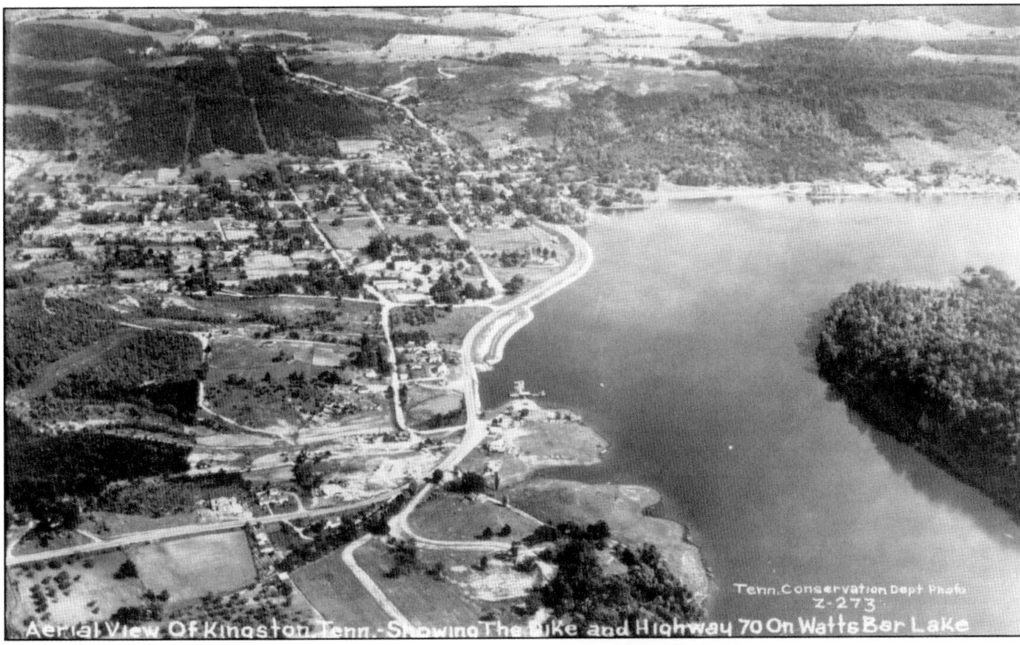

Aerial View Of Kingston, Tenn.-Showing The Lake and Highway 70 On Watts Bar Lake

Kingston, formed in 1799, is one of the oldest cities in Tennessee. It is located on Watts Bar Lake, where visitors can enjoy fishing, swimming, and camping. Watts Bar Lake is one of the largest lakes in the southern United States. Located on the Tennessee River, it has over 700 miles of shoreline. The town's paved three-mile walking trail, starting at Fort Southwest Point and ending at Kingston City Park, offers a scenic view of the lake. Fort Southwest Point is home to the only Colonial-era fort in Tennessee, reconstructed on its original site, and a museum with many interesting artifacts.

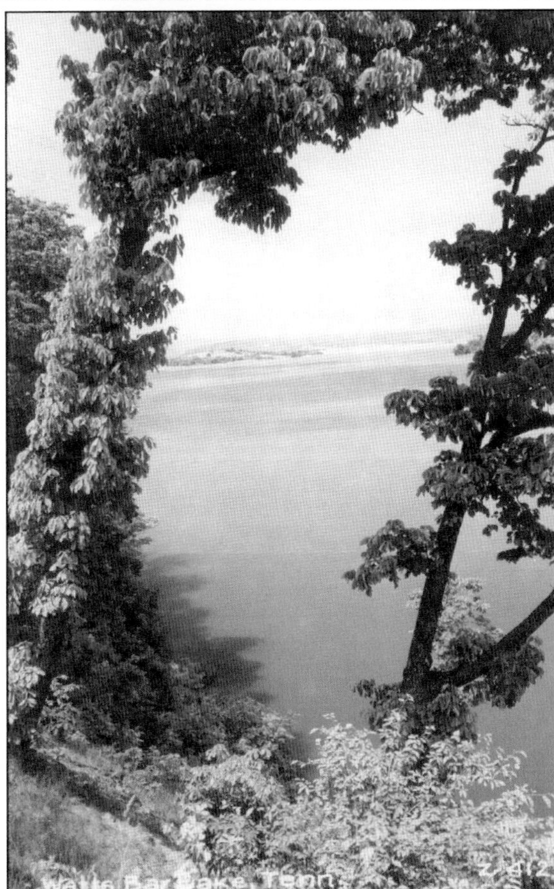
Watts Bar Lake, Tenn.

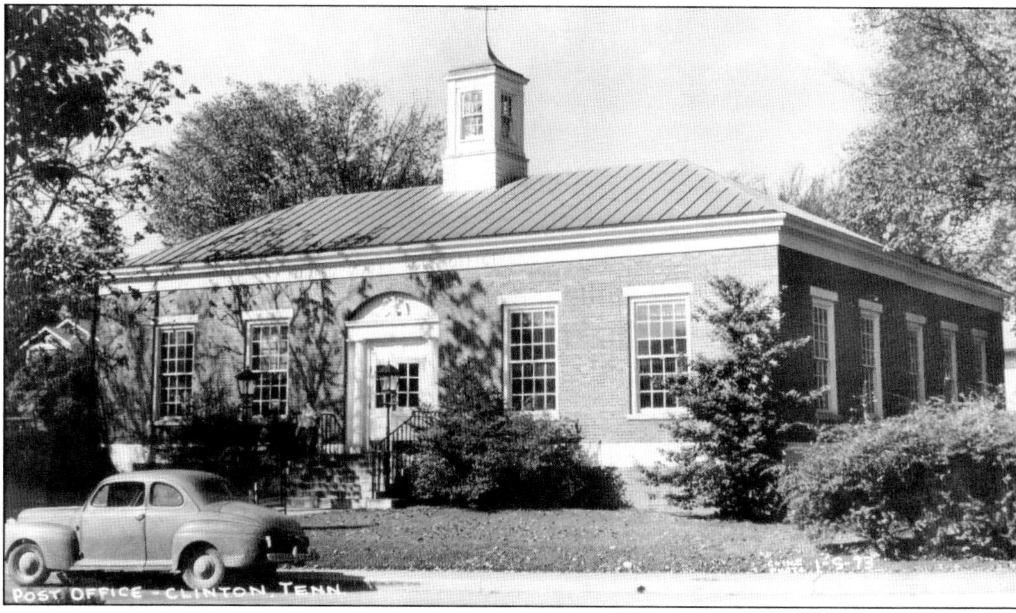

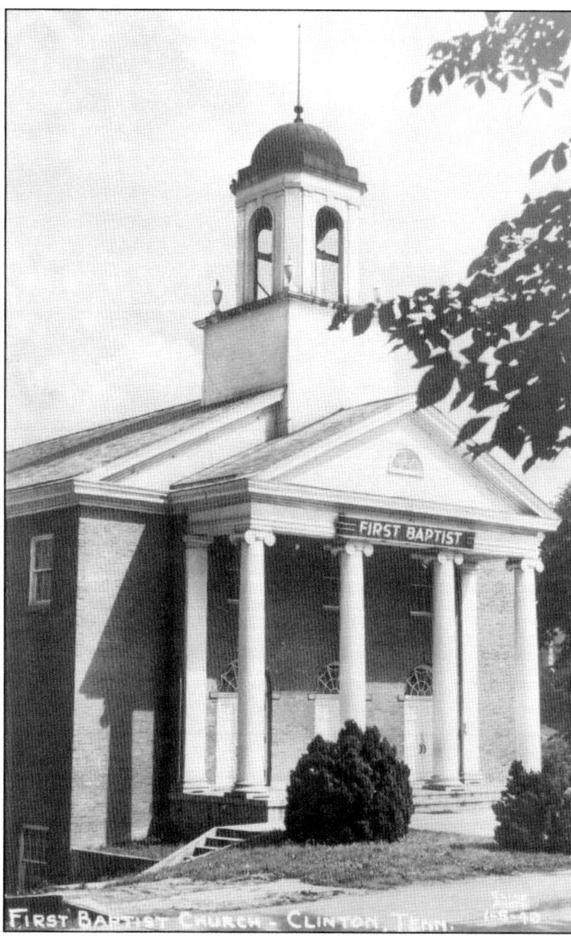

Originally named Burrville, the town of Clinton was established in 1801 and renamed eight years later because of Vice Pres. Aaron Burr's involvement in an infamous, controversial duel. On July 11, 1804, Burr fatally wounded Alexander Hamilton and was indicted on murder charges but not convicted. The town was renamed in honor of George Clinton, a political foe of Burr who served as vice president during Thomas Jefferson's second term. Clinton is located in Anderson County and is the county seat. The post office, shown above, was built in 1937 and now houses a family-owned floral shop called Samuel Franklin. First Baptist Church was built in 1893 and still holds services today. Both buildings are located on Main Street.

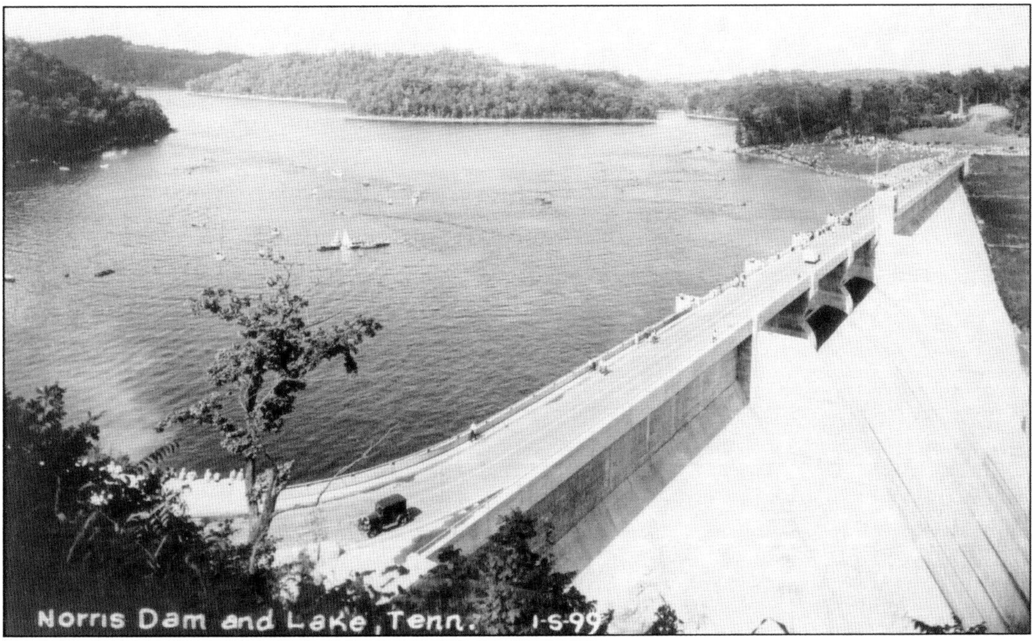

Congress created the Tennessee Valley Authority (TVA) in 1933, and the public corporation's first project, the construction of Norris Dam, began that same year. The dam was built to help control flooding, provide hydroelectric power at a low cost, and improve navigation on the waterways. It was named for Sen. George Norris of Nebraska, who was instrumental in its creation. Completed in 1936, Norris Dam is 1,860 feet long and 265 feet high. Total construction costs were around $36 million, which included buying property for the reservoir. In order to build the dam, over 5,000 graves had to be removed, and nearly 2,900 families were relocated.

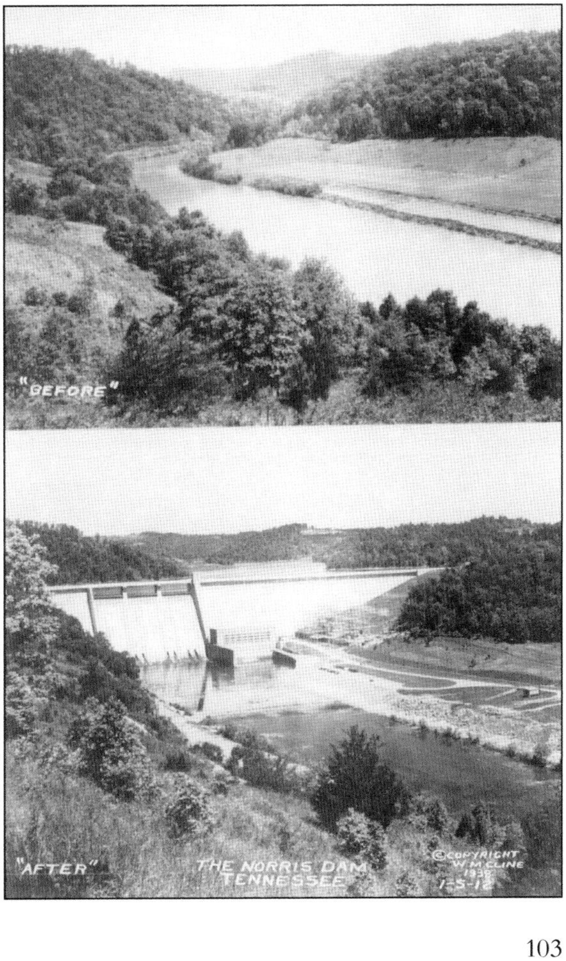

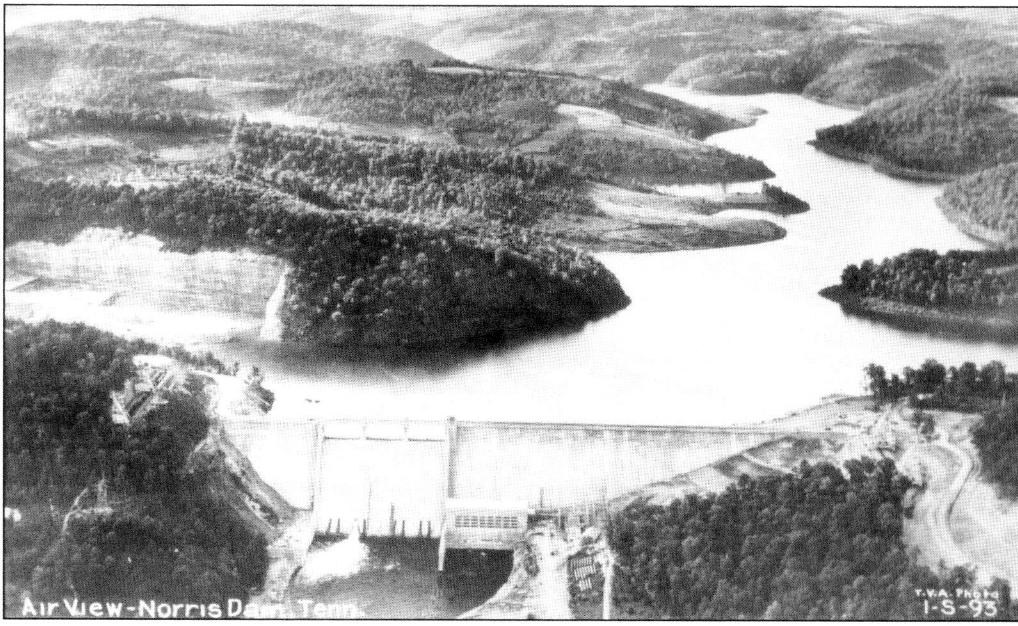

The scenic areas surrounding Norris Dam are owned by several government agencies, including Cove Creek Wildlife Management Area (owned by Tennessee Wildlife Resources Agency), Norris Dam State Park, and the Norris municipal watershed, part of a natural barrier protecting the town of Norris. Norris was a planned community built by the TVA in 1933 to house workers during construction of the dam. The neighborhood was designed to be pedestrian-friendly, and destinations such as schools and stores were located within walking distance of most residences. The TVA sold the town in 1948, and it was incorporated a year later as a self-governing community. Norris is listed as a historic district in the National Register of Historic Places.

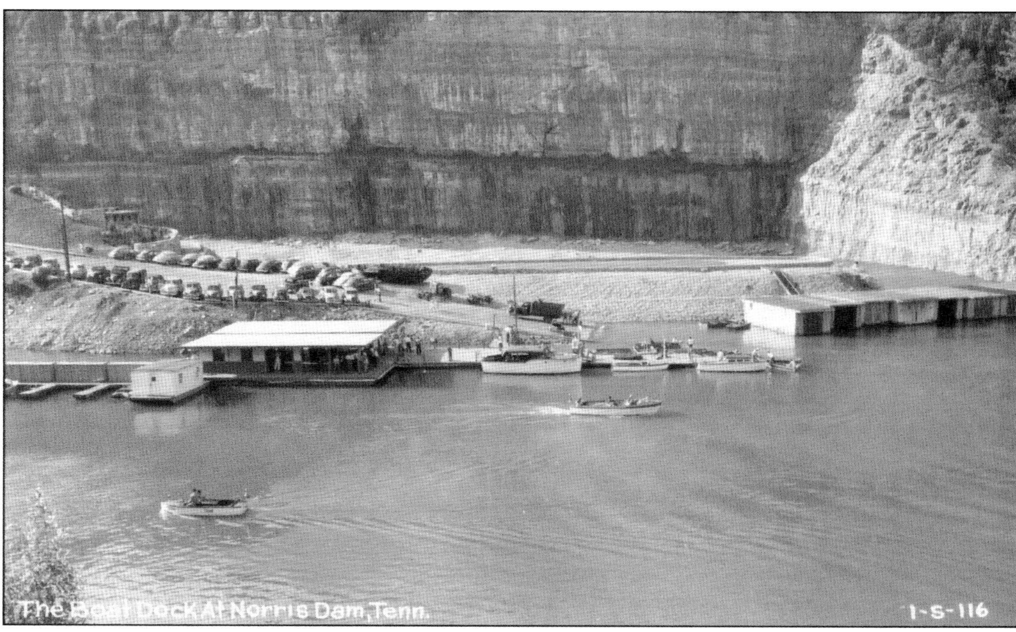

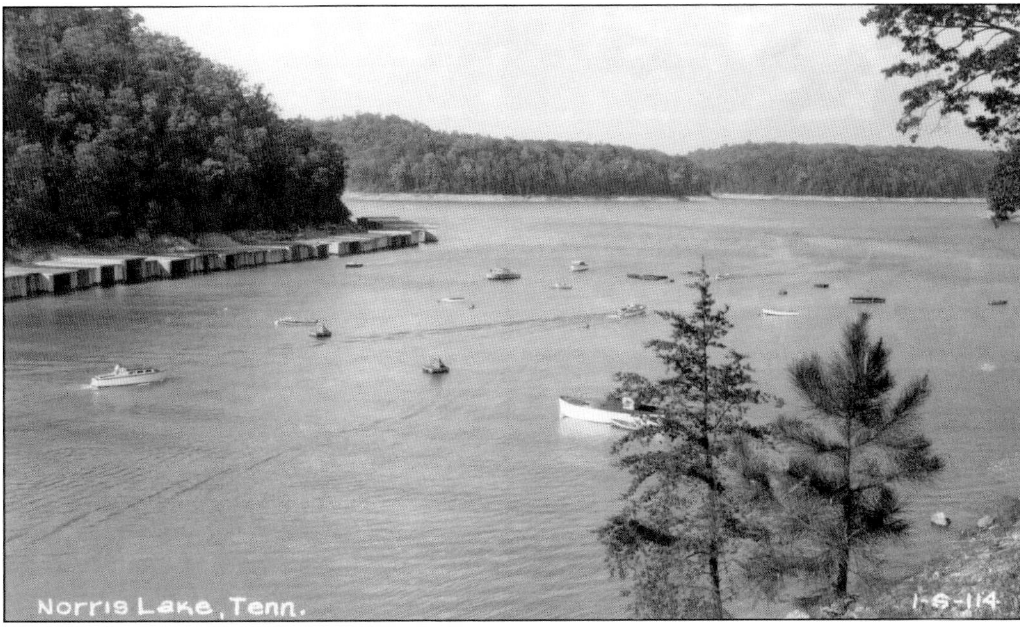

With over 700 miles of shoreline, Norris Lake provides recreational activities for five different counties (Campbell, Anderson, Union, Claiborne, and Grainger). The lake's watershed area covers almost 3,000 square miles. The building shown on the postcard is located at the TVA's eastern observation area of Norris Dam. Formerly a restaurant and gift shop, it is now a visitor center. Numerous hiking trails are located near the dam, as well as campgrounds and a state museum. Just a few miles from the area is the privately owned Museum of Appalachia, which contains artifacts collected by John Rice Irwin, a local resident who wanted to preserve the cultural history of the area that existed before TVA's construction of the dam.

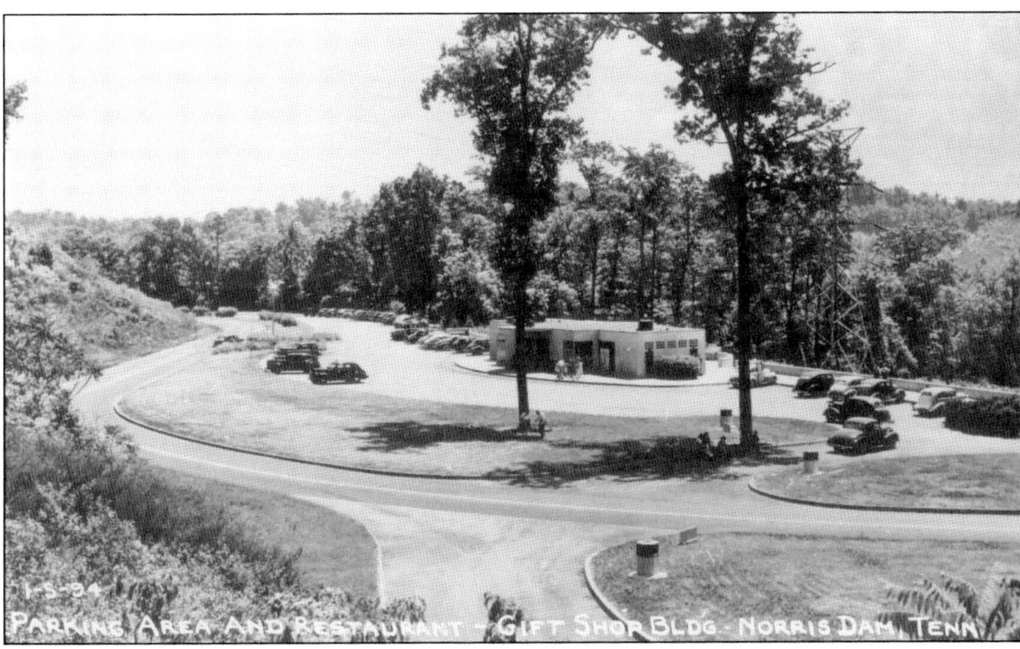

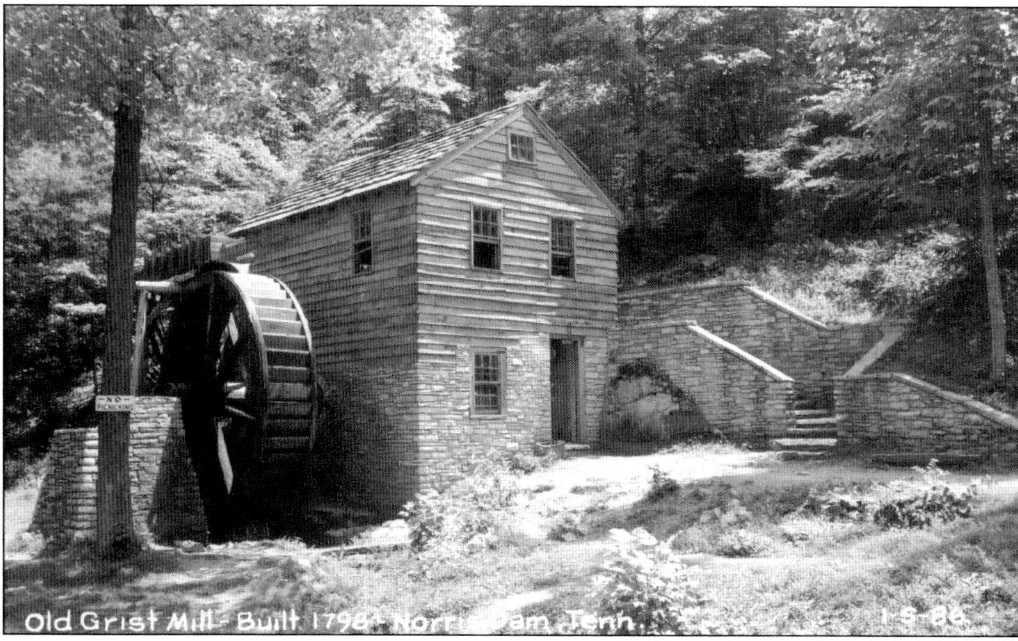

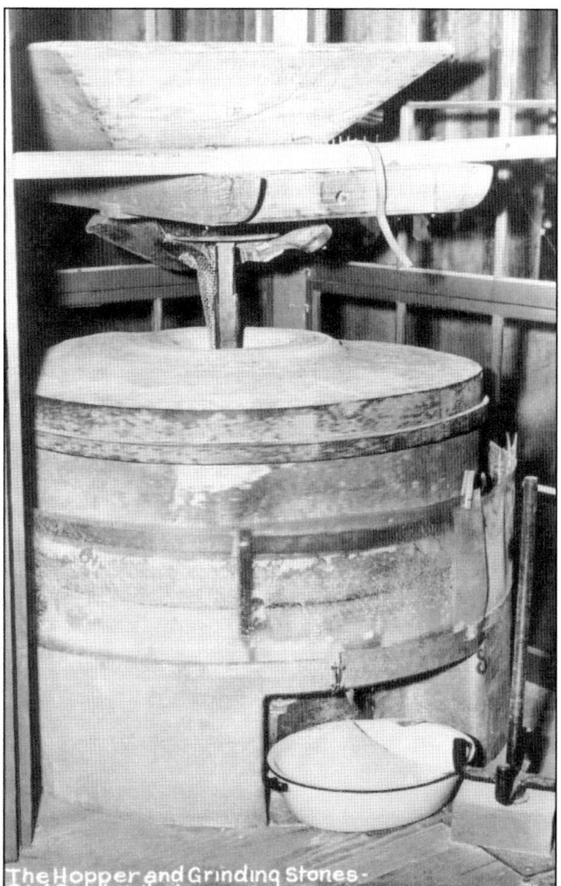

The Rice Grist Mill, originally located at Lost Creek in Union County, was built in 1798. The internal gears of the mill were carved from hickory and the millstones were imported from France. Four generations of the James Rice family used the mill, and not just for grinding grain—over the years, it was also used as a power source for various machines, including a cotton gin and a sawmill. Due to the construction of Norris Dam, the old mill was moved to the TVA's Norris Dam State Park in an area near Lower Clear Creek and reassembled by the Civilian Conservation Corps (CCC). The Rice Grist Mill was later donated to the state of Tennessee and became part of the Lenoir Museum Cultural Complex, where it still operates.

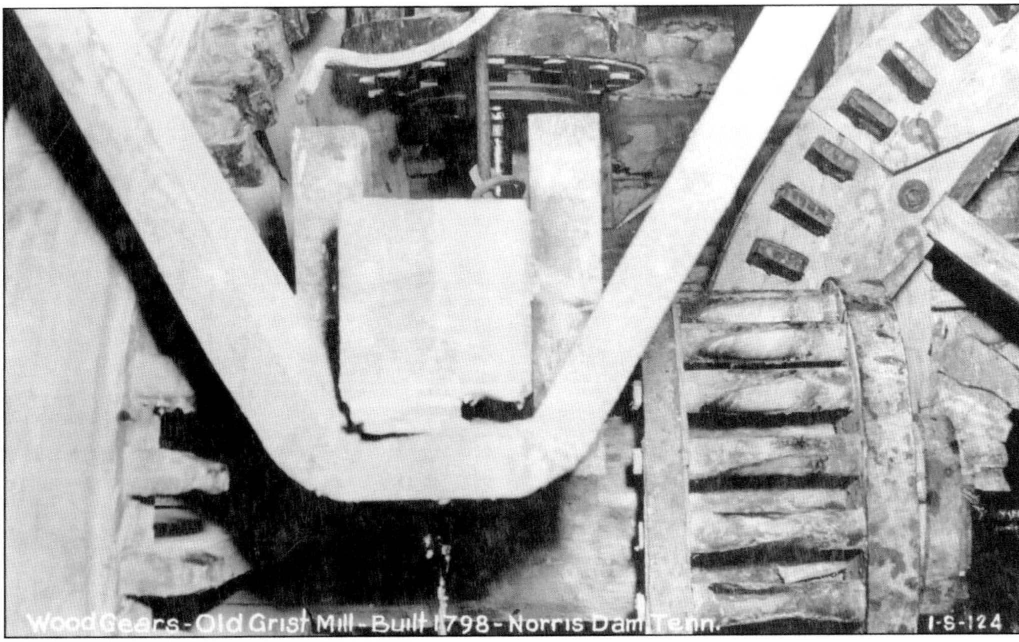

The Lenoir Museum Cultural Complex consists of the Rice Grist Mill (wood gears shown here), a threshing barn, and a museum. Caleb Crosby's grandsons donated the Caleb Crosby Threshing Barn, built in the mid-1800s, to the National Park Service when the TVA announced that it would be flooding the land the barn sat upon. After being stored for 34 years, it was finally reconstructed at the complex. The William G. and Helen H. Lenoir Museum was completed in 1975 and showcases a collection of artifacts and pictures of the area that existed before being submerged by Norris Lake. The museum also houses an antique barrel organ that plays several tunes and has over 40 movable figures, including dancers and marching soldiers.

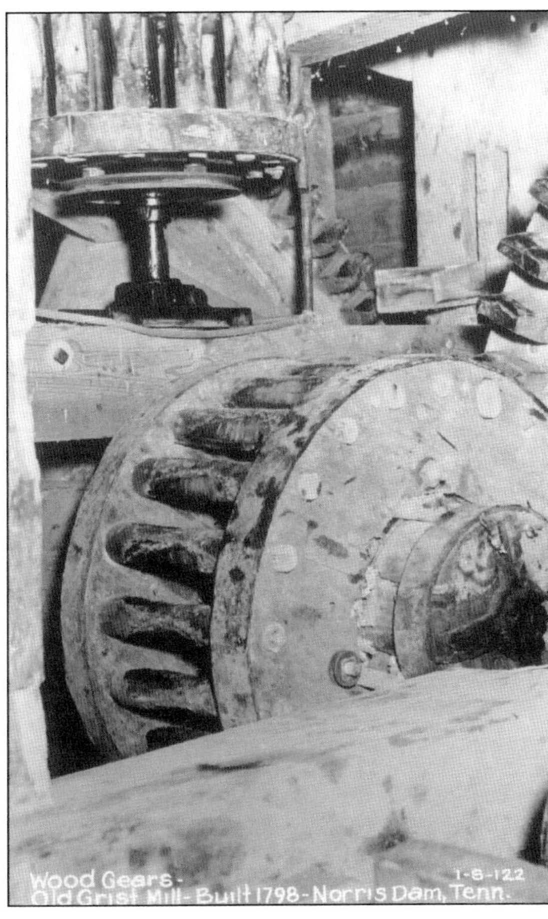

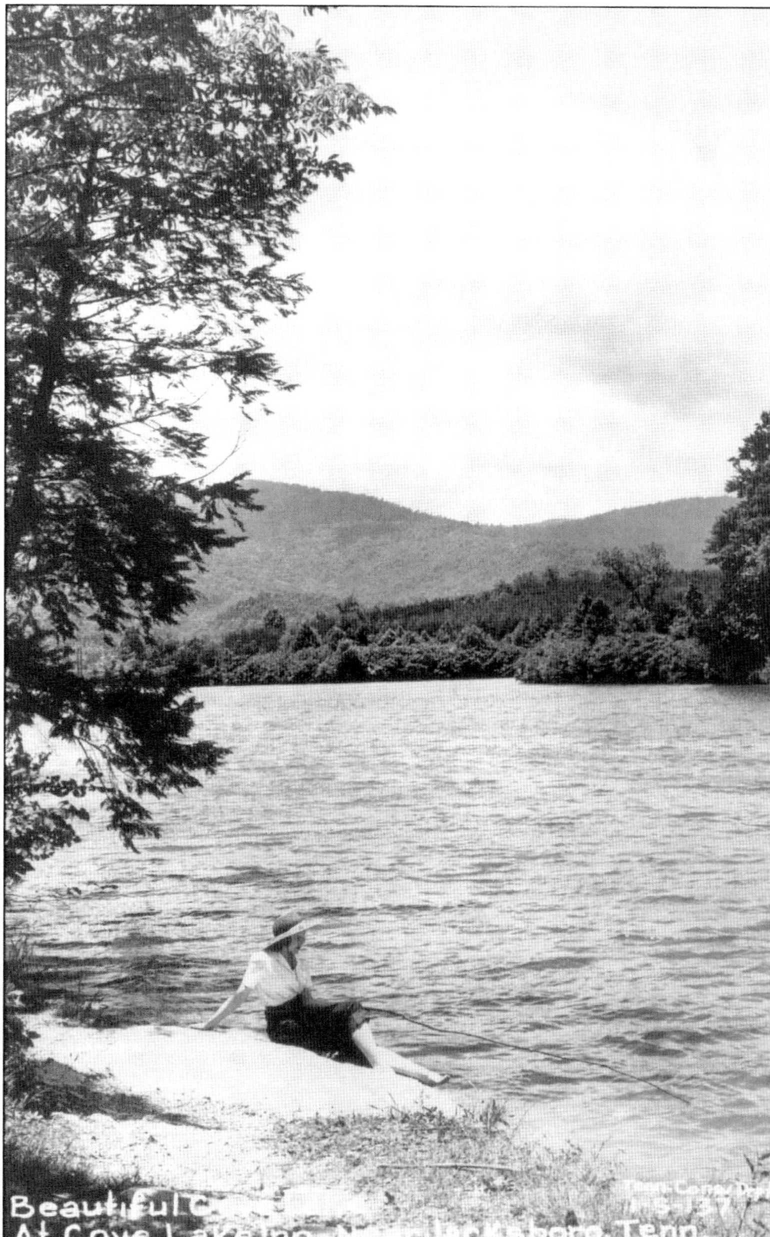

Cove Lake is located in Campbell County, near US 25W (the Dixie Highway) between the towns of Caryville and Jacksboro. The 210-acre lake was formed after the TVA's construction of Caryville Dam in 1936. The purpose of the dam was to minimize the effects of the newly formed Norris reservoir on Caryville, although the town still lost more than 70 buildings. Indian mounds dating from 1000 to 1200 AD (a part of the Mississippian period) were discovered in the area and excavated by the University of Tennessee in 1937. The artifacts included pottery, tools, and weapons. These artifacts, along with others excavated from additional TVA reservoir sites, are on display at the Frank H. McClung Museum at the University of Tennessee campus in Knoxville. Remnants of one of the excavated mounds can still be seen on an island at one end of the park.

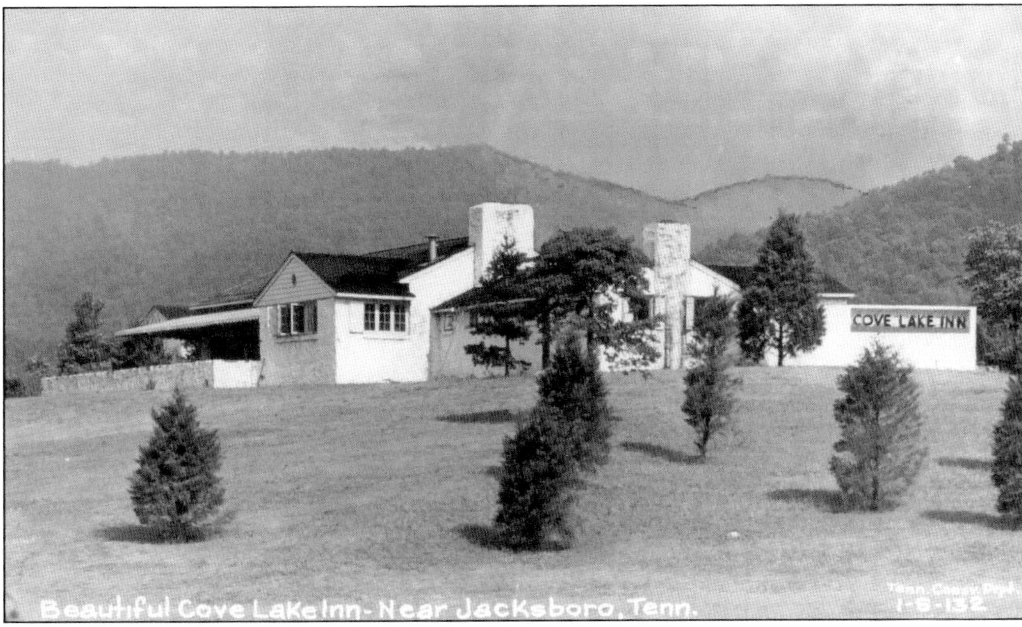

In conjunction with the National Park Service (NPS) and the Civilian Conservation Corps (CCC), the TVA built a recreational park next to Cove Lake in the late 1930s. The Cove Lake Inn, built by the CCC during the park's construction, is no longer operational. However, part of the building still stands and is currently used as a restaurant. The park was deeded to the state in 1950, and Cove Lake State Park now has over 670 acres with 100 campsites, 112 picnic tables and grills, three playground areas, and a swimming pool. To maintain the serenity of the park, no gas-powered boats are allowed, but pedal boats and rowboats are available for rental.

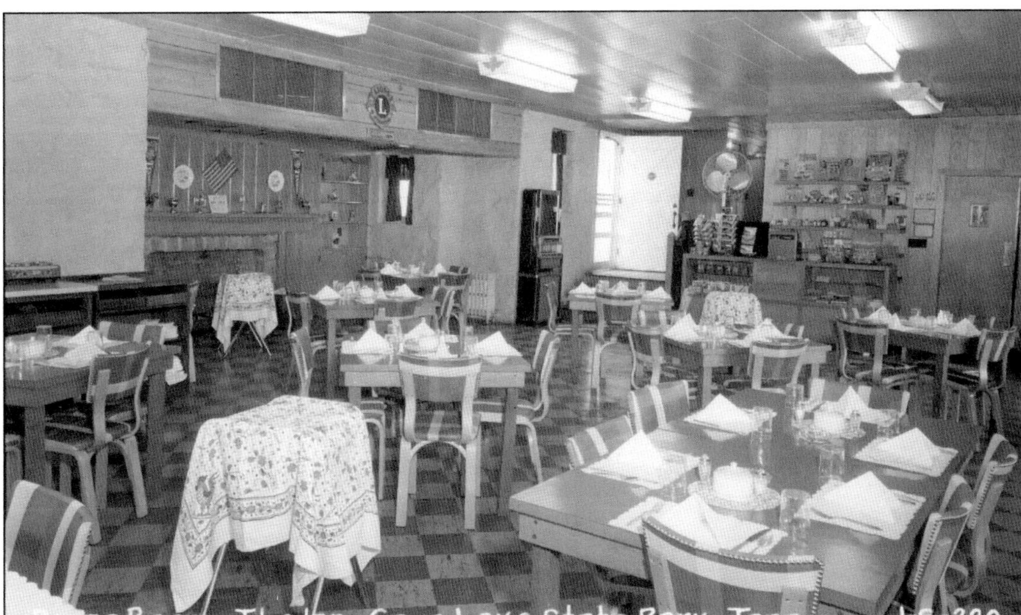

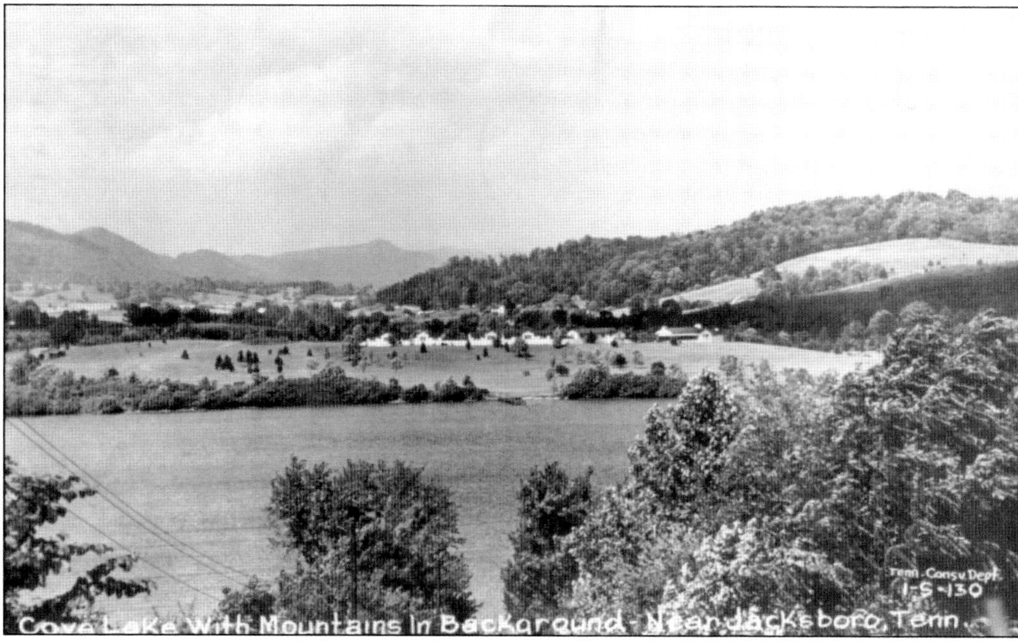

Located in a scenic valley next to the Cumberland Mountains, Cove Lake State Park is the perfect place to enjoy nature. During winter months, several hundred Canadian geese feed on the lakeshore. For the casual walker, the park provides a three-and-a-half-mile paved trail. For the more adventurous visitor, the park offers access to the Cumberland Trail. Though not yet completed, the Cumberland Trail will eventually provide a footpath from Cumberland Gap National Park in Kentucky to Signal Point National Park, located on Signal Mountain in Tennessee. The Cumberland Mountains segment of the trail is approximately 10 miles, from Cove Lake to LaFollette, and provides access to a spectacular rock formation known as the Devil's Racetrack.

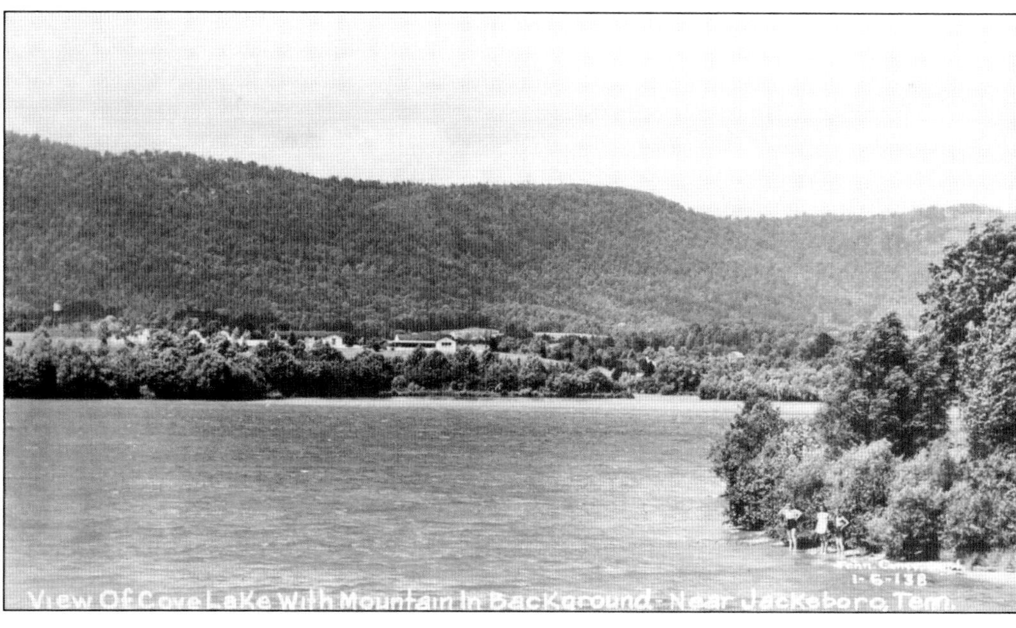

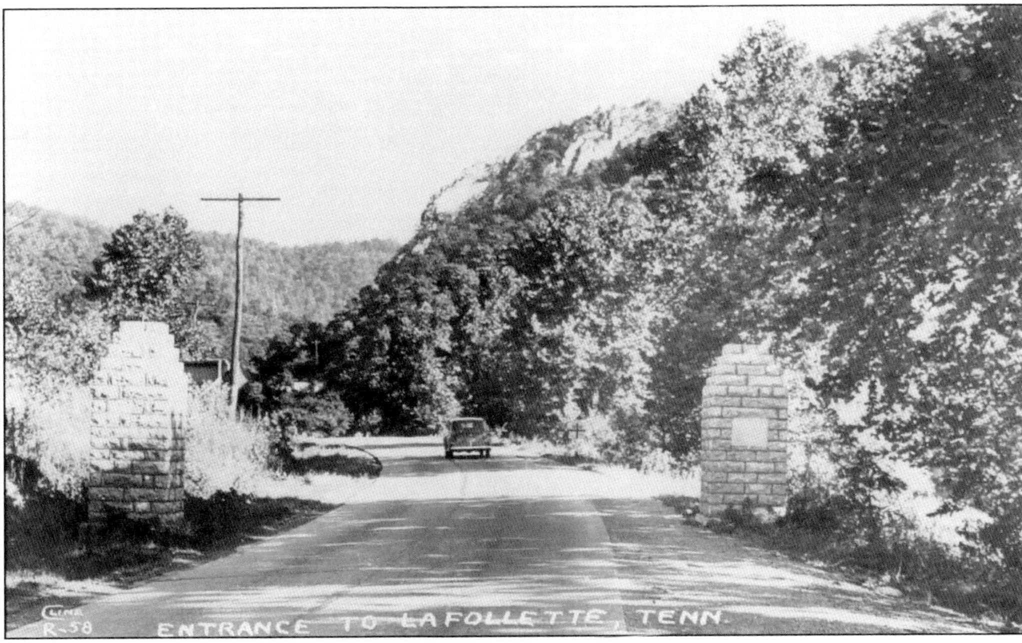

In the 1890s, Harvey and Grant LaFollette purchased over 30,000 acres in an area known as Big Creek Gap and formed the LaFollette Coal, Iron, and Railway Company. The city of LaFollette was incorporated in 1897. Harvey LaFollette's family lived in a beautiful 27-room Victorian home designed by Knoxville architect George Barber and nicknamed Glen Oaks. Located on Indiana Avenue near the Campbell County Museum and Archives, Glen Oaks is listed in the National Register of Historic Places. After the LaFollette coal company ceased operations around 1926, the Dixie Highway (US 25W) helped maintain the town's economy. Tourist courts, such as the one pictured below, were constructed along the Dixie Highway to provide travelers with food and lodging.

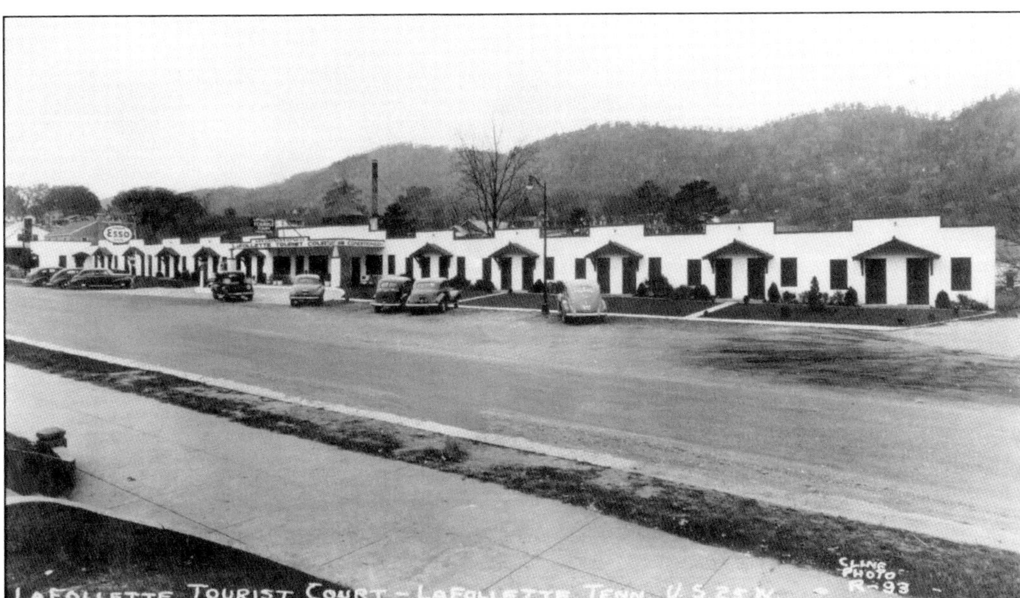

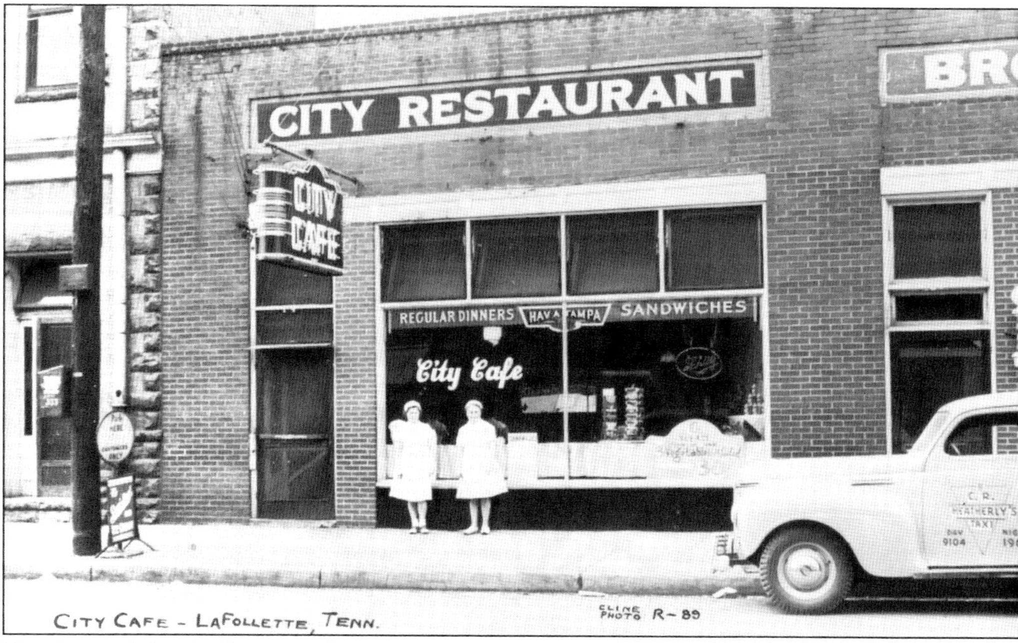

Tourists and locals frequented eating establishments such as the City Café in LaFollette. A young architect named John Fox Jr., who later became a famous author, designed the town of LaFollette in the late 1800s. His novel *The Trail of the Lonesome Pine* was a bestseller in the early 1900s and was later made into a 1936 film starring Henry Fonda.

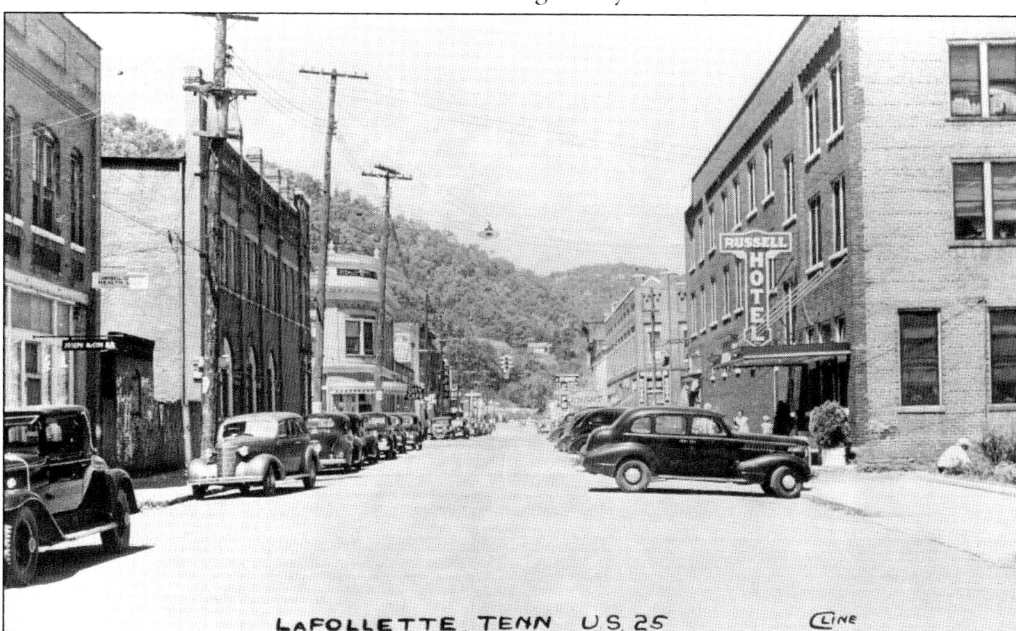

Russell Hotel (first building pictured at right) was built in 1922. William Russell, the major stockholder of the hotel, was involved in a deadly gunfight in August 1936. The altercation occurred at a voting poll over a hotly contested sheriff's race. William Russell was later convicted of killing his brother, Horace Russell, and nephew, Albert Russell, and he spent two years in the penitentiary. The hotel was demolished in 1997.

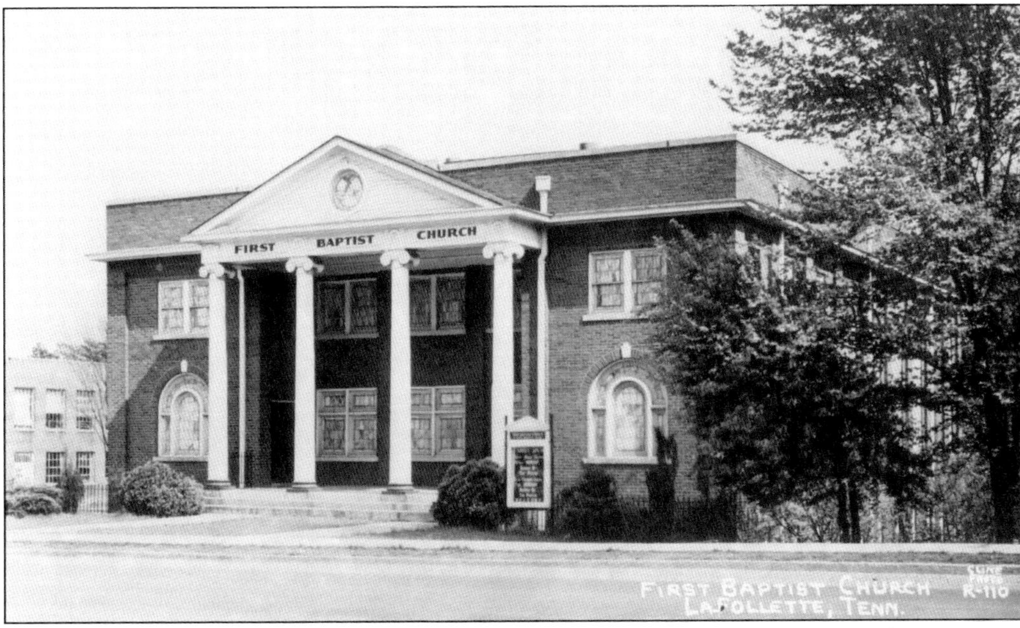

The congregation of LaFollette's First Baptist Church was first known as Big Creek Gap Baptist Church, organized in 1881. The name was changed in 1902. Six years later, the LaFollette church became part of the newly organized Campbell County Baptist Association. The congregation moved to the building shown above in 1928, and services are still held there today.

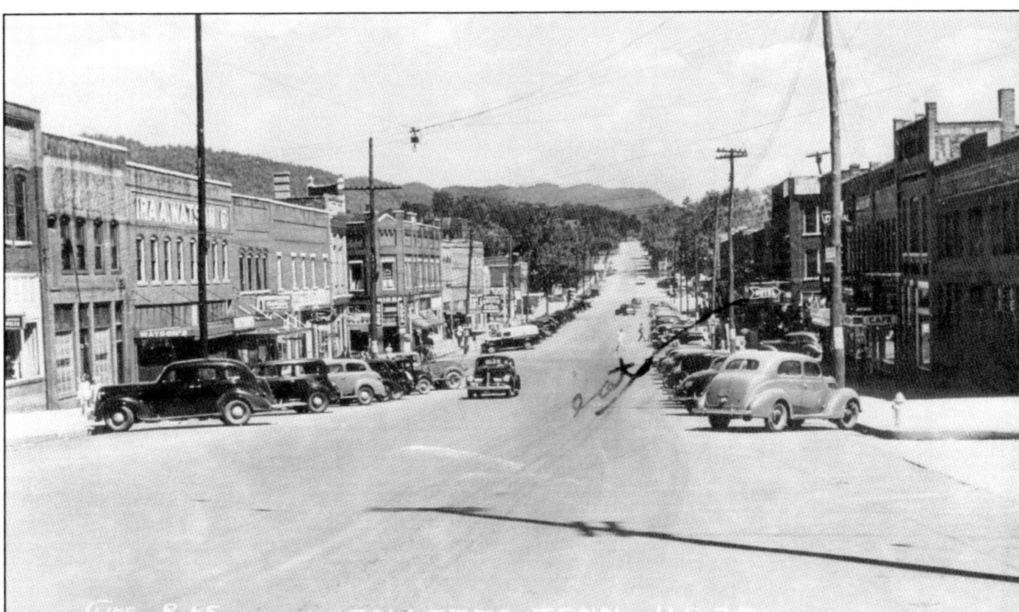

The Ira A. Watson Company (third building from left in the picture) was a department store chain with the majority of its stores located in the Southeast. It was founded in 1907 and based in Knoxville, Tennessee. The company filed for bankruptcy in 1992 and was purchased by Peebles in 1998.

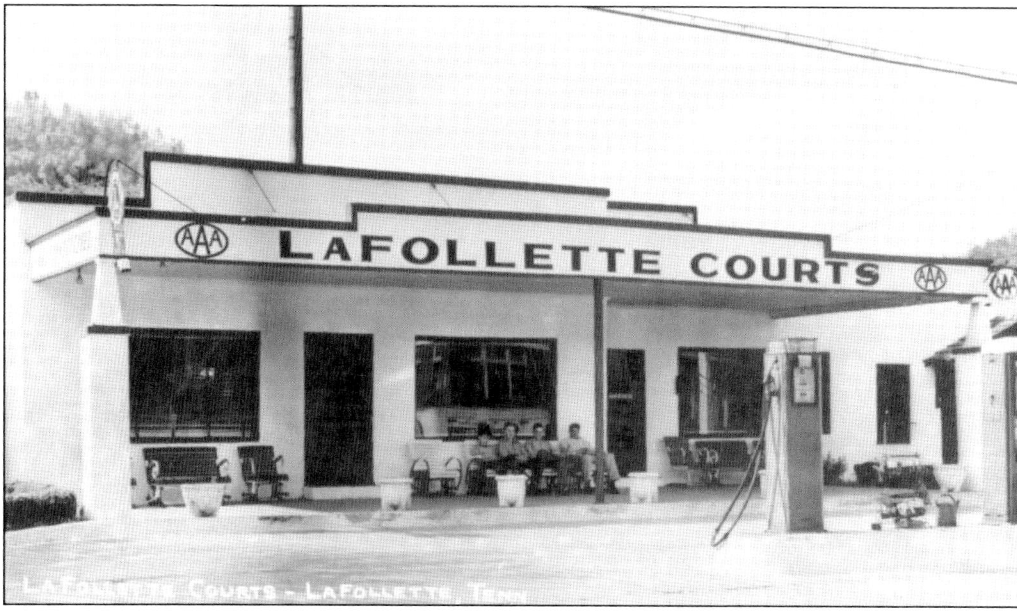

Before the Dixie Highway and other main thoroughfares were built, most people stayed in hotels when they traveled. As better roads were constructed and the popularity of the automobile grew, a need arose for more convenient roadside accommodations. In the beginning, drivers would simply park on the side of the road to rest during travels. Commercial auto camps offered travelers a place to camp and to meet basic needs, with electrical hookups, a community kitchen, and a restroom. Later, motor courts were built and provided travelers with simple cabins; the courts often had a gas station and a restaurant.

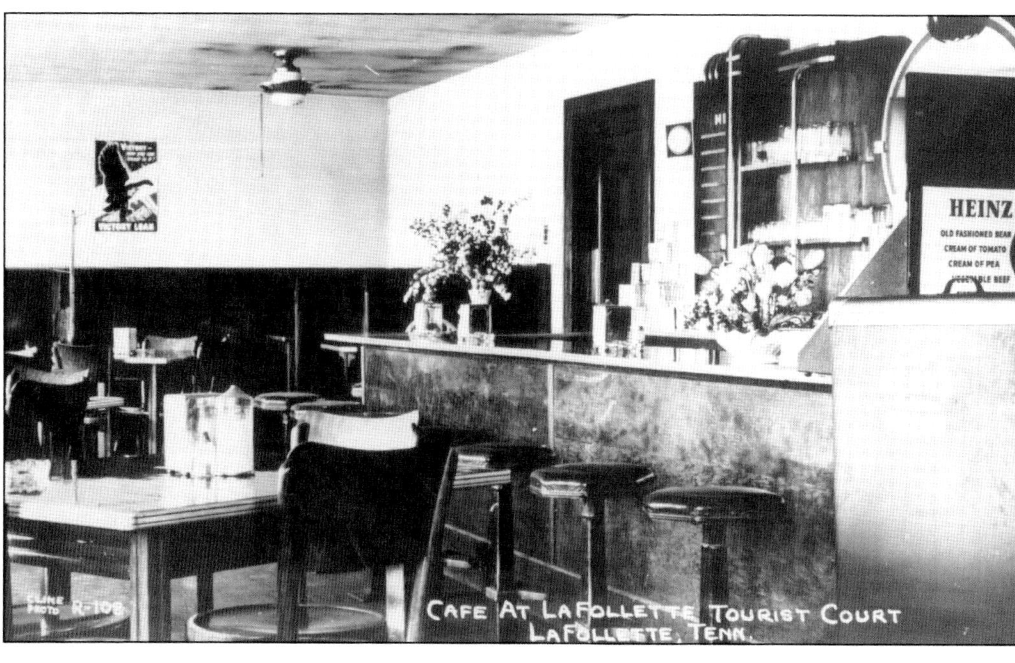

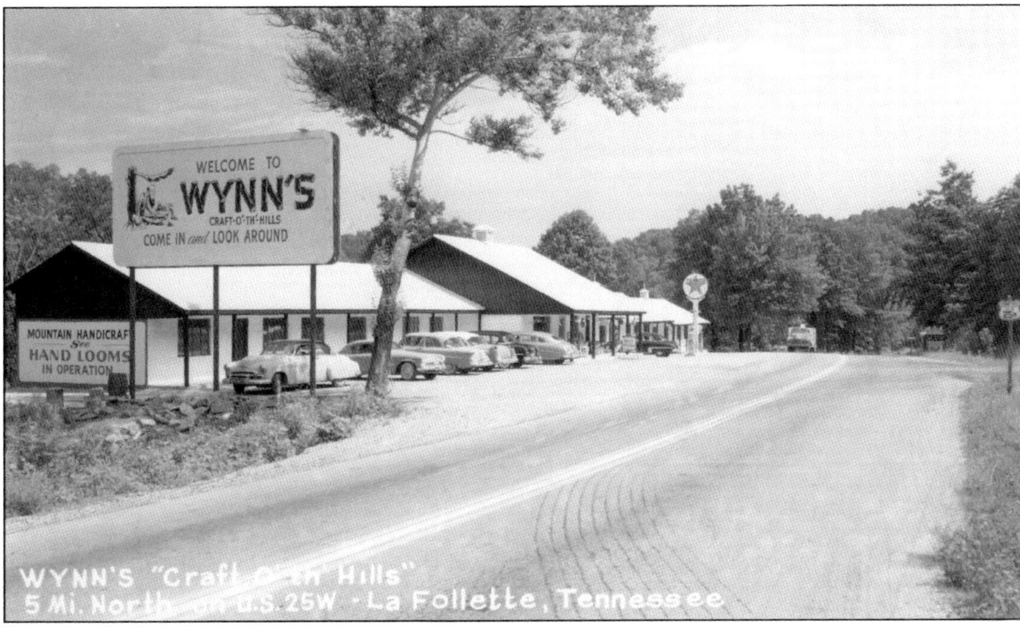

Prior to the completion of Interstate 75 in the 1960s, motorists frequented such businesses as Wynn's Craft-o'-th'-Hills on US 25W. Wynn's, shown in this image, was one of the largest of the roadside-type craft stores in the country. Besides crafts, it also sold picnic supplies and had a picnic area available for customers. The store covered an area of over 8,000 square feet.

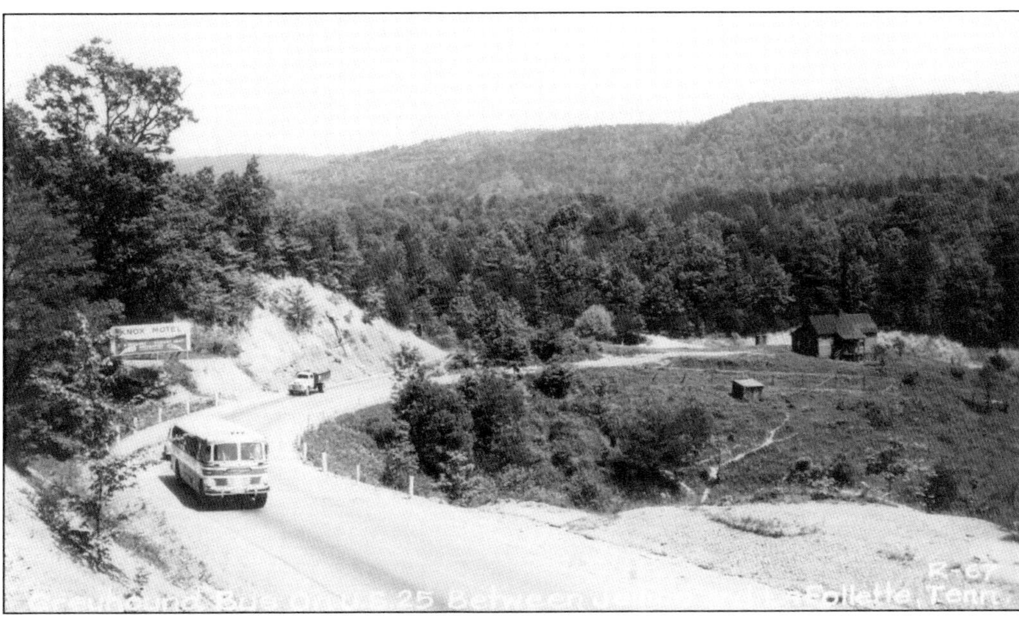

Harlan Sanders, of Kentucky Fried Chicken fame, was a member of the Dixie Highway Association's executive committee for the US 25W route. The section of US 25W connecting LaFollette and Jellico is one of the most scenic drives on Tennessee's Dixie Highway and is still the main route between the two towns.

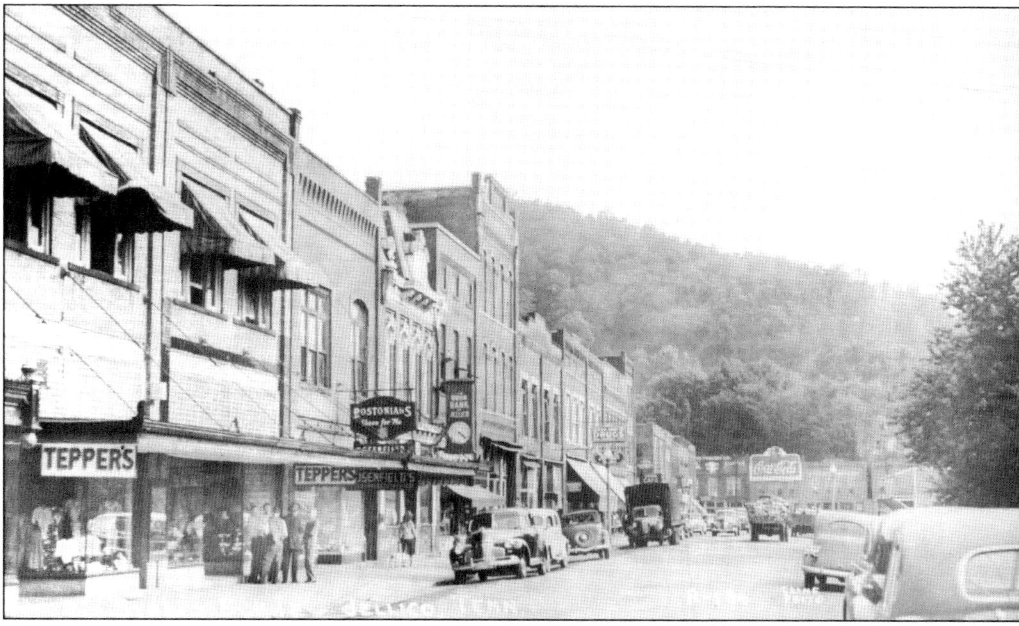

After originally being known as Smithburg when it was founded in 1878, the town of Jellico changed names in 1883. Many stories have been told to explain the origin of the name; a popular theory is that it was named after the bituminous Jellico coal. The coal is supposedly named for the wild angelica plant that grows throughout the mountainside.

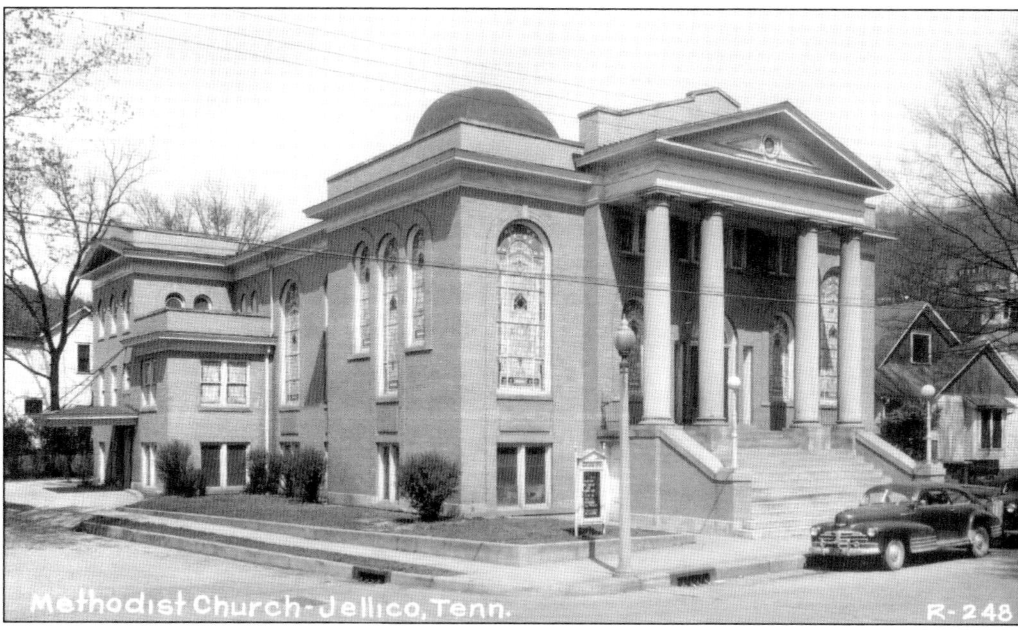

Services for the Methodist church in Jellico were first held in 1886 at the Tannery Hollow School, and the congregation's first building was constructed in 1889. The Jellico United Methodist Church structure pictured here is located on Fifth Street and was completed in 1921; services are still conducted there today. In October 1924, the congregation hosted the Holston Annual Conference of the Methodist Episcopal Church.

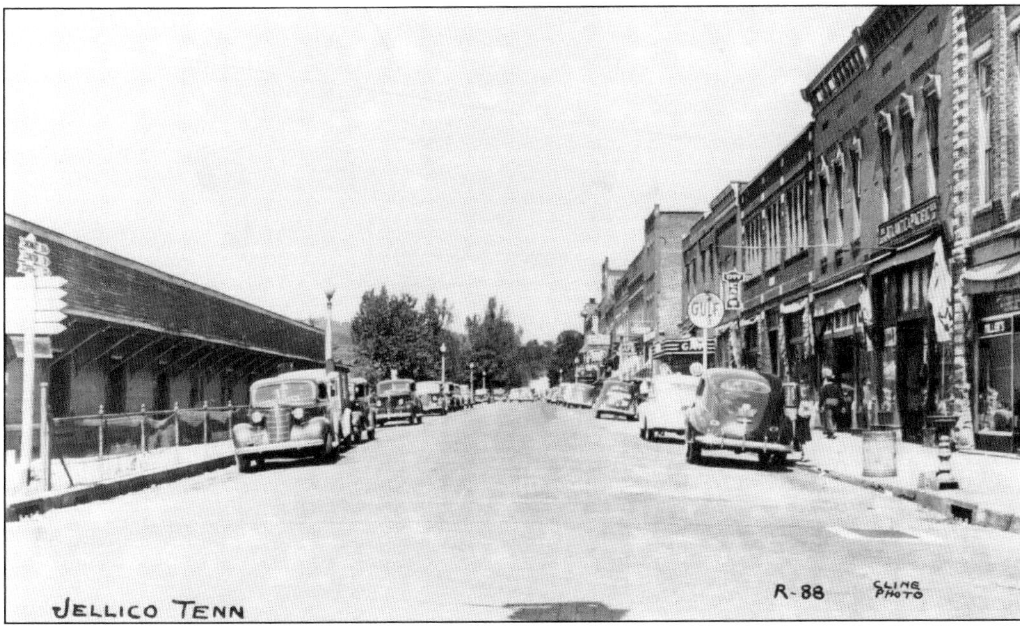

The road through Jellico, now known as US 25W, was added to the Dixie Highway route in 1918 after Judge Michael M. Allison, president of the Dixie Highway Association, found the construction progress through Knox County, Kentucky, to be less than acceptable during his inspection tour. This view of Jellico's North Main Street shows the Gay Theatre just beyond the white car on the right; the theater closed in the 1950s.

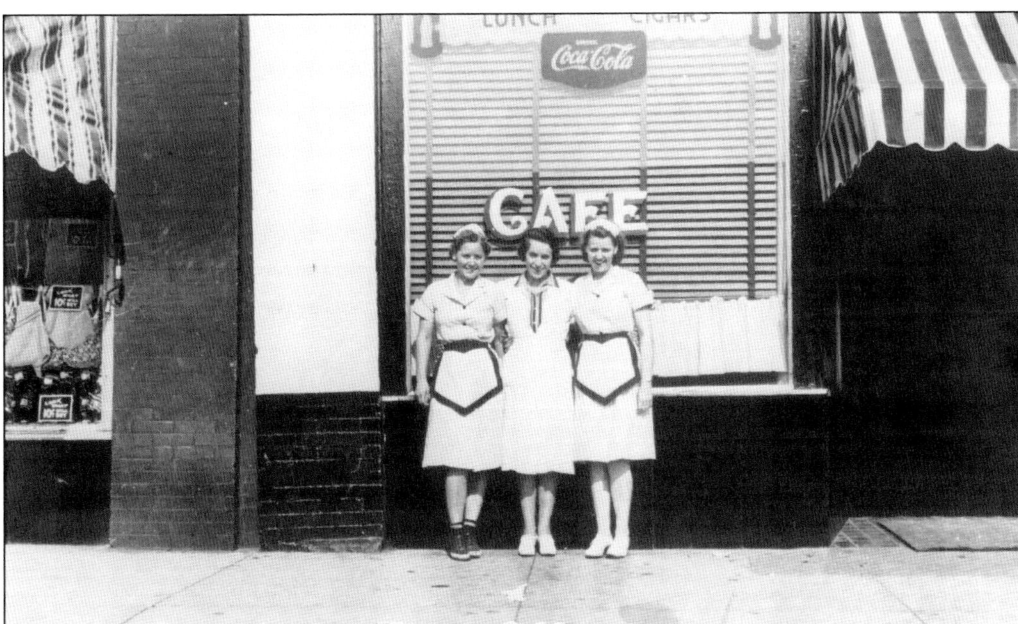

In 1999, Jellico's historic business district along North and South Main Street was added to the National Register of Historic Places. It consists of 30 buildings dating as early as 1875. A few blocks north of the Union Café (pictured) is the old US Post Office and Mine Rescue Station, built in 1915 and added to the register in 1984.

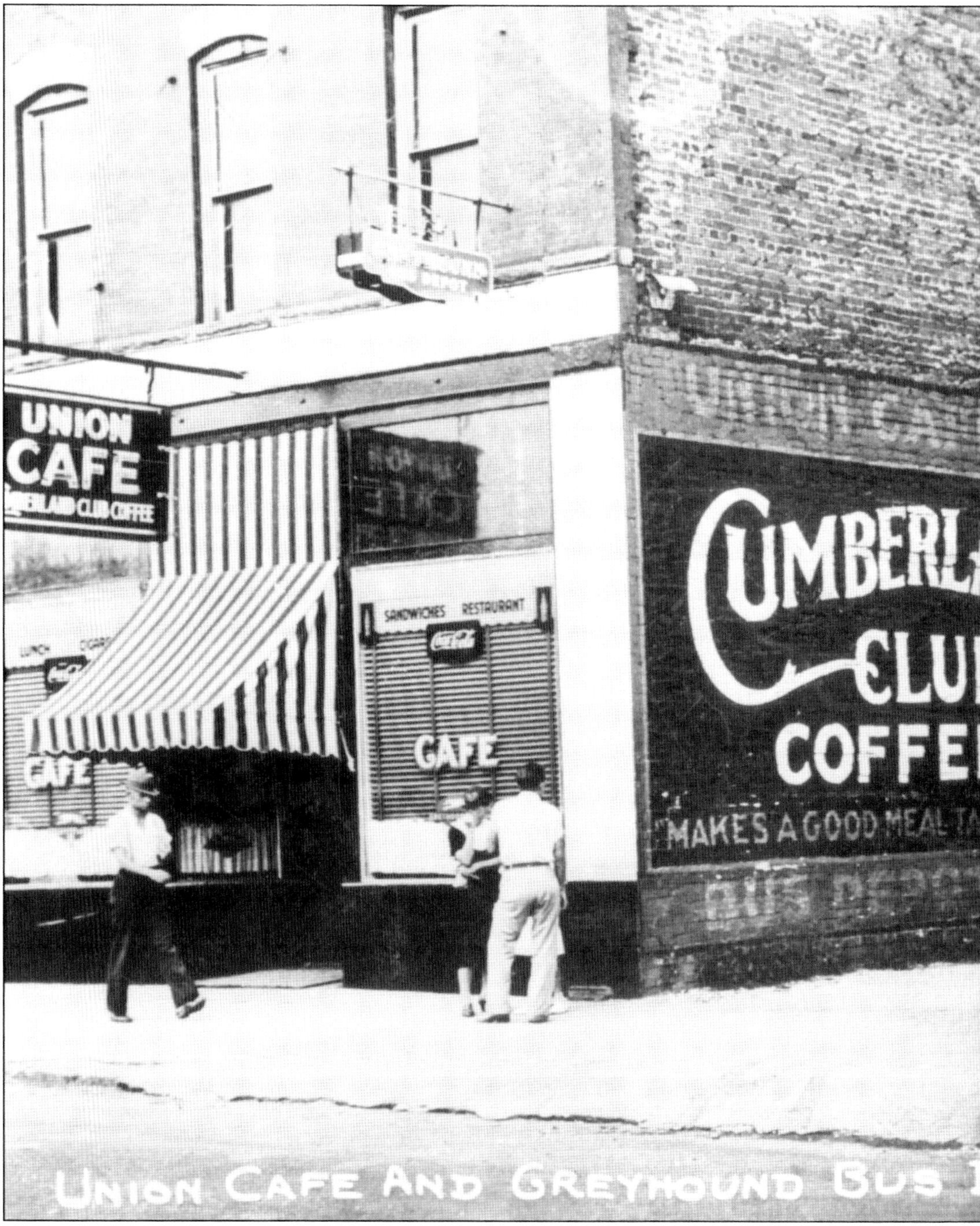

Cumberland Club Coffee, advertised on the side of the Union Café, was packaged and distributed by the Jellico Grocery Company, incorporated in 1903. It guaranteed the quality of the coffee, saying: "If you try a package you will have no other." During its existence, the company had distribution centers in numerous Tennessee and Kentucky towns. In 1975, it was acquired by

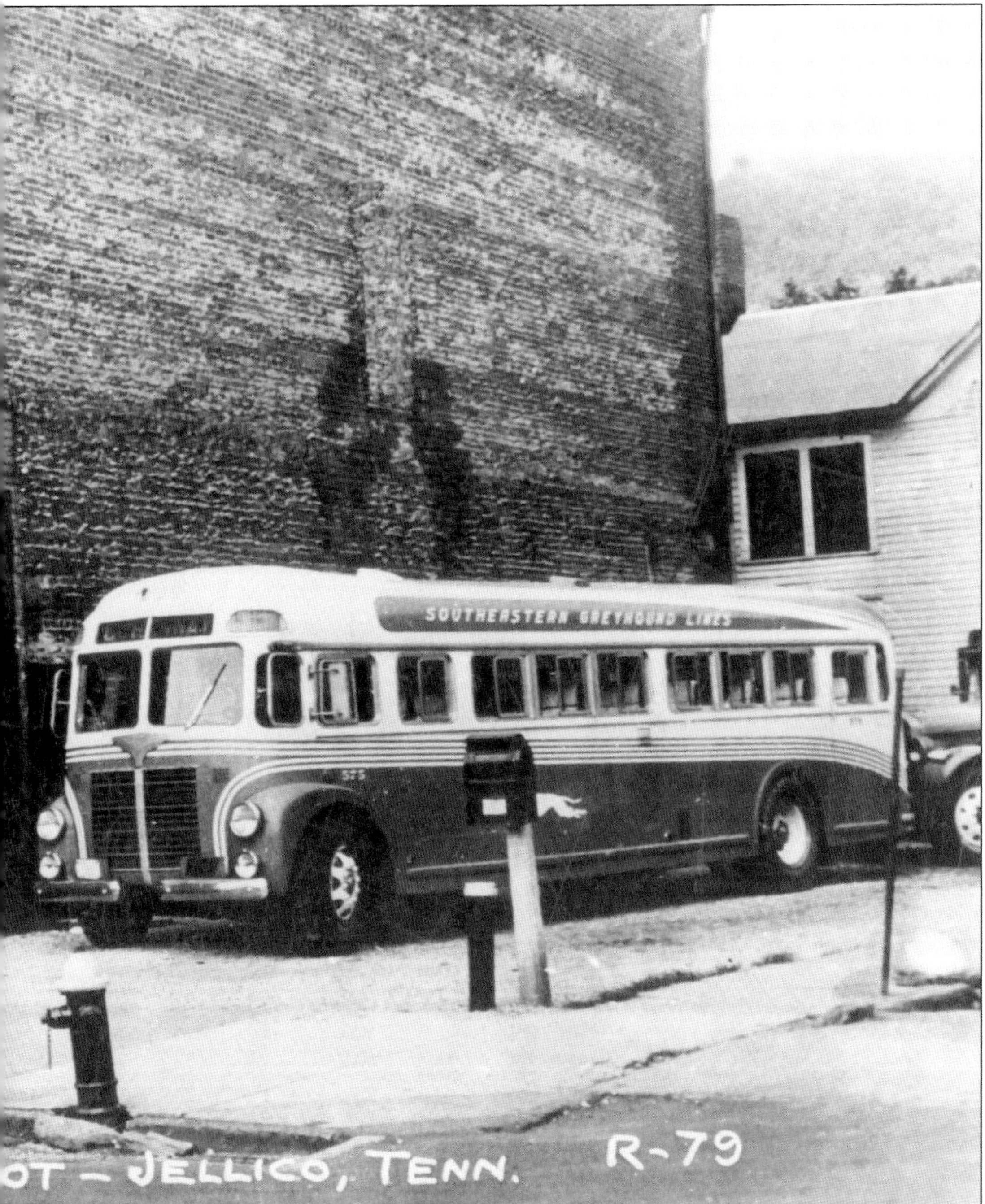

the H.T. Hackney Company of Knoxville, opened by Henry Tate Hackney in 1891. Today, the Knoxville-based wholesale company has distribution centers in 10 states, enabling it to cover more than 20,000 grocery and convenience stores in 21 states.

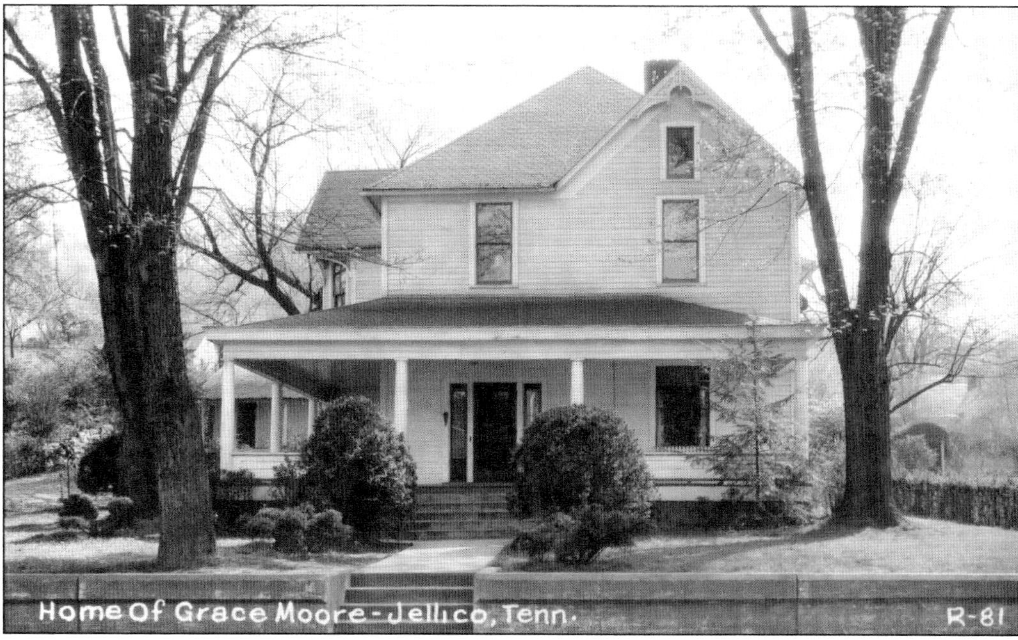

Grace Moore, well known in her day as an actress and opera singer, was born in Del Rio, Tennessee, but grew up in Jellico. Moore debuted in 1928 with the Metropolitan Opera and was nominated for a Best Actress Oscar in 1934 for her role in *One Night of Love*. Sadly, the Grace Moore house no longer exists.

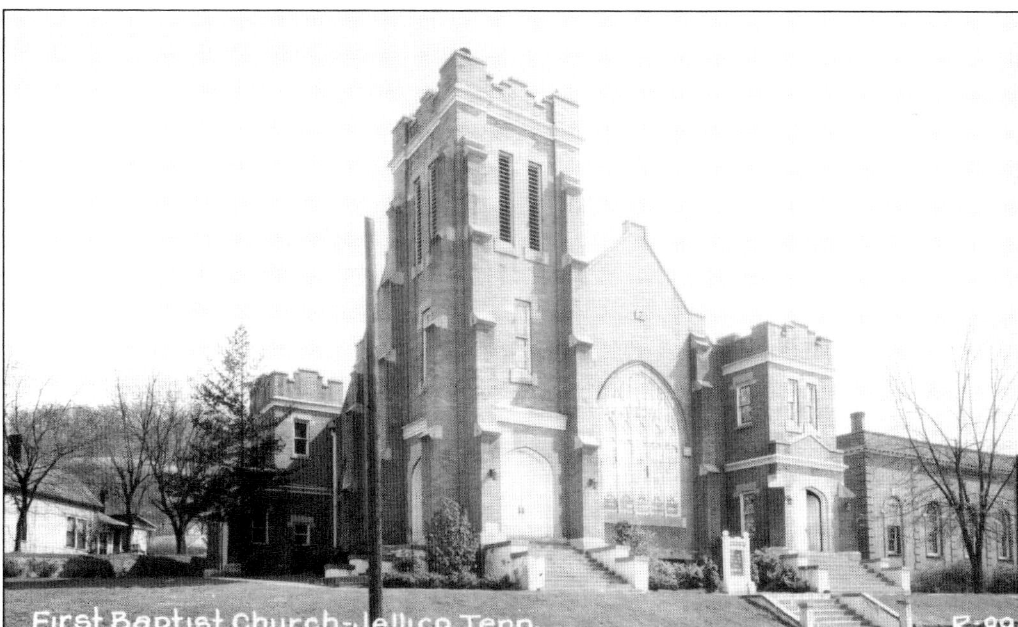

The First Baptist Church, located on South Main Street, opened its first one-room structure on August 24, 1884. The building shown above was the congregation's fourth home. Dedicated on May 4, 1913, it is still used for services. Grace Moore began her singing career as a member of the First Baptist Church choir.

Four

Beyond the Dixie Highway

The Dixie Highway was only one of several highway projects that made traveling easier during the time period of the pictures in this book. Between the two of them, Walter Cline Sr. and Walter Cline Jr. traveled to nearly every state in the South, across the Southwest, and as far north as Canada at Niagara Falls, photographing places that would appeal to the average person. The final chapter explores only a portion of the Clines' work from beyond Tennessee. The journey continues along the Dixie Highway to the Okefenokee Swamp in Georgia, moves to the historic French Quarter in New Orleans, travels through North Carolina's Blue Ridge Mountains, then north to the Capitol and Niagara Falls, southward to the Abbey of Gethsemani in Kentucky, and concludes in Tennessee. The final image appropriately shows the Eastman Corporation (now known as the Eastman Chemical Company), which was established in 1920 to provide raw materials for the Kodak division of the Eastman Company.

The contributions that George Eastman made to the lives and work of photographers like the Clines are immeasurable. In 1883, he introduced roll film with a roll holder, which was much more user-friendly than the cumbersome glass plates previously available and was adaptable to most plate cameras being used at that time. His company, Eastman Kodak, launched the consumer-friendly Brownie camera in 1900 and, shortly after, introduced photographic paper pre-printed with a postcard back, giving birth to the real-photo postcard.

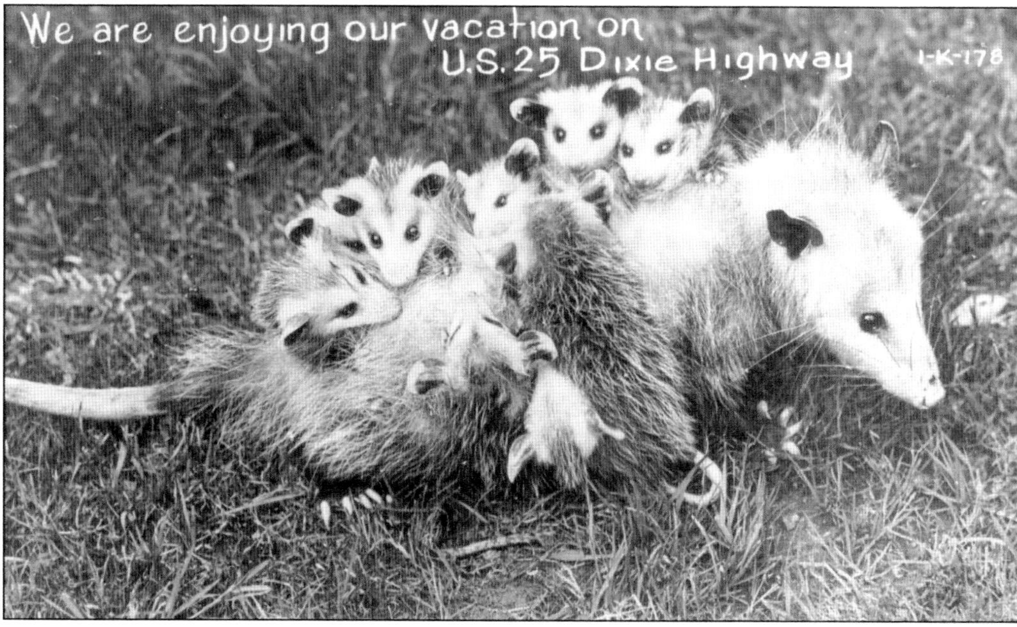

Virginia opossums, also known as North American opossums, are the only marsupials native to North America. Newborn opossums are about the size of kidney beans and stay in their mother's pouch for about two months. They then cling to their mother's back for several more weeks until they are old enough to take care of themselves. When threatened, an opossum sometimes goes into a shock-like state resembling death—colloquially known as "playing possum."

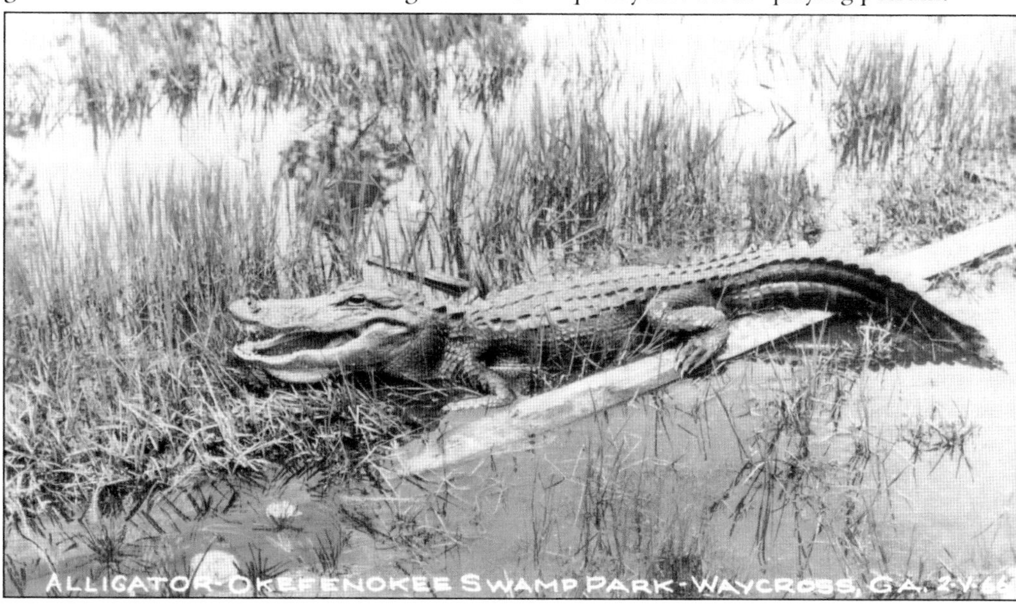

The Okefenokee National Wildlife Refuge, created in 1937, is located in southern Georgia and northern Florida and protects approximately 400,000 acres of the Okefenokee Swamp. The Okefenokee Swamp Park is located just north of the refuge; the 40,000-acre government works project was completed in 1946 and has operated as a nonprofit organization since that time. A variety of plants and wildlife, including alligators, can be encountered on the park's guided tours.

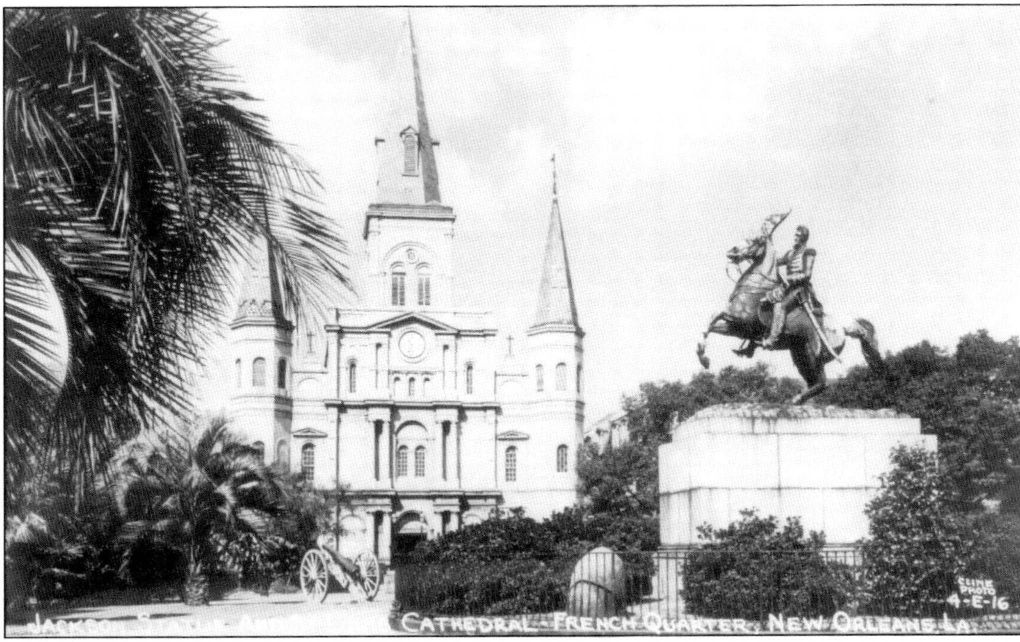

New Orleans's St. Louis Cathedral was built in 1794 and, due to extensive damage, was rebuilt in the 1850s with the addition of its architecturally iconic triple spires. Jackson Square was named in honor of Andrew Jackson for his bravery in the Battle of New Orleans. The image of his statue in front of the cathedral has been used in numerous photographs, movies, and television shows.

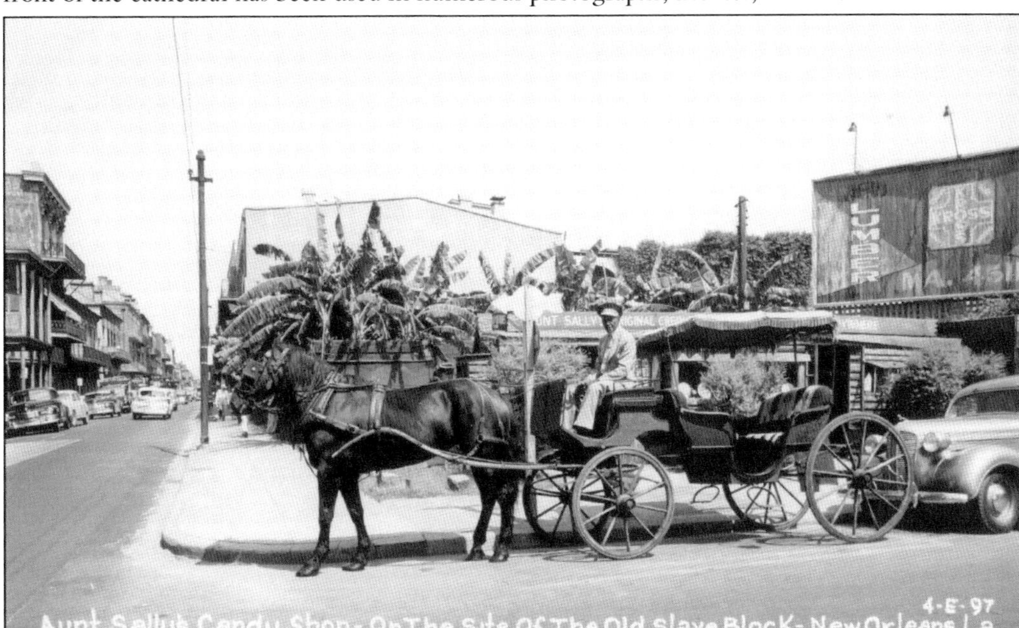

Pierre and Diane Bagur opened Aunt Sally's in the early 1930s and used mule-drawn buggies to transport their goods. They relocated several times during the first few years but always remained in the French Quarter. After the devastating Hurricane Katrina, Aunt Sally's was one of the first businesses in the historic district to reopen. The family-owned candy shop still uses pecans and pure cane sugar from Louisiana.

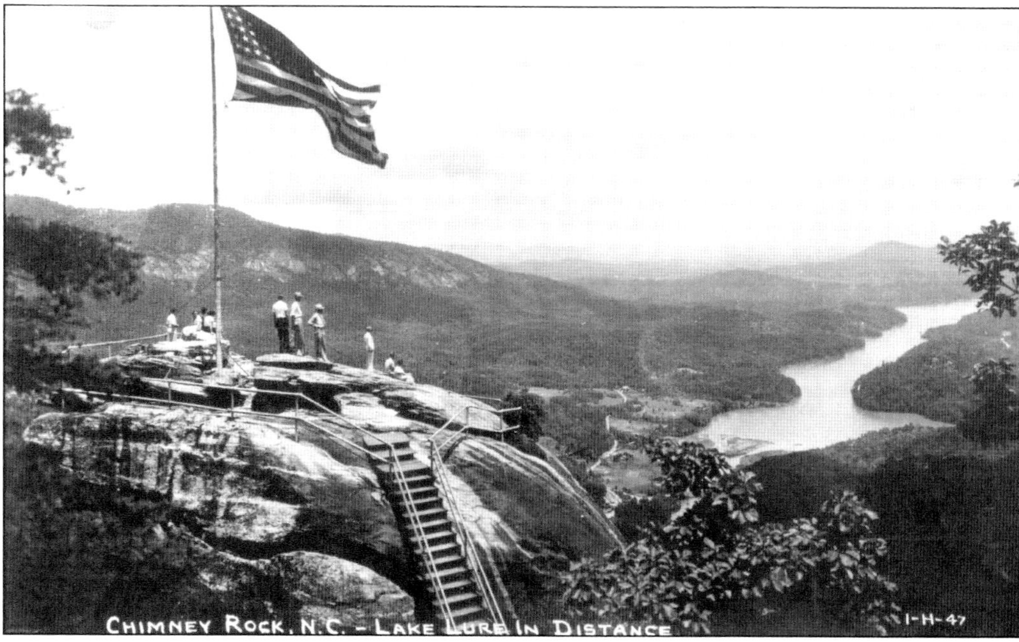

Chimney Rock offers visitors a breathtaking 75-mile panoramic view of Lake Lure, the Blue Ridge Mountains, and Hickory Nut Gorge. It was purchased in 1902 by Lucius B. Morse and remained in his family for over 100 years, until 2007, when the 1,000-acre park was sold to the state of North Carolina to become part of its new Chimney Rock State Park.

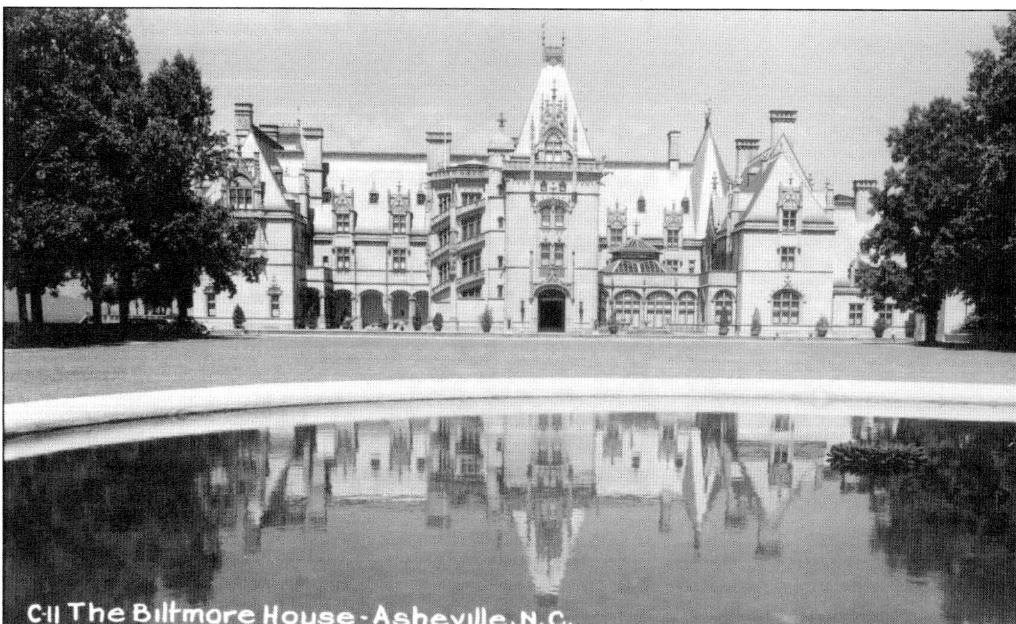

The Biltmore House, constructed in 1895 by George Washington Vanderbilt, was designed by architect Richard Morris Hunt, and the grounds were designed by landscape architect Frederick Law Olmsted. Much of the original 125,000 acres is now the Pisgah National Forest. Built in a French Renaissance style, the four-story home is listed in the National Register of Historic Places. The 8,000-acre estate remains family-owned and hosts over a million guests each year.

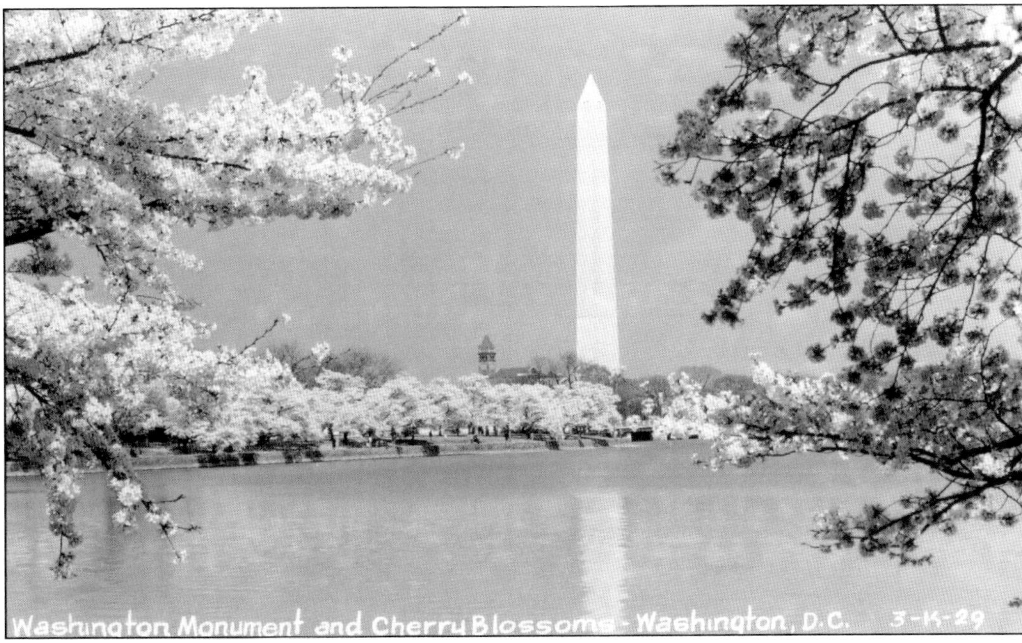

Completed in 1884 to honor George Washington, the obelisk-shaped Washington Monument was designed by Robert Mills and is over 550 feet tall. In 1912, Japan donated more than 2,000 flowering cherry trees, which were planted along the Potomac River. Through donations, a trust fund maintains and replaces the trees in the grove. The National Mall and Memorial Parks Cherry Blossom Festival is held each year in early spring.

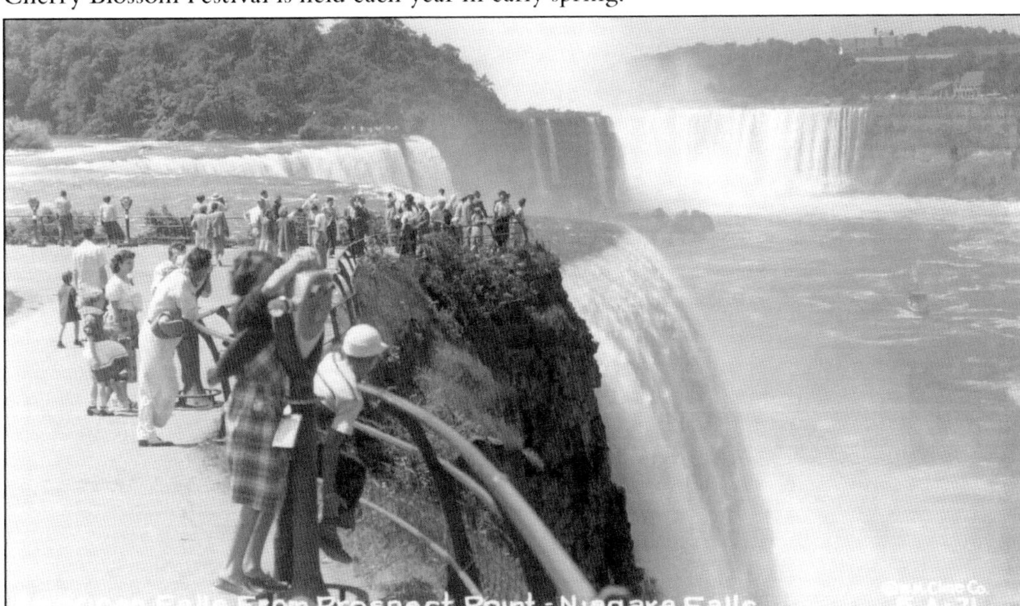

Niagara Falls State Park was established in 1885 and is the country's oldest state park. It was designed by Frederick Law Olmsted, who was also the landscape architect for New York City's Central Park and the Biltmore House. Alternating electrical current was first transmitted in 1896 by electrical engineer Nikola Tesla, and power plants in America and Canada still use Niagara Falls as a major source of hydroelectricity today.

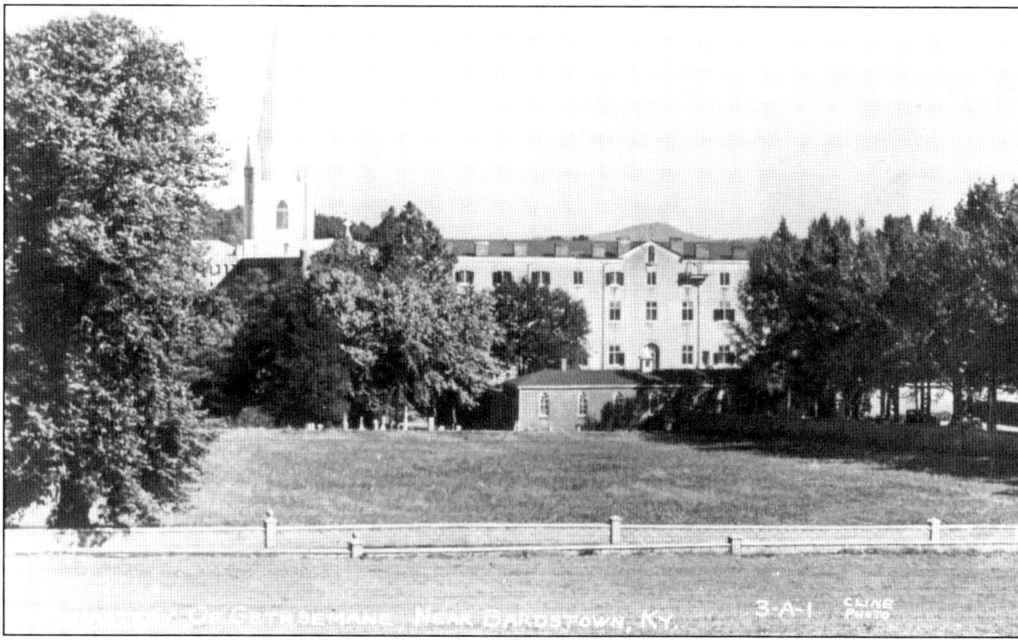

Founded in 1848 by French Trappist monks, the Abbey of Gethsemani is a Roman Catholic monastery located in central Kentucky. Thomas Merton, author of the bestselling 1948 autobiography *The Seven Storey Mountain*, was a member of the monastic community for 27 years until his death in 1968. He left a legacy of over 60 published works covering a variety of subjects, including contemplative prayer, and his books remain popular today.

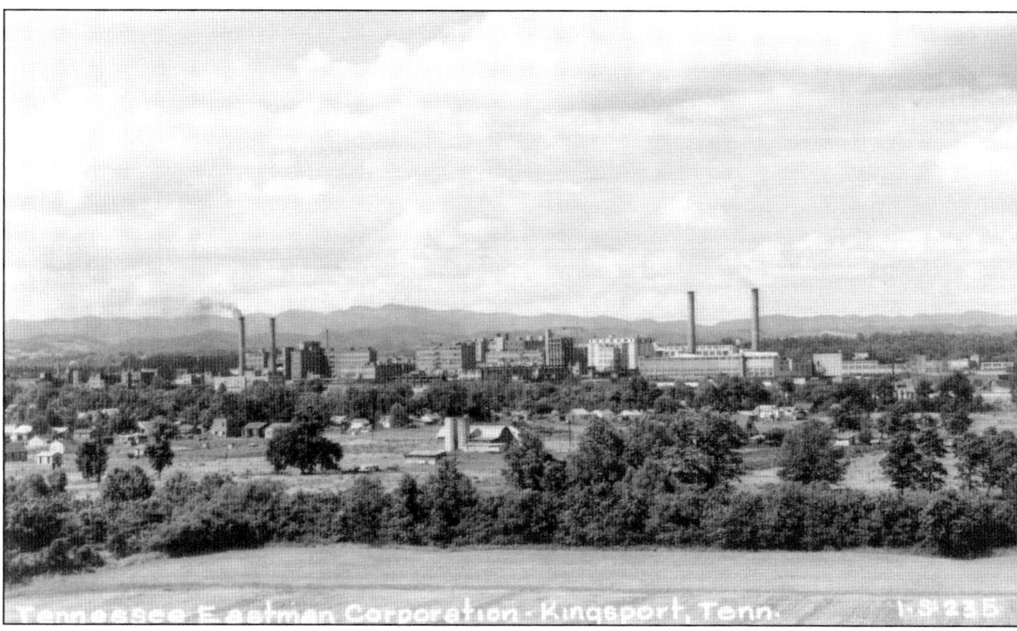

George Eastman invented a simplified camera designed for affordability and convenience. The Kodak camera was first introduced to consumers in 1888 and quickly grew in popularity. Eastman believed in building loyalty and goodwill with employees and achieved this goal by providing factory workers with fair wages and generous profit-sharing opportunities.

Bibliography

Cline, Walter M. *The Muzzle-Loading Rifle: Then and Now.* Huntington, WV: Standard Printing and Publishing Company, 1942.

Grundy County Heritage Book Committee. *The Heritage of Grundy County, TN.* Waynesville, NC: County Heritage, Inc., 2004.

Hollis, Tim. *See Rock City.* Charleston, SC: History Press, 2009.

Jakle, John A., Keith A. Sculle, and Jefferson S. Rogers. *The Motel in America.* Baltimore: Johns Hopkins University Press, 1996.

Manning, Russ. *Scenic Driving Tennessee.* Guilford, CT: Falcon, 2002.

———. *Tennessee's South Cumberland.* Norris, TN: Mountain Laurel Place, 1994.

Matthews, Larry E. *Caves of Chattanooga.* Huntsville, AL: National Speleological Society, 2007.

McDonald, Miller. *Campbell County Tennessee USA: A History of Places, Faces, Happenings, Traditions, and Things, Volume 1.* LaFollette, TN: County Services Syndicate, 1993.

Preston, Howard Lawrence. *Dirt Roads to Dixie: Accessibility and Modernization in the South, 1865–1935.* Knoxville: University of Tennessee Press, 1991.

Pyle, Paul, Allen Parsons, and Jean Smotherman. *Camp Forrest, Tullahoma, Tennessee, 1941–1946.* Tullahoma, TN: Tullahoma Chamber of Commerce, 1984.

Siler, James Hayden. *A History of Jellico, Tennessee: Containing Historical Information on Campbell County, TN, and Whitley County, KY. Jellico Advance-Sentinel,* 1938.

Stager, Claudette, and Martha Carver, eds. *Looking Beyond the Highway: Dixie Roads and Culture.* Knoxville: University of Tennessee Press, 2006.

West, Caroll Van. *The Tennessee Encyclopedia of History and Culture.* Knoxville: University of Tennessee Press, 1998. Revised electronic edition available at http://tennesseeencyclopedia.net/

———. *Tennessee's Historic Landscapes: A Traveler's Guide.* Knoxville: University of Tennessee Press, 1995.

———. *Tennessee's New Deal Landscape: A Guidebook.* Knoxville: University of Tennessee Press, 2001.

Wilson, John. *Scenic, Historic Lookout Mountain.* Chattanooga: R. McDonald, 1977.